THE
STARTUP
CHECKLIST

THE
STARTUP
CHECKLIST

25 Steps to a Scalable, High-Growth Business

DAVID S. ROSE

WILEY

Published by John Wiley & Sons, Inc., Hoboken, New Jersey.
Published simultaneously in Canada.

For general information about our other products and services, please contact our Customer Care Department within the United States at (800) 762-2974, outside the United States at (317) 572-3993 or fax (317) 572-4002.

Wiley publishes in a variety of print and electronic formats and by print-on-demand. Some material included with standard print versions of this book may not be included in e-books or in print-on-demand. If this book refers to media such as a CD or DVD that is not included in the version you purchased, you may download this material at http://booksupport.wiley.com. For more information about Wiley products, visit www.wiley.com.

Library of Congress Cataloging-in-Publication Data:

Names: Rose, David S., 1957- author.
Title: The startup checklist : 25 steps to a scalable, high-growth business / David S. Rose.
Description: Hoboken : Wiley, 2016. | Includes index. | Description based on print version record and CIP data provided by publisher; resource not viewed.
Identifiers: LCCN 2016013847 (print) | LCCN 2016008684 (ebook) | ISBN 9781119163794 (hardback) | ISBN 9781119164050 (pdf) | ISBN 9781119164043 (epub)
Subjects: LCSH: Entrepreneurship. | New business enterprises–Management. | Investments. | BISAC: BUSINESS & ECONOMICS / Entrepreneurship.
Classification: LCC HB615 (print) | LCC HB615 .R656 2016 (ebook) | DDC 658.1/1–dc23
LC record available at http://lccn.loc.gov/2016013847

Printed in the United States of America
10 9 8 7 6 5 4 3 2 1

To Daniel and Joanna Semel Rose,
my unwavering supporters throughout a half
century of entrepreneurship.

Contents

Foreword

BEING AN ENTREPRENEUR is one of the greatest ways to make the world a better place. Building a company the right way with a great product, mission, and structure, unlocks human potential and allows you to have enormous impact in your immediate and extended community.

This book is priceless in helping you do just that. It is a step-by-step guide to taking an idea and turning it into a business.

I have been starting businesses all my life, since I was 12 years old in Junior High School. Since founding Idealab as a technology incubator in 1996, I have started more than 100 companies. The steps shared in this book are so clear and logical, it's painful to think about how wildly useful it would have been to have in my hands 20 years ago.

This book will help you avoid mistakes and make you 1,000 percent smarter in your approach to building a business. I guarantee that there will be at least one chapter in this book which could dramatically change the trajectory of your success and happiness. David describes how to approach your business when it's just a kernel of an idea, how to develop a plan and test your product in the market, how and when to hire the right talent (and importantly, how to think about equity splits and compensation), and takes you through the various administrative tasks that can be seen as tedious but are critical to avoiding expensive mistakes in the future. He outlines how to approach raising money and investors and the different sources of money available for a startup.

Starting a great company is so much more than just a great idea. There are a thousand things you can do to unwittingly undermine your success. This book will help you navigate some of the critical junctures that will make or break your progress. In addition to the actual checklist, David provides a wealth of online resources that will allow you to become fully educated on every aspect of building your company. This book outlines that process better—and all in one place—than any other thing I have ever read.

David S. Rose has seen it all, over many years and across thousands of companies, and then, to the great benefit of the rest of us, has distilled the essence of what it takes to succeed. I can't say strongly enough how much I feel following the checklist David has created will help you make your company more successful.

—Bill Gross

Preface
Why Every Entrepreneur Needs This Book . . . Instead of the Other 93,210 Books on Entrepreneurship

"To open a business is easy, to keep it open is an art."

—Chinese proverb

ENTREPRENEURS HAVE BEEN STARTING COMPANIES without reading instruction books since the first Phoenician trader bought his first ship over 5,000 years ago. And for those who do want some guidance, Amazon would be pleased to sell you any of the 93,210 books listed in its "start a business" category, many of which are quite good. So why is there a need for yet another startup book?

Because this book is designed for a very specific type of business starter: the entrepreneur who is deliberately setting out to create a scalable, high-growth business designed for the twenty-first century, a business that will likely hire employees, issue stock options, raise money from outside investors, grow rapidly, and eventually either be acquired by a larger company or "go public" through an initial public offering. It turns out that starting that kind of business gets very complicated, very quickly. Making even small mistakes at the beginning can cause problems at every later step along the way.

I've been starting companies myself for over 45 years as a serial entrepreneur (more than half a dozen of them), and as an active business angel investor I have personally funded and advised over 100 others. I've founded, taught in, or advised many of the country's leading entrepreneurship training programs, and, as the founder and CEO of Gust,

I've learned from the aggregate experience of providing the tools used by more than half a million startups around the world. I've also answered over 4,000 questions from aspiring entrepreneurs on Quora, the online question-and-answer site, and heard of just about every variety of problem in the playbook.

Along the way, I have learned firsthand the problems that can quickly arise from starting off on the wrong foot. They range from the fundamental (charging off to start a business that just doesn't make sense) to the painful (hooking up with people whose interests are divergent from yours) to the tragic (getting equity allocations wrong at the beginning and never being able to recover), all the way to the really, really expensive (making simple mistakes at the incorporation level that result in five- and six-figure cleanup costs the first time a serious investor is thinking of supporting you).

This book is intended to be your one-stop checklist to starting up right. I assume no prior knowledge on your part about business—just a strong desire to create something seriously big, and to do so in the most effective, most efficient, and least expensive way possible. My goal is to walk along beside you throughout the process, providing the background you need to understand the *whys* in addition to the *whats* and the *hows*. I will take you step-by-step through the nitty-gritty practical tasks of starting up a high-growth venture, introduce you to the latest online tools that will save you time and money, point you to the standard books that should be in every entrepreneur's library, and give you a peek behind the angel/venture curtain so you can understand what potential investors are thinking when they are considering funding your startup.

As my hero, Benjamin Franklin, wrote, "Experience keeps an expensive school, but fools will learn in no other." Having spent a lifetime painfully learning from experience, my goal now is to shorten the time that you will need to spend in Ben Franklin's "expensive school."*

---

*Benjamin Franklin was an amazing entrepreneur. You should read his delightful *Autobiography* for some cool startup experience and tips. (Not to mention his will, which established the first seed fund for entrepreneurs . . .)

Introduction
25 Key Action Steps
(Plus One) for Every Entrepreneur

BECAUSE YOU ARE undoubtedly raring to go out and change the world with your amazing business concept, I'm going to open this book with a crash checklist in "starting smart" so that you can avoid the biggest bone-headed errors made by many bright-eyed and enthusiastic first-time company founders. I'll give you a quick overview of each of the steps that will take you from an idea to an exit, and I'll explain how to use this book as your companion along the way. Even if this Introduction is all that you read, at least you'll know what you should be doing, and where to find an in-depth discussion in the book on each of the following topics.

Now, off we go!

Prepare to Launch

0. Before You Start, Educate Yourself.

Just as you would not start a trek to the North Pole without reading at least *Arctic Exploration for Couch Potatoes*, you should start your entrepreneurial journey by getting oriented to the basics . . . and that's exactly what this book is about. Once you've finished, if you are typical of most hyperactive entrepreneurs, you'll be off getting your parka and snowshoes. But if you can eke out a bit more patience, among the other 93,210 startup books, a few have become known as classics for a reason. They deal with everything from "What is entrepreneurship?" to "How can I start cheaply?" and "How do I turn an idea into a company?"

Therefore, after you finish *The Startup Checklist*, the next thing I suggest you do is take the time to read a few of the other basic books on the "starting a company" thing. While this book deals with the hands-on, practical aspects of starting up, there are others that will provide invaluable context, advice, and theory, as well as detailed help with specific challenges many entrepreneurs face. I realize that the thought of reading even one book, let alone more, may seem boring or painful, or a waste of time. But when you stack the task up against the vital future of your enterprise, it begins to look like the best deal in town. In this book, I have pulled out a few gems of wisdom from the industry's leading thinkers and teachers to get you started, but I have also included in Appendix A my *Startup Reading List* of classics that are full of too much mission-critical information to cover here. Read them.

1. Translate Your Idea into a Compelling Business Model.

A business is created in order to execute on an idea. Not having a clear picture of that idea is guaranteed to result in an extraordinary amount of wheel spinning. While you will spend the rest of your business career refining your idea, there must be something at the core, or you'll have nothing to refine. In particular, it is crucial at the beginning to distinguish the *business concept* from the *product concept*. It is well and good to come up with an idea for a cool new widget, app, or website, but it's more important to understand what value the product brings to which customer, and to understand who will be willing to pay you for your work in developing it. At this point you don't need a full-fledged business plan, but you do need the ability to explain clearly what you're doing and why—and that's your business concept. In Chapter 1, I discuss creating a visual business model using the Business Model Canvas.

Once you have your business concept sketched out, I suggest you invest the time to get prefeedback. Take your nascent idea around and talk to domain experts in your field to see what they think about it. Don't worry, they're not going to steal your idea (they won't!). What they will do, however, is to give you a reality check to see if your idea makes sense to people who know the industry you're preparing to enter. Whatever they tell you shouldn't necessarily be dispositive (sometimes it takes a fresh creative look from outside an industry to make a conceptual leap), but it should absolutely be taken into consideration . . . and not just given lip service. It is far better to find out before you start that your idea has been tried multiple times with no success than it is to learn it after you've spent two years trying fruitlessly to smash a round peg into a square hole.

2. Craft a Lean Business Plan to Serve as Your "Plan A" Road Map.

Assuming the prefeedback you're getting indicates that you may be on the right track, now is the time to start organizing your business concept into a more detailed road map for your venture. In Chapter 2, I discuss how to prepare and use a Lean Business Plan. This is not a lengthy, text-heavy document, but rather the essential framework for everything that you will be doing down the road. It provides the context that will let you assess each new opportunity, product, option, and even employee in light of where you are trying to go and how you plan to get there.

While you will only produce a full written plan in the event that you are specifically requested to by a bank or other interested party, investors will be asking detailed questions of you . . . questions that you can answer only if you have already carefully thought through your business to the level of detail required to do a plan in the first place.

3. Find and Know Your Competitors, and Analyze the Strategic Landscape.

With an idea in hand that seems promising, take a look around to see who else is working on the same thing. That's because—as much as I hate to spoil the surprise—someone else is. Consider this: as of this writing, on the Gust online platform for early stage businesses, there are over 500,000 companies that have created startup profiles. Do you believe that there are 500,000 different business types in the world? No, there are not. How about 50,000? Nope, not that either. 5,000? Maybe, but I don't think so. 500? Yup, that sounds about right. So what does this mean to you? It means that, at this moment, as you are about to pour your soul into a new venture, there are between 100 and 1,000 other founders doing the same (or similar) things!

That being said, just because there are competitors is no reason to assume that they will succeed and you will not. Counterintuitively, experience has shown that a business arena with no competitors is considerably more difficult to conquer than one in which other people have paved the way for you (that's a lesson I learned painfully in the mid-1990s when I had a brilliant, breakthrough product for which we could never actually find a market.) But it is important that you are aware of what the competitive arena looks like so that you won't be unhappily surprised down the road. Chapter 3 is about the competition: who they are, where to find them, and how to analyze them.

4. Draft Your Founding Dream Team.

Talented as you may be, it is unlikely you have all the skills required to launch and build a successful business on your own. And even if you do, you won't have the time and energy to do so, especially as your company begins to grow. Sooner rather than later, you will need to identify a handful of other people who can complement your talents, forming a founding team that can help you launch your venture on a profitable, high-growth trajectory. It is important to consider the skills, background and knowledge that you will need to make the company a success, figuring out which ones you have and which ones you lack. Understanding the role of The Entrepreneur in a startup is the cornerstone of building a high-growth venture, and in Chapter 4 I talk about how to assess whether you *are* one . . . or need to *find* one, as well as how to set clear expectations among the members of your founding team.

5. Allocate the Equity in your Startup.

Once you've joined forces to create a founding team, you will need to have a discussion about equity—how much of the venture each person will own. In the same way that "good fences make good neighbors," a clear, rational, and mutually agreed-upon equity structure sets a company up for success, whereas a poorly thought-out one is a recipe for conflict and failure. I walk through the intricacies of equity allocation in Chapter 5, including why the logical 50/50 split is not in the best interest of the company. The important things to remember are that (1) "equity is forever," so once it's in someone's hands there is no easy way for you to get it back; and (2) equity is all about the future upside of the business, and thus should be held by those likely to be instrumental in making that upside real, rather than people whose services can be purchased on the market for cash.

6. Build a Minimum Viable Product and Validate Your Plan with Customers.

Up to this point, your business concept has existed only in theory. You haven't been trying to sell any products or services to real-world customers. Now it is time for the rubber to hit the road. Your goal is to see whether any of your potential users are willing to pay for what you want to sell.

In Chapter 6, I introduce you to the famous Lean Startup Methodology, and its most important tool, the Minimum Viable Product (MVP). This is a basic version of the product or service you plan to offer that is just "real" enough to make it testable with live customers. The MVP can be a bare-bones prototype, a web page advertisement, or a small-scale service designed to simulate the kind of operation you will use to service hundreds of thousands of customers. It facilitates experiments in the marketplace—tests that will generate feedback you can use to tweak or redesign the offering, each time enhancing the likelihood that your offering will be a huge hit.

If the responses to your landing page, crowdfunding campaign, or other market test come back positive, you're good to go. On the other hand, at any of the above stages, if reality or sage advice suggests you're off target, reformulate the concept or pivot the business model, and try again as many times as it takes to build a truly successful model.

7. Establish Your Brand with Online Public Profiles.

Today's electronic communication tools make it much easier and more affordable than ever before to create a public image and presence for your business—a brand with a meaning and value all its own. Start this process early in the launch phase of your business and it can benefit you in many ways. Individuals and companies that may want to team up with you—talented employees, strategic partners, even investors—will have a way to find you, as you begin to tell your startup story. Chapter 7 outlines the process of creating your online public profiles, with a brand name, logo and website, and discusses the social media platforms that have become essential venues for entrepreneurial ventures.

8. Network Effectively within the Entrepreneurial Ecosystem.

Back in the Dark Ages, around 2000 AD, there was no such thing as an "entrepreneurial ecosystem." Today, entrepreneurs are as highly regarded as baseball players and the world in which you are starting your business is replete with individuals and organizations who can help you nurture your talents. These are the equivalent of Little Leagues, coaches, sporting goods stores and back-lot *Fields of Dreams*. While it is possible to survive as a loner, you will recruit many more allies (and have access to many more benefits) if you proactively put yourself in the middle of the action, as I describe in Chapter 8. Whether it is attending Meetups, applying to an accelerator program, pitching your concept in business competitions, or participating in online forums, embracing the ecosystem will pay off in the long term more than you realize.

Launch and Build Your Company

9. Incorporate as a Delaware "C" Corporation for Protection and Investment.

Everything you have done so far can (and probably should) take place before there is an actual business in existence. But as soon as you are ready to bring on partners, hire employees, develop intellectual property, raise capital, or generate revenues—in short, anything that creates or shares value of any kind—you need to establish an official business entity to be the owner of that value. In Chapter 9, I take you through the various types of possible business structures, including sole proprietorships, partnerships, LLCs, and corporations.

In the real world, however, there is only one serious option. If you plan to do anything involving employee or advisor options, venture capital, or serious angel funding, you need to be established as a C corporation so that ownership of the business is divided into shares of stock. And while the corporation can theoretically be formed in any state in the United States, for practical and economic reasons, it almost always makes sense to set up the "official" home of your company in the state of Delaware.

On one level, incorporating a new entity can be cheap and easy: Read the state's instructions, spend a few hours of do-it-yourself time and $89, and you're all set. Alternatively, there are a number of online services that cater to small businesses that will do much of the work for you for a few hundred dollars more. But that is where danger lies. It is one thing to incorporate a simple, one-person company for a hobby business. It's a different thing entirely to make sure that your company's by-laws, stock option plans, shareholders' agreements, and other documents are drafted correctly to set the stage for the scalable, high-growth business that you are destined to become.

10. "Lawyer Up" the Right Way.

Because a few dollars saved by incorporating "on the cheap" are almost guaranteed to cost thousands—or even tens of thousands—of dollars the minute you begin dealing with investors or option holders, it is critically important that you begin working from the beginning with a good startup attorney. I discuss how to find and work with one in Chapter 10.

11. Recruit Your Boards of Directors and Advisors.

Talent always has a price. A world-class coder? Plan on $150K+ a year. A world-class chairman of the board? Priceless. Unlike employees you will hire for their skills and cofounders you will partner with for their entrepreneurial energy, advisors and board members are typically those you would not be able to hire at any price. Whether they are angel investors in your company, CEOs of other companies of your size, or grizzled veterans in your industry, great advisors and mentors are worth their weight in gold.

In Chapter 11, I explain the roles played by a company's board of directors and its individual members, as well as by other advisors, who can help you keep your company on track. I also discuss how to find great advisors, how to attract them, and how to make the most of their contributions.

12. Select an Accountant and an Accounting System.

You don't need to be an accountant or have a finance degree to be an entrepreneur, but you do need to develop a deep, intuitive understanding of business finance. It is important to master the basic principles that every business uses to manage the flow of funds into, through, and out of the company.

Chapter 12 is a crash course in business finance, in which you will learn the basics, as well as which tasks professional bookkeepers and accountants should handle for your startup, and how to find them. I also introduce Cloud-based software services that can automate and streamline the financial management process for your company.

13. Establish and Manage Your Credit Profile.

As a brand new startup, your business has no history or financial track record, which means that you may find it challenging to do business with other (particularly bigger) companies who might not even be sure that you exist. Because of this, it is important that you think of your company's credit profile right from the start. One of the first things you'll do when you incorporate is to apply to the IRS for an employer identification number (EIN), which is like a social security number for your business. You will be using this to identify your company to anyone who pays you money or receives money from you, to file your taxes, and to open bank accounts.

You will also want to get a D-U-N-S number, which is managed by Dun & Bradstreet, and identifies your company's credit profile. It is a good idea to know what your business credit looks like to potential partners and customers, and D-U-N-S numbers are necessary to do business with companies like Apple, Walmart, and other major players. I talk about the importance of credit and walk you through the most important credit-management procedures in Chapter 13.

14. Open Bank, Credit Card, and Merchant Accounts.

You are familiar with the basic processes of banking from managing your personal finances. But commercial banking is a different kettle of fish. Chapter 14 includes the best ways to select and work with the right commercial bank for your startup. I also discuss the most useful kinds of bank relationships for startup businesses, including checking, credit, and merchant accounts, and provide advice on what features to look for when selecting a mobile and web payment processor.

15. Choose Your Key Technologies, Platforms, and Vendors.

An advantage of starting a company in the twenty-first century is that you will not be operating in a vacuum, but instead can take advantage of an extensive world of Cloud-based platforms for banking, accounting, sales, legal, human resource management, and more. Figuring out which of today's most powerful technology platforms are best for your particular needs—and then how to get started in using them—is something I discuss in Chapter 15, which also includes my personal "best of class" picks.

16. Measure Your Business with Data Analytics.

As quality guru H. James Harrington wrote, "Measurement is the first step that leads to control and eventually to improvement. If you can't measure something, you can't understand it. If you can't understand it, you can't control it. If you can't control it, you can't improve it." While terms like "big data" and "customer analytics" have become so common in the business media as to be almost clichés, in my experience, the power of these tools is routinely ignored by first-time founders. If you are planning to found a high-growth business, I assure you that "analytics," as I discuss in Chapter 16, are crucial: to figure out how to run your business, and to answer the questions that you will hear from the very first (and second, and third . . .) investor when you start looking for funding.

17. Round Out Your Team with Employees and Freelancers.

As the demand for your products or services grows, so will your business, and that means you'll need help. Recruiting, hiring, and training A+ employees is a challenge that many first-time entrepreneurs are not equipped to handle, and mistakes here can have lasting repercussions. In Chapter 17, I introduce you to the New Hire Draft Board, and discuss key things you should be looking for when bringing together your team.

You will want to think about the option of outsourcing particular functions rather than hiring employees to handle them—an alternative that offers both advantages and disadvantages. Some companies get started by outsourcing virtually everything. But to develop real value in your enterprise (the kind that other companies or the public markets will be prepared to pay for), you will have to increasingly bring key parts of your operation in-house.

Whether dealing with employees or freelancers, you will need create and nurture a positive, productive business culture even as your company grows, so you never lose the sense of creative ferment and excitement that is one of the great rewards of running an entrepreneurial venture.

18. Establish a Stock Option Plan to Incentivize Your Team.

As an angel investor, I routinely deal with startups that are just coming out of the "garage" stage. They've hired a few people, and are getting ready to launch their first product. When I ask about salaries, I'll hear "so much in cash, and so much in equity." But then, when I ask how the company actually issued the equity to the employee, all I get is a blank stare. Suffice to say, you can't simply "promise" your team that they'll get equity! Instead, you need to work with your lawyer, set up an employee stock option plan, reserve shares of stock in your certificate of incorporation to back up the options, have all option grants officially approved by the company's board of directors, and then actually issue grants to your employees, as I describe in Chapter 18. There are no shortcuts here!

Raise Funds; Collaborate with Investors; Plan for Your Exit

19. Understand the Funding Process and What Investors Want to See.

While investing your own money or the revenues generated by your first few sales—otherwise known as *bootstrapping*—is a great way to start your business, the more successful your company is (or, conversely, the longer it takes you to find the correct product/market fit with your

Minimum Viable Product), the more cash you will need to fund your growth. Since banks will not lend money to startups (did I mention that a majority of all startups fail?), you will need to attract the right investors, win their support, and work with them to ensure a long and mutually satisfying relationship.

By the time your minimum viable product works and develops marketplace traction, you may be ready to raise money to help fund your venture. For most people, this initially means raising small amounts of cash from friends and family. But if you appear to have a tiger by the tail, you could successfully approach professional angel investors . . . or even, in rare circumstances, venture capital funds. Unfortunately, this is often where I see the biggest disconnect between perception and reality.

If you read the industry blogs and breathless stories in the popular press, you might assume that everyone with a good idea for a startup simply walks in to a venture capitalists' office and walks out with a check. In reality, it is nothing like that. Less than one quarter of one percent of real companies each year that incorporate, hire employees, and open for business actually receive financing from venture capitalists! Before going out in search of funding, you should make it a point to understand how the entrepreneurial financing world really works.

Chapter 19 provides an overview of the investment process, with a behind-the-scenes look at angel investors. It also explains in detail what investors are looking for when considering potential startup investments—crucial information for entrepreneurs who want to know how to portray their businesses in the best light.

20. Nurture Your Investor Pipeline.

The days when a starry-eyed entrepreneur could spin a tale of riches to a well-heeled patron over a napkin in a coffee shop are long gone. Today, the art of the pitch is much more complicated—and is fundamental for anyone hoping to engender outside support for a new venture must master. You'll need different pitches in your arsenal, including stand-up, verbal, and elevator pitches, and the canonical 20-minute PowerPoint presentation aimed at angel investors and venture capitalists. In Chapter 20, I walk you through the basic techniques for identifying investors who may be interested in supporting your business, and lay out what you will need to have in your "presentation wardrobe."

21. Fundraise with Online Platforms.

In the old days, funding for startup companies came solely from founders and the founders' families. By the twentieth century, "angel investors" began to appear—rich business people willing to take risks on startup entrepreneurs. But they were few and far between, and you had to know one personally in order to get funded. After the stock market crash in 1929, the U.S. government established the Securities and Exchange Commission to regulate how companies could raise money. This made the process more organized, but also included a rule saying that you while you were allowed to sell shares of your company privately to rich people . . . you couldn't tell anyone about your company, or ask them to invest. In fact, it wasn't until 2012 that the laws were changed to reflect reality: you can reach a lot of potential investors through the Internet! Today, raising startup funds online through "equity funding platforms" is still in its infancy but already accounts for hundreds of millions of dollars annually. In Chapter 21, I introduce you to the different types of platforms, and discuss which ones make the most sense for a high-growth entrepreneur.

22. Understand Term Sheets and Prepare for Due Diligence.

Although it would be nice if an investor were to walk over, hand you a check for a million dollars and wish you luck, unfortunately that is not the way it works. Investments in startups are governed by extensive, detailed contracts; so extensive that they start with a contract to write a contract . . . known as a term sheet. In Chapter 22, I explain the crucial differences between Convertible Notes and Convertible Preferred Stock, and walk you through the details. For extra credit, Appendix D includes a sample investment term sheet that I have annotated to explain what every line means.

At every stage when you are dealing with third parties who are interested in a company's ownership—whether because they are planning to invest in you, lend to you, acquire you or be acquired by you—they are going to ask detailed, probing questions about everything your company has ever done. I have included an eight-page list of these questions in Appendix B because it will help you eliminate 80 percent of the time and cost of doing any kind of corporate financing or acquisition. That is the time spent cleaning up all of the things that should already have been done, and finding the elusive paperwork that proves you actually did it.

Chapter 22 shows you how to keep the correct kind of records, and get everything ready for your inevitable due diligence examination . . . even before your investor asks. While this may not result in an instant marriage proposal or a bonus on the sales price, it will certainly put you at the top of the investor's "heroes list."

23. Get the Most from Your Investors, Now and in the Future.

One of the biggest mistakes that first-time entrepreneurs make is to think of funding and investors as a "one and done" task, when in reality nothing is farther from the truth. Once an investor puts money into your fledgling venture, that investor is your partner for life (or at least until the company has an exit). As such, the nature, content, and timing of your communications with investors and other stakeholder are critical, and will often determine whether you are able to raise follow-on investment rounds when you most need them. In Chapter 23, I provide pointers on the care and feeding of your investors, from many years of experience on both sides of the table.

24. Determine What Your Company Is Really Worth.

Valuing a business is a lot more complicated than it may appear from watching television's *Shark Tank*. It is also tremendously important. The rewards you will gain from launching and building your business depend on how the company is valued in the marketplace. Business valuation also affects the company's ability to attract investment capital, reward employees and achieve a satisfactory exit for the venture's founders.

In Chapter 24, I explain the ins and outs of business valuation, describing the many factors (logical and illogical) that impact the seemingly straightforward number that encapsulates the worth of your company. I walk you through the most widely used valuation techniques in the startup world, and then explain why automated systems may soon be taking much of the guesswork out of the equation.

25. Keep Your Eye on the Exit and Reap the Benefits of Success.

There are four possible endings for the business venture upon which you are embarking, all of which have to do with turning the value you have created into cash:

1. You can continue running the business in perpetuity and take out cash to fund your lifestyle.
2. You can sell the business to a larger company and walk away with cash.
3. You can register for an IPO and "take the company public," thus converting your ownership to publicly tradable shares that can be sold for cash.
4. You can shut the company down and lose the cash you, and your investors, have put into it so far.

While no one likes to imagine the fourth scenario, which of the first three you aim for can have a significant impact on everything from the type of business you enter to whether and how you finance it, and even what options you have for an exit. In Chapter 25, I walk through the alternatives and provide some insight on what may happen to your company following an acquisition.

That, in a nutshell, is the quick guide to how to conceive, start, and scale a high-growth business. If you have a short attention span, feel free to dive into and out of specific chapters when you need some direction. Otherwise, turn the page and let's get started . . . the right way!

PART

I

Prepare to Launch

1

Translate Your Idea into a Compelling Business Model

EVERY GREAT BUSINESS STARTS with a great idea. You probably wouldn't be reading this book unless you already had at least the glimmerings of a business idea. In this chapter, you'll learn how to take your raw, perhaps unproven idea and measure its likelihood of success—then enhance, improve, and solidify it.

Elements of the Business Model

A business model is the idea that underlies a successful business. It describes how the business creates value for customers, delivers that value to them, and captures a portion of the value for its owners. Every successful business, no matter how large or small, complex or simple, operates according to a business model that makes sense. (Of course, some large, complex companies operate according to several business models at once since they include divisions or departments that create, deliver, and capture value in varying ways. But don't let that confuse you.) Therefore, one of the most important steps you need to take as an entrepreneur is to transform your business idea into a business model that shows how you'll create, deliver, and capture value.

There are many ways to think about a business model. One of the most effective is described and illustrated by Alexander Osterwalder and Yves Pigneur in their best-selling book *Business Model Generation.*[*] In their structure, a business model includes nine basic elements:

- **Customer segments.** The specific, different groups of customers the business serves—that is, the identified customers for whom it will create value.
- **Value propositions.** How the business solves problems and meets the needs of its customers, creating value for them in the process.
- **Channels.** How the business reaches its customers and delivers value to them—for example, through direct online sales, retail distribution channels, value-added resellers, company-owned storefronts, or affiliate programs.
- **Customer relationships.** The ways in which the business connects with, relates to, and retains customers.
- **Revenue streams.** Where the money comes from: how the business generates income from the value propositions it offers to customers.
- **Key resources.** The assets required to create and deliver the value propositions to customers—for example, physical assets such as buildings and machinery, and human assets such as employees with particular skill sets.
- **Key activities.** What the business does to make its business model work, such as inventing, buying, building, distributing, operating, and so forth.
- **Key partnerships.** Outside organizations, such as suppliers and partners, that help the business model work.
- **Cost structure.** The costs that the business incurs in operating its business model.

These nine elements can be mapped in a diagram that Osterwalder and Pigneur call the Business Model Canvas, which provides a standardized, visual way of analyzing, developing, and refining your ideas. You can print out a large-format version of the Business Model Canvas

---

[*]Hoboken, NJ John Wiley & Sons, 2010.

and post it on a wall or spread it out on a table so that you and your cofounders can work on it together.

One benefit of the nine-elements model in the canvas is that it forces you to think through all the key pieces that need to be in place to make a business idea into a viable basis for a profitable, self-sustainable company.[*]

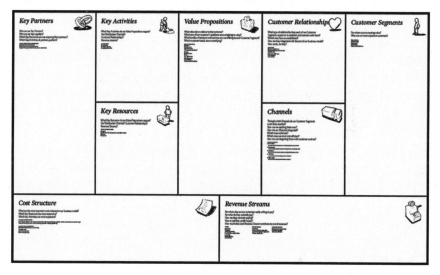

Figure 1.1   The Business Model Canvas

Copies of printed templates for the Business Model Canvas can be downloaded for free from businessmodelgeneration.com. An online, interactive version of the Canvas specifically designed for high-growth startups is available at LeanMonitor.com. Another comprehensive online version is available at Strategyzer.com.

The Importance of Understanding Your Business Model

These days, it seems like everyone is a wannabe entrepreneur—just as everyone used to be an aspiring actor or have the Great American Novel in a back pocket. While I have heard many clever ideas

---

[*]Another good guide to the process of analyzing and sharpening a business model is *The Startup Owner's Manual* by Steve Blank and Bob Dorf (K & S Ranch, 2012), which walks you through the process of developing and refining the Business Model Canvas within the context of a startup.

for products and services over the years, in my experience, the number one differentiator between an aspirant and a real founder is that the former is in love with his product, but the latter is in love with her business model. I have often had discussions with other investors about companies that have approached us for funding, and we all had the same reaction: "I can't wait to buy the product when it comes out . . . but no way would I invest in the company!" A product or service can be cool, or innovative, or beautiful, or even useful, but it only becomes a viable business if the aggregate economics of the value being created are significantly more than the aggregate economics of the costs of operating the business. If you are aiming for a scalable business, then you're looking further for a viable business that gets better—not worse—as it gets bigger.

How can you determine whether your business idea has the potential to become a multi-billion-dollar unicorn? In general, there is a simple math equation that estimates basic viability by multiplying four factors:

Number of potential purchasers ×

Percentage of capturable market share ×

Absolute dollar amount of each sale ×

Percentage margin of net profit =

$$\overline{\text{Total potential profit}}$$

The perfect new business idea would be one that would check all four boxes—that is, it would be appropriate for a large number of potential purchasers, be attractive to a high percentage of those possible customers, generate sales with high dollar value, and promise a high profit margin on each sale. To make it truly scalable, you'd want to check a fifth box—the business would need to get even better as it got bigger.

For example, if you were trying to evaluate a concept for a house-cleaning business, it would be great if everyone in the world needed their house cleaned; if you had a way of locking up the entire global market and servicing every house in the world; if everyone would be willing to pay a large amount for this service; and if your cost to clean a house was low, and dropped with every additional customer. I assume you would take that business, right?

Unfortunately, these five propositions turn out not to be true in regard to housecleaning—which explains why no one has yet ascended to the top of the *Forbes* list of the world's richest billionaires by launching an international housecleaning business.

As you might imagine, business concepts that check all the boxes are exceedingly rare. However, when you look at successful businesses, you'll discover that even three out of the five can make for a viable—and even potentially scalable—business.

For example, take the business of sending tourists up for a visit to the International Space Station. There's obviously not a giant market for that, since it can only accommodate one visitor every few years. But it so happens that one of my portfolio companies actually does that. Why? Because the ticket price is around $50 million per person, it has decent margins, and it has 100 percent market share. (It was also a business, believe it or not, that could be started relatively inexpensively, because its customers paid in full, in advance, before the company was required to pay the Russian government for the actual experience.) And while it's not scalable *per se*, the company has leveraged its experience into allied areas, such as zero-gravity airplane flights, astronaut training, and jet fighter missions.

Furthermore, when you do the analysis, it's important to be clear about what the business is actually doing. Let's go back to the idea of a housecleaning business. It would be very problematic to try to grow housecleaning into a truly large business. The logistics of service delivery around the world would make it extremely difficult to eke out a decent profit margin, and the minimal cost of entry by competitors (who need only a van, some tools and supplies, and a few employees to set up a rival cleaning company) means that you would probably never develop a large market share.

But if we're talking about something like Angie's List or HomeAdvisor, the first thing we need to realize is that the business these companies are in is not actually housecleaning. Instead, it is lead generation and/or booking and intermediating payment for house cleaners. Looking at in that way completely changes the equation. Your marketing and service delivery costs are at Internet scale, and therefore low and decreasing the larger you get. On the other hand, the value you are delivering to the people willing to pay for it (the actual house-cleaner) is high relative to their opportunity costs (which means you can extract a decent margin), and because you can target everyone on the Internet, you have a sizable addressable market (even if only the top one percent would be willing to pay to have their houses cleaned).

This is also the case for other apparently small or low-margin businesses, such as urban taxis (Uber), errands (TaskRabbit), cups of coffee (Starbucks prepaid cards), and free radio (Pandora, Spotify, iHeartRadio, etc.). Once you add the dozens of potential future revenue streams for each of these enterprises based on their existing infrastructure (Uber providing just-in-time delivery services, online music sites selling concert tickets and memorabilia, Starbucks selling music and coffee machines, etc.), these seemingly quixotic businesses become potentially very large profit centers.

One way to develop the right mind-set is to study the business models that have been employed by other company founders—including both successes and failures. Some great companies have been launched by adapting a business model from one industry to another, or by tweaking a familiar and proven model in a way that unleashes a flood of new resources, customer demand, or technological creativity. In certain circumstances, it is possible to create a successful new company by simply altering one of the nine business model elements in the Business Model Canvas as applied by competing businesses in the same market sector— for example, by discovering and applying a new channel for delivering value to customers; by devising a new way of forging intimate, lasting relationships with customers; or by identifying ways of improving the cost structure of the business and thereby making it more profitable.*

Developing a Scalable Startup Business

The subtitle of this book is *25 Steps to a Scalable, High-Growth Business*, and the word **scalable** is included for a good reason. There are many enterprises that are successful, profitable, and contribute much to society,

---

* A great place to examine other companies' business models in an easily digestible form is businessmodelgallery.com, which has re-created over 100 well-known models in Business Model Canvas format. Browse through them by industry or type of company to be inspired.

but which would be unrealistic, unprofitable, or at least overly challenging for you to start building as a one-man or one-woman startup on your way to becoming a unicorn.*

If you are reading this book, then you are unlikely to be building a Death Star, opening a barbershop, or offering xylophone master classes in your living room. That's because, while those might be interesting opportunities, for different reasons none of them are scalable.

There are three characteristics that together make a startup business model truly scalable:

1. *You have to be able to start small.*

    Unless you happen to be the long-lost daughter of Emperor Palpatine, the odds are that you do not have enough capital to build your first Death Star, nor will you be able to raise the funds to do so.† The ideal startup is one that can be bootstrapped from its own early revenues—or at least funded from the founder's personal savings account.

2. *Your marginal costs must drop over time so that each additional dollar of revenue costs less than the previous dollar.*

    This is the core of what most people mean when they discuss business scalability. For example, Amazon's Kindle publishing business is scalable because, after the cost to Amazon of selling the first digital copy is taken into account, each additional copy is almost pure profit. In contrast, if you wanted to expand your barbershop, the second shop would cost you almost exactly as much as the first one (for rent, equipment, and barber salaries). Since no business is infinitely scalable (that is, there is no business where all costs drop to absolute zero), an associated consideration is relative scalability, which means that a business needs to be scalable over a longer range than its competitors.††

---

*A "unicorn" is a term coined by venture capitalist Aileen Lee, used to describe a company with a market capitalization of over $1 billion.

†In case you are curious, students at Lehigh University worked out that the cost to build the Death Star would be about $8,100,000,000,000,000 ($8.1 quadrillion), which is 13,000 times the world's GDP.

††For a longer discussion on scalability, see the article by my fellow New York angel investor Christian Mayaud at http://www.sacredcowdung.com/archives/2005/06/what_is_a_scala.html.

3. *Your scalability needs to be built into your business model, rather than relying on any special exogenous factors.*

Subway, for example, currently has 45,000 sandwich store locations around the world. And it is opening more than six new stores every single day, including weekends! It would not be able to do that if it had to find world-class cordon bleu chefs for each location. Similarly, if your business depends on recruiting a never-ending supply of xylophone virtuosos who are also good teachers, I'm afraid that it is simply not scalable.

2

Craft a Lean Business Plan to Serve as Your Venture's Road Map

MENTION THE TERM "business plan" and the image that likely comes to mind is a thick document generated by a business consultant for you to give to a banker or investor and then forgotten about. But since these days everyone worships at the altar of the lean startup, it's common knowledge that a business plan is old-school and completely useless. All you need is a slide deck and a great team, right?

Wrong! That's because, while you weren't looking, the old-school business plan was superseded by something that is critically important, intended for you instead of other people, developed by you instead of other people, and constantly reviewed and updated. It is called "The Lean Business Plan," and in this chapter I will (with permission) borrow liberally from the work of Tim Berry—the world's leading expert on business planning—to give you a quick overview. For a complete hands-on lesson, you will want to read Tim's definitive book, *Lean Business Planning* (Motivational Press, 2015, and LeanPlan.com), which is available both in book form and for free as a series of detailed posts on his website.

The Principles of Lean Business Planning

1. Do Only What You'll Use.

Lean business means avoiding waste and doing only what has value. That means starting with a lean plan instead of a giant document, and continuing with a planning process involving regular review and revision. You keep it lean because it's easier, better, and, in practice, really all you're going to use.

The lean plan is about what is supposed to happen, when it is supposed to happen, who does what, how much it costs, and how much money it generates. It is a collection of decisions, lists, and forecasts that does not necessarily exist as a single document somewhere. You use it to track performance against your plan, review your results, and revise regularly so the plan is always up-to-date. It will be more useful if it is gathered into a single place, but it doesn't have to be. And it is only as big as you need for its business function.

The main output—and therefore the main purpose—of the lean business plan is a better business. Forget the additional descriptions and verbiage for outsiders until you need them. Wait for that until you have what Tim calls a "Business Plan Event," where someone else needs to understand where you're going. At that point, you can take your core updated plan and add a small bit of contextual and formatting material, and you'll be all set.

You need to know your market extremely well to run your business. What you do not have to do, however, is to include everything you know about it in your lean business plan.

Your lean plan is about what's going to happen, and what you are going to do. It's about business strategy, specific milestones, dates, deadlines, forecasts of sales and expenses, and so forth. It is not a term paper.

2. It's a Continuous Process, Not Just a Plan.

Lean business planning isn't about a plan that you do once. Like lean manufacturing and lean startups, it's a process of continuous improvement.

With lean planning, your business plan is always a fresh, current version. You never finish a business plan, heave a sigh of relief, and congratulate yourself that you'll never have to do that again. With lean planning, the plan is smaller and streamlined so you can update it easily and often, at least once a month. Your lean plan is much more useful than a static plan because it is always current, always being tracked and reviewed, frequently revised, and a valuable tool for managing.

Because of this, a business plan is not a single thing. It's not something you can buy, or find prewritten. You don't do it and forget it, and you can't have one written for you. If you don't know your plan intimately, then you don't have a plan.

3. It Assumes Constant Change.

One of the biggest and most pervasive myths about planning is that it reduces flexibility. In fact, when done the right way, it builds flexibility. Lean business planning manages change. It is not threatened by change.

Running a business effectively requires minding the details but also watching the horizon. It's a matter of keeping your eyes up (looking at what's happening on the field around you) and your eyes down (dealing with the ball), at the same time.

4. It Empowers Accountability.

It is much easier to be friends with your coworkers than to manage them well. Every startup founder has to deal with the problem of management and accountability. Lean business planning sets clear expectations and then follows up on results. It compares results with expectations. People on a team are held accountable only if management actually does the work of tracking results and communicating them to those responsible.

In good teams, the negative feedback is in the metric itself. Nobody has to scold or lecture, because the team participated in generating the plan, and the team reviews it. Good performances make people proud and happy; bad performances make people embarrassed. It happens automatically.

It is important, however, to avoid the "crystal ball and chain." Sometimes—actually, often—metrics go sour because assumptions have changed or unforeseen events occur. You need to manage these times collaboratively, separating the report from the results. Your team members will see that, believe in the process and continue to contribute.

5. It's Planning, Not Accounting.

One of the most common errors in business planning is confusing planning with accounting, and this is true for lean planning too. Although they look like accounting statements, your projections are just projections. They are always going to be off, one way or another. The purpose of projections isn't to guess the future perfectly, but rather to set down expectations and then connect the links between spending and revenue. Think of it like this: Accounting goes from today backward in time, in exact detail. Planning goes forward into the future, in ever-increasing summary and aggregation.

The reports that come from accounting—called statements—must accurately summarize the actual transactions that happened in the past. But projections, unlike financial statements, are educated guesses about the future. They aren't reports of a database of actual transactions. While accounting reports on records are in a database, for projections we guess what the totals might be.

So don't try to imagine all the separate future transactions in your head and then report on them. Estimate the totals. That's not only easier but better as well. It's a better match to how the projections help you manage, and how we humans deal with numbers.

How to Make a Lean Business Plan

1. Set Your Strategy.

If you've been following this book so far, you will be well on your way to having defined your venture's strategy because that's what you worked through in the last chapter with the Business Model Canvas.

You should now have a clear focus on the core of your business that will be used as the context as opportunities arise and decisions need to be made. It is in the entrepreneurial DNA to want to enter every new market to please everyone. But a good strategy summary helps to frame new opportunities correctly without emotion.

Finally, the strategy as it currently stands, as well as potential revisions in response to real-world conditions, should be reviewed in the monthly review sessions that are an integral part of lean business planning.

2. Plan Your Tactics to Implement the Strategy.

You should think of your business plan as a pyramid, with strategy at the top, tactics in the middle, and concrete specifics at the base. The middle of the pyramid, which connects the *whys* to the *whats*, is your tactical plan.

When it comes to your lean plan, the tactics should be as simple as possible—ideally just bullet point references. Don't worry about writing descriptions and explanations or compiling background information until you have a real business need to explain them to outsiders. Do worry about thinking through your marketing and product plans, and planning them well.

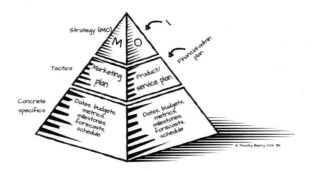

Figure 2.1   The Lean Plan Pyramid

Marketing Tactics   Marketing, in essence, is getting your customers to know, like, and trust you. To do that, you must understand them inside and out. Know how and where to find them, how to help them find you, and how to present your business to them in the way that best matches your strategy and business offering. You have to make choices about pricing, messaging, distribution channels, social media, sales activities, and so forth. For your lean plan, these are mainly bullet points—for your internal use only.

Product/Service Tactics   Product and service tactics are the decisions you make about pricing, packaging, service specifications, new products or services, sourcing, manufacturing, software development, technology procurement, trade secrets, bundling, etc. Your lean plan contains your decisions on these items as bullet points. You probably already know your tactics by heart so all you have to do is list them briefly in your lean business plan.

Other Tactics   Tactics often include financial tactics, team building, hiring, recruitment tactics, or the logistic tactics related things such as taking on a new office or manufacturing space. Tactics are easier to recognize than to define. Focus on content and what's supposed to happen. Think of tactics as absorbing the traditional marketing plan, product plan, and financing plan. Your next step will be to set these tactics into a plan with concrete milestones, performance metrics, lists of assumptions, and so on.

3. The Concrete Specifics

Once you have the strategy and tactics clear, it's the specifics you need to track progress, identify problems, and make changes. These include milestones, measurements, assumptions, and a schedule for regular review and revisions.

Review Schedule   The single most important component of any business plan—lean, traditional, or any other kind—is a review schedule. This sets the plan into the context of management. It makes it clear to everybody involved (even if that's just you) that the plan will be reviewed and revised regularly. All the people charged with executing a business plan must know when the plan will be reviewed and by whom. This helps make it clear that the plan will be a live management tool, not something to be put away on a shelf and forgotten.

Identify and List Assumptions   Identifying assumptions is important for getting real business benefits from your business planning. Planning is about managing change, and in today's world change happens very fast. Assumptions solve the dilemma about managing consistency over time without banging your head against a brick wall.

Assumptions may be different for each company. There is no set list. What's best is to think about the assumptions as you build your twin action plans.

If you can, highlight product-related and marketing-related assumptions. Keep them in separate groups or separate lists. The key here is to be able to identify and distinguish later (during your regular reviews and revisions) between changed assumptions and the difference between planned and actual performance. You don't truly build accountability into a planning process until you have a good list of assumptions that might change.

Milestones   There is no real plan without milestones. Milestones are what you use to manage responsibilities, to track results, and to review and revise. Without tracking and reviewing, there is no management and no accountability.

Just as you need tactics to execute strategy, so too you need milestones to execute tactics. Look for a close match between tactics and milestones.

Take your milestones list and categorize what's supposed to happen—and when—for ongoing tactics related to products, services, marketing, administration, and finance. These include launch dates, review dates, prototype availabilities, advertising, social media, website development, programs to generate leads, and traffic. These milestones set the plan tactics into practical, concrete terms, with real budgets, deadlines, and management responsibilities. They are the building blocks of strategy and tactics. And they are essential to your ongoing plan (vs. actual management and analysis), which is what turns your planning into management.

Give each milestone the following:

- Name
- Date
- Budget
- Person responsible
- Expected performance metric
- Relationship with specific tactics and strategy points

Milestones Table

Milestone	Due Date	Who's Responsible	Tactics, Details
Reconfigure social media accounts	Completed	Terry	Marketing tactics
Investigate inventory turns	Completed	Garrett and Leslie	Financial review
Meet with Caroline to review market strategy	Completed	Garrett and Terry	
Top 10 customer list	November 13, 2014	Terry	Tactic: focus
Social media program	January 14, 2015	Terry	Let's make sure we're all on the same page with the new year. Social media priorites, context, emphasis, specific plans.
Monthly review	February 19, 2015	Garrett	
Spring promotion plans	March 18, 2015	Terry	Bicycle season coming again. Review general marketing, specific sales and event schedules.
Host bike repair workshop	May 02, 2015	Terry	Tactic: more per customer
Summer marketing programs	May 20, 2015	Terry	Time to establish specific social media content and events for the summer. Participation in community bicycle events.
Summer finance strategy	May 20, 2015	Leslie	Annual financial checkup on cash flow, working capital, and financial needs during the summer slow season.
Review summer inventory plan	June 20, 2015	Garrett	Financial review
Back-to-school programs	August 19, 2015	Garrett	Special sales, promotions, events, and social media spin for the next school year
Annual strategy review session	October 07, 2015	Garrett	SWOT session, strategy and tactics review.

Figure 2.2   Sample Lean Plan Milestone Table

Metrics   Developing performance metrics is a critical part of developing accountability, one of the principles of lean planning. Make metrics an explicit part of your lean plan. Show them to the management team as part of your planning, and then show the results again and again during your monthly review meeting. Management often boils down to setting clear expectations and following up on results. Those expectations are the metrics.

The most obvious metrics are in financial reports: sales, cost of sales, expenses, and so on. However, with good lean planning, you can look for metrics throughout the business, in addition to what shows up in the financial reports. For example, marketing generates metrics on websites, social media, e-mails, conversions, visits, leads, seminars, advertisements, media placements, etc. Sales should track calls, visits, presentations, proposals, store traffic, price promotions, and so on. Customer service has calls, problems resolved, and other measures. Finance and accounting have metrics that include collection days, payment days, and inventory turnover. Business is full of numbers to manage and to track performance. When metrics are built into a plan and shared with the management team, they generate more accountability and more management.

A going business is always revising its plan. Change is constant. Follow your review schedule monthly. A real business plan is never done. If your plan is done, your business is done.

Experts know that planning is *managing* change, and not *voided* by change. As your business evolves, so will your business plan. You will add pieces to fit your needs. You will need to add product and marketing information to coordinate development, deployment, messaging, and timing. You will have to add to your financials to account for loans and capital equipment, which become part of a balance sheet.

The normal lean planning process is what Tim Berry calls the PRRR cycle—"plan, run, review, and revise." It is a lean planning version of the traditional lean business technique, and is one of the most critical tools in managing your high-growth startup.

The workable lean business plan is the first step in a planning process that will help you steer your business and optimize your management to be sure your business does what you want. Follow up with the review schedule: review plan vs. actual results every month, and keep your plan alive and growing. Keep it lean, and keep it live.

3

Find and Know Your Competitors

IN PLANNING AND LAUNCHING your startup, it is important to develop a clear, detailed sense of the companies that you will be competing with. Customers almost never make a buying decision in a vacuum. Instead, either consciously or unconsciously, they measure the value to them of a particular product or service by comparing similar offerings from one or more competing firms. Doing this as a company founder is known as competitive analysis and should be an ongoing activity for every business.

Identifying Your Competitors

You may think that you are familiar with most of the leading competing firms, particularly if you are launching a business in a field in which you've already worked. However, in this era of fast startups and the long tail of entrepreneurship, I can virtually guarantee that you have competitors about whom you don't have a clue. To put things in perspective, there are currently over 500,000 startup companies on the Gust platform that are working with or seeking angel investors.

The odds that none of those startups is competitive with your startup is (quite literally) one in half a million! So before you get too cocky, check your knowledge and expand your awareness of competitors who may be off your radar screen by employing some or all of the following techniques:

Survey Potential Customers.   As part of the planning process before launching your business, consider conducting a survey of your potential customers. One topic to ask about is competing providers. Ask customers where they currently obtain the product or service you plan to offer, and use follow-up questions to measure their level of satisfaction and to identify ways in which you can improve on what's now available.

Look for Competitors' Advertisements and Marketing Efforts.   Scan all the relevant media and do a thorough online search. When you find ads or promotional mentions of competing goods or services, try to determine the value proposition being offered, the major points of differentiation, and their potential marketing weaknesses.

Attend Trade Shows, Conventions, Conferences, and Business Forums.   Seek out gatherings where companies like yours meet. If you are launching a business-to-business (B2B) company, find shows and conventions attended by companies like the ones you plan to sell to. It's likely that the firms you will be competing with will be present to market themselves to the attendees.

Join Industry Associations.   Almost every significant industry has one or more of these organizations. Consider joining those that are relevant to your marketplace. These can be great sources not just for competitive intelligence, but also for news about industry trends, educational and informational programs, and networking opportunities.

Evaluating the Competition

The second step is to learn as much as possible about your competitors, as well as to evaluate the strengths and weaknesses of your competitors' business models, which may be relevant and perhaps even crucial to their long-term competitive position. For example, one or more of the companies you compete with may be much larger and have significant revenue streams from products, services, or customer segments that are not directly competitive with you. These may give them an underlying financial strength that would make them harder to beat in a price war. Another may have figured out a way to reduce some of its costs to zero . . . or even less!

There are many ways to learn about your competitors. Here are a few competitive research techniques:

Conduct Shoe-Leather Research (or Let Your Fingers Do the Research). Visit competing companies and study their operations firsthand (if they're a brick-and-mortar company), or sign up for their product on their websites (if they're completely online). There's no substitute for direct observation and getting a personal "feel" for the way rival firms do business. The best way to get a sense of the customer experience is to actually *be* a customer—buy the competitor's offering and find out for yourself what the competitor's product quality, sales techniques, delivery processes, and customer services are like.

In doing this, it is very important to avoid deceptive practices. Don't lie about your identity, submit false documents, or do anything that might be ethically or legally questionable. If you personally are not a member of the target customer segment—for example, if you are older, younger, or a different sex from the typical potential customer—ask an employee, team member, friend, or family member to do the research for you.

Interview the Competitors' Customers. Try to find a number of people who have been using the competing product or service, and interview them to discover the strengths and weaknesses of the competitor. Ask the customers how they discovered the competing product, why they chose to use it, what they like and don't like about it, what other similar products they have tried, and what it would take to get them to change providers.

Read Online Reviews. Virtually every product or service will have detractors as well as fans, and the tenor of the reviews is likely to be a more accurate guide than the comments of individual users (who might be either "ringers" from the company, or customers with an unfair axe to grind.)

Talk with Present or Past Employees of Competing Businesses.   You can learn a lot about the product and service quality, customer relationships, management practices, and other characteristics of competing firms by interviewing those who have worked for them. Whatever industry or market in which you are operating you will find it is a small world, and you may find yourself networking with people who know the competing companies from the inside. You can find out a lot about those firms through open conversations, and without inducing anyone to violate confidentiality agreements or to betray proprietary information.

Examine Competitors' Online Hiring Practices.   Chances are good that you will be using online job posting sites, like Monster or Indeed, as part of your own recruiting practices. Take advantage of these sites as sources of information about the personnel activities and practices of your competitors. What types of people are they hiring? What background traits, educational qualifications, and professional skills do they seem to prize?

Study Professional and Business Websites, Such as Linkedin and Glassdoor.   Read the profiles, comments, blogs, and messages posted by professionals in your industry on social media sites dedicated to business. Many will contain clues—overt or subtle—about the culture, business practices, strategies, and methods of the companies with which you compete.

Common Mistakes in Competitive Analysis

As you gather competitive information from these and other sources, be as methodical, accurate, unbiased, and thorough as possible. Don't give extra weight to data that reinforces what you already want to believe. Researchers refer to this tendency as confirmation bias, and it is very easy to fall prey to this tendency without realizing it.

A sure sign of amateurism—even naiveté—in a business plan document is the claim "Our business has no competition." You may think this makes your business concept particularly attractive to potential investors, but actually the opposite is true. Remember those 500,000 other startups on Gust? A savvy investor knows that claiming you have no competition indicates that either you have failed to study the market carefully (and have simply overlooked the existence of competing firms), or you've developed a business concept that meets no genuine human need, and is therefore unlikely to attract customers. Keep in mind that, in addition to direct competitors, your business will be competing with other companies that are meeting the same underlying need or providing the same kind of value by using other methods.

It is easy to misidentify the array of companies with whom you compete if you define the competing firms too broadly—including companies that aim at a different customer segment, for example, or whose value proposition is so fundamentally different from yours that no customer is likely to find herself choosing between you and the competitor. Or you can make the mistake of defining the competing firms too narrowly, excluding companies whose offerings may be nominally different from yours, but that meet underlying customer needs that are fundamentally the same as yours.

To make sure you are focusing on true competitors (and only on true competitors), ask yourself the following question: Is this company's product or service something that a particular customer seeking to satisfy a particular need at a particular time could choose in place of a product or service from me? If the answer is yes, then you are dealing with a true competitor.

Developing a Competition Visualization

Once you've gathered information about your leading competitors, find a way to display it visually that will enable a quick and easy comparison between your offering and the offerings of your competitors.

Competitive Grid

The simplest way is a straightforward comparative grid of the competition, which you would fill in by ranking each competitor on a point scale (for example, from 10 highest to 1 lowest) to reflect its performance in a particular category (see Figure 3.1). The competitive grid simulates, in a schematic way, the decision process potential customers will go through. Most of those potential customers won't go to the trouble of creating a written competitive grid of their own, but many of them will have much of the same information in mind as they approach a buying decision. Drawing up a competitive grid will enable you to read the minds of potential customers and identify the strengths and weaknesses of your own offering. Studying the grid will tell you where you need to improve your product or service to ensure that it is at least as attractive as the others your potential customers are likely to consider.

Competitive Factors	Your Offering	Competitor A	Competitor B	Competitor C
Product Quality				
Product Price				
Ease of Purchase				
Service Quality				
Brand Reputation				
Operational Strengths / Weaknesses				
Access to Resources				

Figure 3.1   Competitive Grid

The competitive grid can also serve as a simple one-stop source for the information you need when you are drafting the section of your business plan that describes your main competitors and the advantages or disadvantages you face in doing battle with them.

Quadrant Chart

This is something that appears in many investor pitch decks because it makes crystal clear the two or three most important areas in which you intend to compete with others in the industry. It typically plots two important attributes against each other, and positions various competitors relative to each other (see Figure 3.2).

While this is sometimes useful to explain the market, all too often your company somehow winds up standing alone as the hero in the upper right quadrant. Be sure that you don't delude yourself when analyzing the competition.

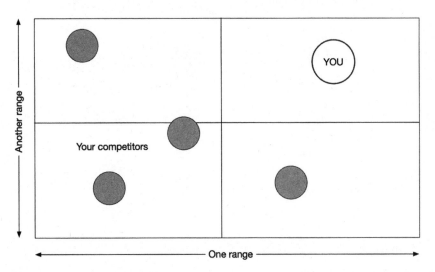

Figure 3.2   Quadrant Chart

Petal Chart

The newest competitor visualization is one suggested by Steve Blank in a 2013 blog post: the petal chart. This acknowledges that in a fast-moving, interconnected world, a company may have many different competitors across many different products and lines, and simple grids or quadrants won't fully capture the picture. Instead, the petal chart puts your company at the center of the universe, and positions all other competitors in "petals" based on the areas, products, or markets in which they are competing:

Figure 3.3   Petal Chart

Source: From "A New Way to Look at Competitors," Nov. 8, 2013, by Steve Blank; reprinted with permission from Steve Blank.

Professional Services and Online Tools for Competitive Analysis

Many consulting firms and specialized companies provide competitor analysis as a customized service. If the size, complexity, and growth potential of your startup justify it, you may want to consider engaging one of them to help you conduct a thorough and professional competitor analysis program.

For many startups, however—especially ones competing primarily in the online world—a more affordable alternative is to use cloud-based tools. These services can automatically track your competitors' websites, traffic, advertisements, social media profiles, and other online activities, and alert you to any major shifts in a competitor's profile. Among the leading online competitive analysis tools are kompyte.com, similarweb.com, SEMrush.com, and the free Alerts service from Google.

One unusual offering comes from eDataSource.com, which specializes in tracking competitors' e-mail marketing campaigns. The company regularly tracks 24 million daily e-mail campaigns from 50,000 brands and can provide fascinating intelligence about things your competitors are doing in your customers' e-mail inboxes.

Whether you keep your competitor analysis activities in-house or employ the resources of an outside company, you'll want to be sure your knowledge of the players in your market is detailed, accurate, and current. Knowing what your rivals are doing is the essential prerequisite to outcompeting them for the hearts—and the pocketbooks—of your customers.

4

Build Your Dream Team

STARTING AND BUILDING any business other than the tiniest one-person shop is a complicated task. Thus, the majority of businesses that aspire to become high-growth companies of the future are launched by a founding team of two, three, or more people. Combining the strengths, insights, experiences, talents, connections, and resources of a few people often gives a new business a greater chance of success than having it rest entirely on the shoulders of a talented single individual. That said, there is a real difference between founding a business and being part of the founding team.

The Crucial Talents Required to Launch a New Venture

Since Bill Hewlett joined Dave Packard in 1939 to create what became the world's largest personal computer company, there has arisen among the denizens of Silicon Valley an evergreen debate as to who is more important in starting a tech company: the techie or the business guy? Steve Jobs or Steve Wozniak? Bill Gates or Steve Ballmer? Jim Clark or Marc Andreessen?

Tech ventures represent a fraction of the thousands of new businesses launched every year, and a similar debate exists in most other business arenas, pitting the creative partner against the business-oriented partner. In the world of fashion, it's the designer vs. the marketing and manufacturing expert; in the food business, it's the chef or flavor expert vs. the processing and packaging expert; in tourism or hospitality, it's the front person who can charm high-rolling guests vs. the back room person who can handle logistics, facilities management, and other unglamorous details.

My response to this debate is to propose that it is time to reject the notion of the business guy or business gal entirely. The problem is that there are really three different components here—and like the classic three-legged stool, they are all essential for success, albeit with differing economic values. What makes for confusion is that the components can all reside in one person or in several. What gets people upset is that there are different quantities of the components available in the economic marketplace, and the law of supply and demand is pretty good about assigning a value to them.

Surprisingly, the components are not the traditional coding/business pieces, nor are they even coding/user interface/business/sales. Rather, the way I see them—from the perspective of a serial entrepreneur turned serial investor, listed in order of decreasing availability, are:

The Concept. A given business starts with an idea. While the idea may (and likely will) change over time, it has to be good on some basic level to succeed in the long run. How excited am I likely to be when I see a plan for a twenty-first-century buggy whip or yet another me-too social network? The base concept has to make some kind of sense given the technical, market, and competitive environment; otherwise nothing else matters. Good ideas are not hard to find. Not at all. There are millions of them out there. The key to making one of them into a homerun success brings us to:

Execution Skills. It is into this one bucket that all of the traditional pieces fall. Here is where you find the superb Rails coder, the world-class information architect, the consummate sales guy, the persuasive business development gal, and the brilliant CFO. Each of these functions is necessary to bring the good idea to fruition. In our fluid, capitalistic, free-market society, the marketplace is generally efficient about assigning relative economic value to each of these functional roles, based upon both the direct result of their contribution to the enterprise and their scarcity in the job market.

That is why it is not uncommon to see big-enterprise salespeople making high six-figure or even seven-figure salaries or commissions while a neophyte coder might be in the low five-figure range. Similarly, a crackerjack chief technology officer (CTO) might be in the mid six figures, but a kid doing inside sales may start at the low end of the spectrum. Coding, design, production, sales, finance, operations, marketing, and the like are all execution skills—and without great execution, success will be hard to come by.

As noted, each of these skills is available at a price; given enough money, it is possible to assemble an all-star team in each of the above areas to execute any good idea. That, however, will not be enough. Why? Because it is missing the final vital leg of the stool, the one that will ultimately reap the lion's share of benefits when success does come:

The Entrepreneur. Entrepreneurship is at the core of starting a company, whether tech based or otherwise. It is not any one of the functional skills above, but rather the combination of vision, passion, leadership, commitment, communication skills, hypomania, fundability, and, above all, willingness to take risks that brings together the forgoing pieces and creates from them an enterprise that fills a value-producing role in our economy. This function is the scarcest of all.

It is thus crucial to note that the entrepreneurial function can be combined in the same package as a techie (Bill Gates), a sales guy (Mark Cuban), a user interaction maven (Steve Jobs), or a financial guy (Mike Bloomberg).

For a successful company, one needs to bring together all of the above pieces, to realize that whatever functional skill set the entrepreneur starts out with can be augmented with the others, and to understand that the lion's share of the rewards will (after adjusting for the cost of capital) go to the entrepreneurial role, as has happened for hundreds of years.

Which Pieces Do You Have? Which Pieces Do You Lack?

Answering these questions will tell you who are the ideal partners to help you launch your business. The single most important question to ask is: Are *you* The Entrepreneur? While in our fast-moving, high-growth world many people would like to think of themselves as entrepreneurs, in reality, only a tiny, tiny percentage of people truly are. Despite the glorification of entrepreneurs on TV shows and in the blogosphere, there is nothing right, wrong, good, or bad about being—or not being—one. They're just . . . different. The crucial thing is that you be honest with yourself, because correctly answering this fundamental question will let you know the type of cofounder(s) you are seeking, and will set the venture up for success. Getting it wrong, however, will at best cause seriously painful restructurings down the road, and at worst doom the enterprise from the outset.

The best description of what the life of the entrepreneurial founder is really like, I've ever seen was written as a Quora answer by Paul De-Joe, the founder of Ecquire.com:

> Very tough to sleep most nights of the week. Weekends don't mean anything to you anymore. Closing a round of financing is not a relief. It means more people are depending on you to turn their investment into 20 times what they gave you.
>
> It's very difficult to "turn it off." But at the same time, television, movies and vacations become so boring to you when your company's future might be sitting in your inbox or in the results of a new A/B test you decide to run.
>
> You feel guilty when you're doing something you like doing outside of the company. Only through years of wrestling with this internal fight do you recognize how the word "balance" is an art that is just as important as any other skill set you could ever hope to have. . . .
>
> You start to respect the duck. Paddle like hell under the water and be smooth and calm on top where everyone can see you. You learn the hard way that if you lose your cool you lose.

You always ask yourself if I am changing the world in a good way? Are people's lives better for having known me? . . .

You start to see that the word "entrepreneur" is a personality. It's difficult to talk to your friends that are not risking the same things you are because they are content with not pushing themselves or putting it all out there in the public with the likelihood of failure staring at you everyday (*sic*). You start to turn a lot of your conversations with relatives into how they might exploit opportunities for profit. Those close to you will view your focus as something completely different because they don't understand. You don't blame them. They can't understand if they haven't done it themselves. It's why you will gravitate toward other entrepreneurs. You will find reward in helping other entrepreneurs. . . .

You have to be willing to sleep in your car and laugh about it. You have to be able to laugh at many things because when you think of the worse (*sic*) things in the world that could happen to your company, they will happen. Imagine working for something for two years and then have (*sic*) to throw it out completely because you see in one day that it's wrong. You realize that if your team is having fun and can always laugh that you won't die, and in fact, the opposite will happen: You will learn to love the journey and look forward to what you do everyday (*sic*) even at the lowest times. You'll hear not to get too low when things are bad and not to get too high when things are good and you'll even give that advice. But you'll never take it because being in the middle all the time isn't exciting and an even keel is never worth missing out on something worth celebrating. You'll become addicted to finding the hardest challenges because there's a direct relationship between how difficult something is and the euphoria of a feeling when you do the impossible.

You realize that it's much more fun when you didn't (*sic*) have money and that money might be the worst thing you could have as a personal goal. If you're lucky enough to genuinely feel this way, it is a surreal feeling that is the closest thing to peace because you realize it's the challenges and the work that

(*continued*)

(*continued*)

you love. Your currencies are freedom, autonomy, responsibility, and recognition. Those happen to be the same currencies of the people you want around you.

You feel like a parent to your customers in that they will never realize how much you love them and it is they who validate you are not crazy. You want to hug every one of them. They mean the world to you.

You learn the most about yourself more than any other vocation as an entrepreneur. You learn what you do when you get punched in the face many many times. You learn what you do when no one is looking and when no one would find out. You learn that you are bad at many things, lucky if you're good at a handful of things and the only thing you can ever be great at is being yourself which is why you can never compromise it. . . .

You become incredibly grateful for the times that things were going as bad as they possibly could. Most people won't get to see this in any other calling. When things are really bad, there are people that come running to help and don't think twice about it. . . . I will forever be in their debt I and you can never repay them nor would they want or expect to be repaid.

You begin to realize that in life, the luckiest people in the world only get one shot at being a part of something great. Knowing this helps you make sense of your commitment.

Of all the things said though, it's exciting. Every day is different and so exciting. Even when it's bad it's exciting. Knowing that your decisions will not only affect you but many others is a weight that I would rather have any day than the weight of not controlling my future. That's why I could not do anything else.

Does this resonate with you? Or does this seem somewhere between scary and masochistic? If the former, then you may indeed be The Entrepreneur, and the partners you need to find are those whose strengths are in execution: coding, design, sales, marketing, and operations. But if you are the latter, you may find that you are better suited to the role of a cofounder, and the partner you need to find is the crazy entrepreneurial CEO. In either case, as founder or cofounder, you had better be prepared to sacrifice everything else in your life for the years it will take to establish your company. Remember, no one ever promised this would be easy.

Establishing Expectations Among the Members of Your Founding Team

Before you and your would-be cofounders embark on a startup together, you'll face some tough challenges that are as much personal, psychological, and emotional as they are business-related.

If you are hoping to launch your new business in partnership with one or more people you consider friends, there is a hard truth you need to face: Be prepared to lose the friendship. Starting a business is one of the most emotionally draining activities you can possibly engage in, right up there with marriage and parenting. Given the odds that the new startup will fail (a majority do), try to envision whether your friendship could survive a bankruptcy. It's not necessarily essential that it can (we're not talking about going into business with your spouse), but understand that bankruptcy is a real possibility.

For the rest, do your best to ensure that everyone is coming to the table with similar expectations. These expectations should include answers to the following questions:

- What kind of business are we launching? What is our profit-making model? What kind of growth expectations do we have?
- What role will each member of the founding team play in building the business?
- How much time will each member of the team be expected to contribute? Is this a full-time work commitment for all of the team members?
- What other resources will each member of the team contribute? These resources could include specific talents and skills; individually owned pieces of intellectual property (such as product designs, software code, written documents, patents, copyrights, trademarks, and so on); personal contacts and networking abilities; access to physical assets (such as work spaces, machinery, or tools); and financial resources.

- How will decisions affecting the business be made? Ultimately, even in equal partnerships, one member of the founding team must have the ultimate decision-making authority, otherwise the company risks being locked in indecision . . . and that is the one thing it cannot afford. So which member of the founding team will be the entrepreneurial CEO?
- What personal goals does each member of the founding team bring to the business? How many months or years does each member expect to remain engaged in the business? How do the team members' personal life goals fit with the growth expectations for the business?

In addition, you'll need to develop a clear understanding about how the rewards from the business will be divided among the founding members. In particular, you'll need to decide how equity in the business will be shared. We'll discuss equity allocation and the company's capitalization in greater detail in Chapter 5, but for now, think of equity as "ownership and control of the company." So dividing up equity in a way that is fair and creates effective incentives for all members of the founding team is one of the toughest challenges you will face in the early days of your business.

Caution: It is absolutely imperative that all cofounders have "reverse vesting" on whatever equity they are allocated. This means that even though ownership of the company starts out being divided up among the founding team, if one or more of them leaves the venture before it reaches its full flowering, the company is able to recapture part of their equity. While this may initially seem unfair to the founders, I have seen more companies blow up because they didn't have this in place than for any other reason.

In considering the questions of time commitment, compensation, equity, and other contributions, everything needs to be thoughtfully and honestly customized for each member of the founding team. Everyone can have different goals—that's fine—but differences need to be laid on the table and discussed fully and openly. Once the business is under way, if the team members are surprised to discover that one person is working at the new business 24/7 while another is working only 4 hours a day, the team is likely to fracture into arguments and recriminations. Therefore founders of a startup need to work hard to be honest with one another about what exactly they are willing to commit.

At the same time, it is desirable at this early stage of the process to leave room for some flexibility in your founding plans. The necessary balance is complicated to reach. On the one hand, if you don't make things explicitly clear up front, you are begging for a future disaster by kicking the can down the road. On the other hand, if everything is set in stone before you start, you may find yourself with a completely untenable structure even 6 or 12 months out, when it becomes clear that not everyone is contributing as much as you envisioned at the outset.

One of the best "agreements to agree" for cofounders that I've seen is the Founder Accord from McCormick & O'Brien, which is included, with their permission, in Appendix F. It is intended to provide entrepreneurs with the comfort they need to take risks, while sparing them the effort and expense required to complete a customary corporate formation and capitalization before knowing that they actually have a viable business, or have even formed a company. Note, however, that it should not be viewed as a substitute for the long-form legal documents that will memorialize the points sketched out in it (any more than a term sheet is a substitute for customary financing documents). It is a temporary fix—the intermediate step between the proverbial handshake and a stack of legal documents. It may help create the conditions necessary to set the larger company formation process in motion, but it is not a substitute for that process.

Once you are clear that your business idea has the potential to turn into a company (not just a fanciful project), you absolutely, positively need to incorporate legally and structure a real company, as I'll discuss in Chapter 9.

5

Allocate the Equity in Your Startup

DEVELOPING AN EQUITY-SHARING plan that fairly recognizes, honors, and rewards the contributions of multiple cofounders is a challenge faced by every startup with more than one founder, and one that has probably caused more grief than any other issue. As such, there are many good blog posts and articles on the subject that can help provide perspective.[*]

Allocating Equity

The one thing that all these experts agree on is that the most obvious, simple, and seemingly objective way to divide the equity in a startup business—namely, an equal split of the equity among the members of

---

[*]"DO NOT Split Equity Between Founders Equally" by Martin Zwilling (http://www.businessinsider.com/splitting-startup-equity-for-your-piece-of-the-pie-2010-11), "The Only Wrong Answer Is 50/50" by Dan Shapiro (http://www.geekwire.com/2011/wrong-answer-5050-calculating-cofounder-equity-split/), and "Founder's Dilemmas: Equity Splits" by Eric Ries (http://www.startuplessonslearned.com/2012/04/founders-dilemmas-equity-splits.html).

the founding team—is the wrong way. Instead, the founder(s) need to do the fairest job they can of assigning relative value to what everyone is bringing to the table.

One factor that makes this difficult is the huge variation in what differing team members may contribute. Founder A may be the creator of the original business concept. Founder B may have the greatest level of industry knowledge and experience, and the practical skills required to turn the concept into a working reality. Founder C may be willing and able to work incredibly hard at the business, keeping the company running under tough circumstances and providing a huge amount of "sweat equity." Founder D may provide strong personal connections to key business partners who can make the difference between success and failure. And Founder E may invest a significant amount of personal money that helps get the business off the ground. How do you compare and balance these varying contributions and value them appropriately?

Unfortunately, there are no hard-and-fast rules for resolving this dilemma. For example, there is no specific valuation ratio between sweat equity and cash in a venture, and that's not even a good way to think about the issue. The bottom line is that cash is cash is cash, and everything else is not cash. The reason for this is that cash is *fungible*, which means it can be interchanged for everything else, from programming skills to vacations on the Riviera. Other things, such as your particular time and effort, are not.

A better way to think about this is to separate two aspects of the "sweat" that one puts into a new venture. These are critically different and have very different economic attributes attached to them.

The first is the entrepreneurial value of the founder(s) in a new venture. This is what happens when someone starts an enterprise and creates something of value. If you start a company and then raise a round of angel investment at, say, a $2,000,000 valuation, the entrepreneurial value of the time and effort it took you to get to that point is . . . $2,000,000. The value created has nothing to do with the quantified effort that it took to get there. You might have created that value by slaving 18 hours a day, seven days a week for five years (in which case, the value of the sweat equity is $8.70 per hour), or you might have created that value by having a brilliant concept, execution plan, and team that you pulled together in two weeks of leisurely work (in which case, the value of the sweat equity is $25,000 per hour).

The second component is the replacement cost of the specific skills and effort that are involved in the particular work. If the same tasks could have been achieved by paying a programmer (or marketer or part-time CFO) $2,000 on a short-term contract, then that is what the replacement cost value of the work would be.

In practice, once a company has been funded and a valuation established, sweat equity contributed after that point is usually compensated based on its replacement cost number, that is, the salary the employee would have been paid if the cash had been on hand. The employee either is credited with that amount of equity or is credited with that amount of equity plus a bonus (say, 25 percent or 50 percent extra) in recognition of the fact that the employee is willing to take the risk of never being paid if things don't work out.

This is just one example of the complicated, somewhat subjective calculus involved in figuring out how to reward the varying contributions of members of the founding team.

Frank Demmler has worked up a model for doing this in a blog post titled *"The Founders' Pie Calculator."**

Demmler suggests looking at each of the factors that should be considered, as follows:

Idea. The company wouldn't exist if it weren't for the original idea, and that is certainly worth something, but there's a lot of truth in the saying, "A successful business is 1 percent inspiration, 99 percent perspiration."

Business Plan Preparation. The development of an initial business plan [or useful Business Model Canvas] is a difficult and time-consuming effort. To pull together and organize all the thoughts of the founding team—fill in blanks, identify and reconcil differences, and produce a document that captures the essence of the business and helps to persuade banks, investors, board members and others to support the company is a mammoth undertaking, as anyone who has done it will attest. Again, the

---

* https://www.andrew.cmu.edu/user/fd0n/35 Founders' Pie Calculator.htm.

plan is a necessary element of starting the business, but execution against the plan is where the real value lies.

Domain Expertise.   To what degree do you and your partners have meaningful experience in the [industry] of your business? Knowing the industry, having relevant experience, and having a Rolodex of accessible contacts can greatly improve the company's probability of success and will speed its growth rate. Otherwise, it will take longer to get commercial traction and you will have to pay for these assets, usually by hiring someone and including equity in their compensation package.

Commitment and Risk.   You've probably heard the old saying that "a chicken is *involved* with a ham-and-egg breakfast, but a pig is *committed*." Similarly, the founders who join the company full-time and are committed to making it a success are much more valuable than founders who are going to sit on the sidelines and be cheerleaders. In addition, the opportunity cost for those who join the company instead of pursuing another career is not trivial.

Responsibilities.   Who is going to do what? Who is going to stay up at night when you can't make tomorrow's payroll? Where does the buck stop?

Analyzing each area of contribution is the first step in drawing up an appropriate equity-sharing arrangement. The next step is assigning a weighting value to each factor, assessing each founder on each factor, and, finally, working out the math. The result (explained in more detail in Frank's post) will give you a reasonable starting point for determining a fair equity split. In a typical case, you might end up with a table that looks something like Figure 5.1.

As Demmler's system suggests, splitting the equity pie among members of the founding team is not a minor undertaking. Take the time to do it carefully and as accurately as possible, and make sure you talk through the rationale behind the division as thoroughly and openly as you can. Otherwise, you will probably pay a price months or years later—when member(s) of the team reveals that he or she has never been satisfied with the equity split and has harbored resentment and anger the whole time. Many a company has foundered as the result of such a conflict.

	Founder 1	Founder 2	Founder 3	Founder 4	
Idea	70	21	21	0	
Business Plan	6	16	2	0	
Domain Expertise	30	20	30	20	
Commitment & Risk	0	49	0	0	
Responsibilities	0	36	0	0	
Total Points	106	142	53	20	321
% of Total	33.0%	44.2%	16.5%	6.2%	100.0%

Figure 5.1   Sample Founder Equity Table

Equity Control and the Rights of the Founder

Many business founders feel strongly about wanting to control the business as long as possible—or at least to retain a large enough share of equity so that they can exercise a significant degree of control (as well as commanding a major share of the financial rewards generated by the company's growth).

Unfortunately, there is no practical way that a founder can guarantee that he or she will retain a given share of the company's equity throughout its growth. In fact, the concept of "percentage of equity ownership" is probably the single most misunderstood notion in the startup world because it is used by entrepreneurs when they are really talking about something else. Technically, the phrase itself has zero meaning other than as a bald accounting fact. It has nothing to do with economics, control, employment, value, or anything else . . . which means that entrepreneurs who tie themselves in knots aiming for a certain percentage of equity are focusing on the wrong thing.

So, let's put aside this specific issue and look instead at the two major issues usually conflated with equity percentages.

Control

Ultimate affirmative control of a company, including which strategic direction it chooses, the decision to sell itself to an acquirer, who the CEO is, what the CEO is paid—in short, everything—rests with the company's board of directors. Regardless of what percentage of equity the founder owns, if he controls a majority of seats on the company's board, he gets to decide who the CEO is going to be (including hiring himself). Period. The number of members of a company's board is determined by its corporate documents, and technically each share of common stock gets one vote for each seat.

In practice, as you will see in a later chapter, every investment round overrides this "one common share, one vote" structure by way of a vehicle called a shareholders' agreement. That agreement, which is signed by all significant shareholders as part of the closing, provides that everyone will vote for directors according to an agreed-upon set of terms.

However, it is critically important to understand that the investors in any serious investment round (not necessarily a friends and family round, but certainly a Series Seed or Series A from professional angels or venture capitalists) will unquestionably also have *negative control provisions* as a means to protect their investment from the actions of a board they don't control. This means that—regardless of what the board chooses to do *affirmatively*—there are specified things that will require the agreement of the investors (either all the investors voting as a class or the approval of the director they appoint to the board). This means that the investors will effectively have veto power over things like:

- Selling, liquidating, dissolving, or winding up the affairs of the company
- Amending, altering, or repealing any provision of the certificate of incorporation or bylaws
- Creating any other class of equity having rights, preferences, or privileges senior to or on parity with the current investors
- Increasing the authorized number of shares
- Purchasing, redeeming, or paying any dividend prior to the investors
- Authorizing the company to take on any debt greater than $X

In the actual investment documents, these provisions will be spelled out carefully and clearly, so there is no wiggle room or way to game the system. In the real world of early stage companies, though, these protective provisions can often become affirmative control provisions when the going gets tough . . . provided that the investors are willing to play hardball. If, for example, the company needs to take in another round of investment, but the investors want the company to pivot its business model, they can simply refuse to approve accepting the new investment unless the board votes to pivot the model.

Which brings us to the second big issue underlying equity ownership.

Value

The important thing to understand about the relationship between equity percentages and economic value is that 10 percent of a company worth $1 million is worth less than 1 percent of a company worth $100 million. So if you're bringing on board a world-class partner, or taking in an investment that brings in money and expertise to help the company grow to that level, the trade-off is good, even if the founder's equity percentage is significantly reduced. The secret is that the *value* of the reduced percentage is actually a much larger number.

The bottom line: Don't worry about specific equity percentages in the case of a startup. Instead, sit down with your cofounder(s), lawyer, and mentors and discuss what things are most important to you. Making money? Remaining in control? Having the title of founder/CEO/chairman? Bringing in a value-adding partner? Once you know what you want, you can negotiate rationally and calmly for your interests while being flexible on your positions.

6

Build a Minimum Viable Product and Validate Your Plan with Customers

By this point, the word "lean" has been used so frequently and in so many contexts that you may be forgiven for thinking that it is meaningless. It is actually quite the opposite. The reason the term—and the thinking that it represents—has swept the startup world is that it makes fundamental sense. Originally used to describe innovative manufacturing practices at Toyota in the 1980s, the approach was developed for the startup world by Steve Blank and brought to popular attention by Eric Ries in his best-selling book* and subsequent series. The core philosophy of the Lean Methodology boils down to a loop that cycles through three steps:

Build.

Measure.

Learn.

Instead of spending months or years thinking and planning and writing about a business (that's what "wantrepreneurs" do), the essence

---

*Eric Ries, *The Lean Startup* (Crown Business, 2011).

of the Lean Startup Methodology is to start by just getting off your seat and doing something! Based on the initial modeling that you've done with the Business Model Canvas or the lean business plan, you'll come up with a testable hypothesis for a particular product designed for a particular market. You'll get something into the real world (even if it's only something that looks like your product) and see how people react to it. You'll measure what happens, adjust your approach, and go back into the market. With a few cycles of this, you will have figured out the perfect fit . . . at which point, you'll be ready to scale.

Conducting Marketplace Experiments

One of the best ways to learn about what your potential customers really want is to test the appeal of your proposed product or service through carefully planned experiments. As I discussed in Chapter 1, the lean approach to business development is built around the concept of using experiments to test a business idea and rapidly, inexpensively modify it as dictated by real-world outcomes.

The steps in the marketplace experimentation process (as defined by Eric Ries) include the following:

Create a Minimum Viable Product (MVP).

Rather than engage in a lengthy, painstaking process to make your product as perfect as possible, start the experimentation process by creating a simple, basic version of the product that is suitable for testing the core idea with customers. Depending on the nature of your product, the nature of the minimum viable product (MVP) will vary. It may be a prototype—a simple version of the product with its essential features. It may be a video demonstration of the product that can be made available online, enabling customers to react to what they see (either with interest or disdain).

Another alternative is what Ries calls a concierge MVP, which is a custom-made version of the product whose creation and delivery is unrealistically labor-intensive. For example, Ries tells the story of a startup called Food on the Table that uses software algorithms to develop weekly menus and grocery shopping plans based on customer preferences, then link them to supermarkets that deliver the products to customer homes. To test the concept, the startup team created a concierge version of the service that required a company employee to perform all the individual steps by hand. This would be an absurdly expensive way to serve a significant number of customers, but the point of the concierge MVP experiment was simply to test whether customers would like the service and to identify ways it could be improved. Once these issues were resolved, the team set about bringing the product to scale through automated, high-tech tools.

Test the Value Hypothesis.

The value hypothesis is the belief that customers will find the product attractive, useful, and desirable—in short, valuable. The way to test this is by offering the MVP version of your product for purchase to a select group of potential customers and seeing how many people buy it. You can offer your product for sale through any channel that makes sense, but preferably the same one you intend to use once your company is running at full blast—online sales and distribution, retail sales through brick-and-mortar stores, business-to-business sales through visiting sales reps, or what have you.

At this point, remember that it is more important to see if anyone is *willing* to pay for your product than if he or she actually *does* pay for it. That means you can test your value hypothesis without even having a product! One approach that many lean startups take is to craft a clear, pithy online advertisement and then place it alongside targeted keywords through paid search engine marketing. Clicking on the ad leads the customer to a landing page, where you describe the product, perhaps provide illustrations and pricing, and include a "Buy Now" button. At that point (since of course you don't yet actually have a product), the prospective purchaser can be asked to sign up to be notified as soon as the product is available.

With no cost involved on your part, it is possible to construct elaborate test campaigns with different marketing messages, different price points, and different value propositions. You can easily create your own landing page with a simple web page editor, but there are several online services that specialize in managing the process for you, including QuickMVP.com, Instapage.com, landerapp.com, Optimizely.com, and Unbounce.com.

While some people may view this as a form of bait and switch, at best it will give you a mailing list of interested prospective purchasers, and at worst it simply costs the purchaser a minute or two of time.

Test the Growth Hypothesis.

The growth hypothesis is the belief that, once a few customers discover and use the product, their enthusiasm will spread to others—through word of mouth, recommendations, or online virality. The way to test this is by opening up the possibility of purchasing the MVP version of the product to a larger market of potential customers, and watching how many new customers buy it over a reasonable period of time—say, a few weeks.

Watch How Customers Actually Use the Product.

A powerful step in the marketplace experimentation process is to watch customers using the product. How you accomplish this will vary depending on the nature of the product. The key is to pay close attention to how the product is used, to make detailed notes, and, in particular, to notice anything that is unexpected or surprising. You may discover that some features of the product go completely unnoticed or unused by some customers, which suggests that those features are poorly identified, inadequately explained, or simply unappealing. You may also discover that customers use the product in ways you never thought of, which may suggest new applications, and even new markets to be developed.

One way to gain insights into the attitudes, values, preferences, and beliefs of customers is by conducting surveys, whether in person, by telephone, or online. Keep the number of questions to a minimum to avoid discouraging participants; make sure the vocabulary used is clear and universally understandable; avoid writing questions in a way that suggests there is a right and a wrong answer; and, where appropriate, provide a simple answer scale that makes it easy for participants to respond quickly and precisely to any qualitative questions. There are a number of good online tools that can make customer surveys easier to conduct and analyze, including SurveyMonkey and Google Forms.

Anther way to measure the success of your MVP is through focus groups, in which you interview 5 to 10 customers at the same time. This can be a convenient way of gathering views from a group of people at once. The group discussions are recorded so that comments and observations by the participants can be studied later, and they are often facilitated by trained moderators (which can be expensive). With serious dedication, you can also try doing it yourself; the results can be interesting and sometimes valuable. But take them with a grain of salt. Focus groups have been criticized for encouraging groupthink, in which the entire group follows one or two particularly vocal or articulate participants rather than offering independent judgments more reflective of the broader population.

The focus group discussion should be carefully planned to focus on the key questions you want to investigate about your product. Typically, a focus group will last around an hour and a half and will sometimes be observed by researchers and members of a wider project team from behind a one-way mirror.

Nowadays, focus groups can be conducted online or via social media, which can be a more cost-effective approach than the traditional in-person method.

Iterate on Your Initial Product.

Regardless of how you measure the response to your initial product deployment or test, you will probably want to refine your product offering in some way. Then you can conduct a new experiment to test the new hypothesis you develop. If you keep the process simple you can do it rapidly—perhaps running through the entire cycle of defining your hypothesis, developing the MVP, conducting the market experiment, and analyzing the results within a few weeks. This can make it economically feasible for you to repeat the experimentation process as often as necessary to a point where you have a product that a large number of real-world customers respond positively. At this point, your business should be off to the races.

Later in the history of your company, there will be times when you will want to re-enter the experimentation phase—for example, when you develop a new product idea that you want to test, when sales of your existing product begin to falter, or when a new competitor enters the market and threatens to take away some of your customers. Customers and markets evolve continually, so smart, sustainable businesses make experimentation and learning a continual process, not just a one-time activity.

Along with online tools for creating and managing Business Model Canvases and lean business plans, there are some solid tools online for

helping you manage your lean startup cycles. LeanMonitor.com provides online tools that make it easy for you to apply the lean startup
approach to your business (including its experiment tool) as a way of
planning and conducting scientific tests to determine how a product
idea is resonating with customers. Other useful sites with online tools
supporting the lean cycle are LeanStack.com and LaunchPadcentral
.com.

The Wisdom of the Crowd

Over the past few years, the explosion of online, rewards-based crowdfunding sites, like Kickstarter and Indiegogo, has put a potent tool in
the hands of lean entrepreneurs with physical products. Running an
online crowdfunding campaign for your MVP can combine a complete
set of tests for your hypotheses into one nifty package, including product, value, and virality, with full seed funding thrown in as well . . . and
all before you've actually produced your MVP.

In your crowdfunding campaign listing, you can provide detailed
descriptions and prototype photos, offer different levels of rewards at
different price points, and track how many of your supporters pass on
word of the product to their friends. And you are not committing to
delivering the product unless you get enough interest (and purchase
commitments!) to make it economically feasible to go into production.

This type of crowdfunding (unlike the equity fund-raising I will
discuss in Chapter 21) can also be a great way to convince potential investors that the market for your product is viable. While most
crowdfunding campaigns are not successful, if you are using it to test
your lean idea, that could actually be a good thing. You will avoid
wasting effort and money developing a product that customers are not
willing to pay for. Although even the successful campaigns (and there
have been well over 100,000 of them) usually raise less than $10,000,
a growing number have successfully raised six, seven, and even eight
figures.

The ultimate example, of course, is Oculus Rift, the virtual reality headset that started as a Kickstarter campaign, raised $2.5 million
to fund its development and then was purchased by Facebook for $2
billion. (No, that's almost certainly not going to happen with your
product, but it's nice to know that it happened to someone . . .)

7

Establish Your Brand with Online Public Profiles

As you have seen in the preceding chapters, you can go a long way toward starting up your company without actually being a company. You can figure out your business model, start your lean planning process, research the competition, team up with potential cofounders, create your minimum viable product (MVP), and even track how customers react to it, all from your bedroom if you like.

But why stop there? Although you might not yet be incorporated (tackled in Part II) or actually taking money from customers, it's a good idea to establish an identity for your venture. That way, when people hear about the new thing you're working on, they can tell their friends, "Hey, take a look at Project X, it's really cool!" Besides, how can you be a startup CEO without a startup? Seriously, though, having an identity for your startup, whether or not you're actually a legal entity, means that you are in play. Employees might want to work for you, other companies might want to work with you, customers might beat down your door to buy from you . . . and if you're really hot, investors might even come calling.

There's an old joke in the software field that the very first thing an entrepreneur does with a new company is to design the T-shirt. But in fact, it's not a joke! The days of having to go to a Madison Avenue advertising agency for "corporate identity development" and pay Don Draper hundreds of thousands of dollars for a logo are gone. Instead, a quick web search will return over 20 million results for "logo design," of which 383,000 offer "free design services." So get yourself a nice logo, come up with a name for the company, and get going. (By the way, if you'd like to start out fancy with corporate logoware and swag, there is an entire industry just salivating to help you. Check out CafePress.com, TshirtExpress.com, Vistaprint.com, or CustomInk.com.)

Yes, You Need a Website

Because of the extraordinary amplification powers of the Internet, many scalable, high-growth businesses these days are Internet based; that is, they exist only on—and are critically empowered by—online technology. These include e-commerce platforms, online gaming and entertainment, enterprise software-as-a-service solutions, and many others. For these companies, the website IS their product and is fundamental to their existence. But what is just beginning to become apparent to off-line ventures is that a website is now fundamental to every other type of business as well. The universal assumption of every customer, supplier, potential partner, or prospective investor is that your business has a website, and that the website will fill every possible need that anyone interested in your business might have, 24 hours a day.

Websites vary enormously in scope and sophistication. At a minimum you are expected to have an *About* page that describes what you do, a *Contact* page so people can reach you, and a *Product* section so potential buyers can browse through your products and/or services at their leisure. If you are truly aiming for high growth and scalability, you will ultimately need much more, including pages dedicated to real-time, immediate customer service; online ordering (or reservations/booking for off-line ventures); account management; etc.

But for now, while working on your logo and T-shirt, be sure to get a bare-bones website up and running. One of the easiest and most powerful website creation tools for a wide variety of business types is the Squarespace.com platform. For a few dollars per month you can create and publish a complete, beautiful, mobile-optimized website, including unlimited bandwidth and storage, website metrics tracking, and e-commerce. They will even arrange a custom web domain for you (such as "NewCo.com") at no additional cost. Spend an afternoon working with one of its templates and you will create your toehold in cyberspace, available to anyone who wants to check you out.

(By the way, as nifty as its offering is, you're certainly not limited to Squarespace. Some other high-quality hosting partners you can check out are GoDaddy.com, Weebly.com, 1and1.com, and Wix.com.)

Help People Find Your Site

With your website up and running, you now need to be found. For the low-hanging fruit, spend a few minutes making sure that the major search engines (including Google, Bing, and Yahoo) know your website exists. You can submit your site's URL manually,* but you may find it easier to make use of one of the multisearch engine submission sites, such as selfpromotion.com. This platform gives you the opportunity to create the exact descriptions, keywords, and metadata by which you would like your site to be searchable. Then they will automate the submission process to a wide variety of search engines.

Help People Find Your Company

While the search engines are great at generic, horizontal searches for people searching for things like the products and services you offer, they are not necessarily the best tool for someone looking for information about your company. Because company searchers are often strategic partners, future employees, or potential investors, you want to create profiles for your new company on the most important directory sites where those people go searching. Some of these directories are

---

*https://www.google.com/webmasters/tools/submit-url;
http://www.bing.com/toolbox/submit-site-url.

wikis (that is, collaborative data sites) into which anyone can enter information; others are sites that conduct and present original research; still others offer public profiles that you (and only you) can edit and update. For a company looking to grow and scale, here are what I consider the most important platforms on which to create a profile:

CrunchBase

Originally created by the people behind the *TechCrunch* blog, and eventually acquired by AOL, this directory provides descriptions of 100,000 companies, primarily in the technology/online industry. While this site would not be appropriate for a restaurant, spa, or widget-manufacturing company, if you are in the tech-related world, you should definitely create a profile here. Note that CrunchBase is a wiki, which means that other people may add and update data about you over time . . . even if some of that is information you would prefer not to show or to be associated with your profile. You should make it a point to monitor your company's CrunchBase profile regularly, adding the latest information on your team, products, and financing, and deleting information that was incorrectly added by others.

LinkedIn

LinkedIn is best known as the ultimate professional resume website where you can find everyone's work history and see how you are connected to them. For businesses, it is a great way to tell your company's story, engage with followers in a more professional environment than Facebook, post career opportunities, and drive word of mouth at scale. Once you have created a company page on LinkedIn, your profile, and profiles of your employees, will be automatically connected to it through links on your personal profile pages. You can also use the site for blogging, active and passive job recruiting, and to develop a base of followers who can spread your messages and updates.

Glassdoor

This is a specialized web directory of companies in relation to their employees. It posts job listings that can help you recruit new employees, provides anonymous comparative (and detailed) salary surveys so that you can benchmark the salaries you are offering, and allows current and former employees to post anonymous reviews of your company . . . and you. While you can not get negative reviews taken down, what you can do is claim your company's profile yourself and be recognized as the company's official spokesperson. That allows you to control the general descriptive information about the company, see which users are viewing your company, and, most important, respond immediately to reviews.

Gust and AngelList

Finally, if you are planning to seek funding from angels or venture capital investors (or if you are thinking about applying to an accelerator program or business competition), there are two sites on which you should create investor-ready profiles. Unlike CrunchBase and Glassdoor, both of these give you control over your listing, including what information is public and what you want to share with investors or other authorized viewers. Gust (gust.com) and AngelList (angel .co) are used by many different participants in the business ecosystem to connect with each other. As of early 2016, roughly 200,000 companies and 25,000 accredited investors have created profiles on AngelList, and about twice as many of each have created profiles on Gust. In Chapter 21 we will explore using these platforms, and others, to actually raise funds for your venture. But for now, let's focus on creating a profile that will effectively position you in the eyes of potential investors. In both cases, you can upload information about your venture, products, team, business model, and so forth; choose what to display publicly; and choose what to make available only to specific potential investors whom you authorize. To illustrate I will walk you through creating a Gust profile, but the steps are similar for AngelList.

The first thing to notice is that your Gust profile starts out in stealth mode. That means you can spend as much time creating and revising it as you like, without it being visible to the public (although at any time you may choose to provide access to one or more specific potential investors). When you're ready to announce yourself to the world, the fun begins. Your Gust profile has two major areas. The first

Figure 7.1   Gust Public Profile

page (where you land when you start creating the profile) is the **public** page (see Figure 7.1). Once it is published, this is the ONLY page that the public will see. Therefore, what you want to put on this page is all the nonconfidential, cool stuff about your venture that you would like everyone to know.

The public page starts with eye candy for your fans, including a header image (don't forget to include one—it will help your profile stand out!), your logo, and an optional short video that can be your teaser or intro video for your website. The page also includes the basic information that will let people find you in public searches; information about your team, advisors, and investors; and, if you like, your social media links, such as Twitter and LinkedIn. Finally, it provides two opportunities to publicly position your pitch: short and shorter.

Once you have your page the way you like it, click the Publish Profile button at the top of the page, and voila! You will be discoverable. Your profile will be searchable from the main Gust directory, and will automatically be available to a wide range of sites and platforms that support entrepreneurship. Most notably, if you are in an area with an online entrepreneur ecosystem hub that is powered by Gust, such as New York City, London, or Boston, your profile will soon show up there as well.

At this point, you can close your browser and pat yourself on the back for a job well done. If investors come across your profile through browsing, searching, or having it referred by a mutual friend, and after viewing your public page are interested enough to want more information, all he or she needs to do is click on a button, and you will be informed of his or her interest and have a chance to respond immediately.

Note that the typical next step would be to share with the investor all of the plans, pitch deck, financials, and other confidential material that your company needs to provide to any investor with whom you're serious about discussing participation. That's the kind of data you will upload to the rest of your private profile . . . but since that is in the context of raising funds, we need to wait until Chapter 21 to come back and learn how best to reel in a hot investor.

8

Network Effectively Within the Entrepreneurial Ecosystem

WHILE IT MAY take a village to raise a child, every entrepreneur knows that founding a startup can be one of the most intensely personal and lonely challenges on the planet. As Tara Hunt wrote in her classic presentation "So You Wanna Do a Startup, Eh?":[*]

- Startups are hard.
- Startups are really hard.
- Startups are heartbreaking.
- Startups are soul crushing.
- Startups are life shortening.
- Fact: You will wake up in a puddle of your own sweat several nights a week because you realize you are completely fucked.
- So why are we doing this again?
- (Because) I can't imagine doing ANYTHING else. It's an unhealthy, but beautifully necessary obsession.

---

[*] www.slideshare.net/missrogue/so-you-want-to-do-a-startup-eh.

It is precisely because the startup game is so personal and lonely that you must take it upon yourself to reach out and connect with the rest of us who are pursuing parallel paths. While it is not unusual for a startup founder to feel isolated and alone, we are actually surrounded by a much larger ecosystem.

The entrepreneurial ecosystem is the collection of people, companies, organizations, venues, activities, and government agencies that surround and support high-growth startup companies in a given region.

It includes startups themselves (and their founders, employees, and contractors), the angel investors and venture capitalists who fund them, and the incubators, coworking spaces, and accelerators that house them, along with the business plan competitions, universities, educational classes, bloggers, community groups, Meetups, and other support organizations that bring them together. It additionally includes the professional service providers they engage (law firms, accountants, investment bankers, and so on) and the larger corporations who serve as their customers, partners, and, in many cases, eventual acquirers.

On the government side are economic development agencies, labor and employment departments, regional technology centers, entrepreneurial assistance programs, and business resource centers. It also includes government grant programs and publicly funded venture capital funds, government tax and financing incentive programs, government purchasing and procurement programs aimed at small businesses, and a host of tech- and startup-focused job skills, training, and education programs.

While these "others" by themselves cannot guarantee that your venture will be successful, I've found that most successful founders have been smart enough to take advantage of the array of resources and support that surround them.

The world's major tech and startup centers, like Silicon Valley, New York, Boston, and London, have so much happening in the way of entrepreneurial support that it is possible to spend 100 percent of your time talking about startups instead of starting up. In even the tiniest town or rural area, you are likely to find one or more kindred spirits who can provide support and encouragement along your entrepreneurial journey.

Here are some resources you should explore:

Meetups

In 2001, soon after the dot-com crash, New York entrepreneurs Scott Heiferman and Matt Meeker founded a website with an unusual premise: to persuade people to turn off their computers and meet off-line. Meetup was born, and today it is used by more than 15 million people in over 150,000 groups to organize nearly half a million local, in-person get-togethers each month. Thousands of these Meetups relate directly to new ventures, startup entrepreneurs, and innovative companies. In most cases, the program for the Meetup will include demonstrations (often the first public showing) of products or services from one or more intriguing local startups.

Our local group in New York is the NY Tech Meetup, which now has over 50,000 members (making it the single largest group on the Meetup platform). Of course, we can't fit all our members into a lecture hall at the same time, so competition is tough for the 800 inexpensive tickets available each month. During the two-hour meeting, a dozen companies will demonstrate their new products, and the "after-party" following the demos is a great place to meet not only the demonstrators but also the many other attendees who have cool startups themselves. Regularly attending one or more of your local tech/startup Meetups is a fine way to discover kindred spirits (including potential cofounders and team members) and to integrate yourself into the fabric of your local entrepreneurship ecosystem. You can find a schedule of all local Meetups at www.Meetup.com.

Business Plan Competitions

With entrepreneurship having become mainstream, most business schools and many universities have integrated business plan competitions into their academic programs and extracurricular activities. In the old days, these were just what the name implied: events at which students would present theoretical plans for new businesses. In recent years, however, they have evolved into pitch events for real companies that have already been started, and often are already generating revenue. In many cases, the organizations that run the competitions use them as the centerpiece of a larger program designed to help and mentor startup founders. For example, at the New York University (NYU)

Stern School of Business, the W. R. Berkeley Innovation Lab runs an eight-month program that starts with team-building events, moves through multiple sessions where startups can practice their pitching, involves over 100 outside mentors, and culminates in a final competition that provides hundreds of thousands of dollars in prizes to the winner. (If you think that sounds cool, the 43North competition in Buffalo, New York, hands out $5 million in prizes each year!)

Startup Conferences and Launch Events

The big brothers of the business plan competitions are major industry events where new companies apply to be selected for introduction to investors, the press, and potential corporate partners. Some of these events are specifically focused on new company introductions, and the audience sees every presentation. Others are general industry conferences that include a startup competition or launch segment as one part of the scheduled program. Along with the companies presenting or competing, thousands of other startups, founders, investors, and industry participants come to watch and mingle. Among the annual industry events that you may find worth traveling to are:

DEMO.   This is the matriarch of launch conferences, where I introduced my first tech company, Ex Machina, in 1991, and Gust, 20 years later. Produced by the computer industry media giant International Data Group (IDG), DEMO has high production values and is a good way to be up front at 50–75 company or product launches at the same time. The audience tends to be corporate, investor, and press focused, but there are always lots of other founders around as well.

TechCrunch Disrupt.   When it was first held in 2008 under the name of TechCrunch40, Disrupt was the brash newcomer, taking on DEMO head-to-head. In the years since AOL acquired the TechCrunch website and conference, Disrupt has grown in size and spread to other cities, becoming an expected stop on the launch path of many startups. With companies exhibiting in Disrupt's Startup Alley, presenting on stage, or competing in its Startup Battlefield, these conferences can showcase over 200 startups, with an energy level so high that you'll come away exhausted.

South by Southwest.   SXSW, as it is universally known, began as a spring music festival in Austin, Texas. It soon added a film festival before the music events, and then layered on an interactive conference, showcasing panels, sessions, and exhibits from tech and media companies. The interactive festival includes a multiday startup competition known as the Accelerator (for which I have served as a judge on several occasions) and hundreds of lectures, panels, launches, and other activities throughout Austin for an entire week. SXSW is a rapidly growing powerhouse on the startup scene.

Other events that showcase new and exciting startups and are places to learn firsthand about what is happening in the ecosystem include the LAUNCH Festival in San Francisco, produced by Jason Calacanis; Vator Splash, from the team at Vator.tv; SOCAP, presenting social ventures "at the intersection of money and meaning"; Ingenuity, from the New York Venture Capital Association; and events produced annually by SIIA, the Software & Information Industry Association. There are also specialized conferences in every industry segment, from financial services to clean technology, publishing to fashion, education to enterprise software.

Accelerators and Demo Days

One of the more interesting recent additions to the entrepreneurial ecosystem has been the rise of the accelerator. Accelerators usually provide coworking space, mentorship, intense peer support, regular presentations, and visits from industry experts and investors . . . and stipends of tens of thousands of dollars to support a team's expenses during the three months you are working with them. There has been an explosion of these programs in recent years, most modeled after the successful Y Combinator in Silicon Valley founded by Paul Graham. Accelerators such as those offered by networks such as Techstars, Wayra, Dreamit Ventures, LaunchPad, Founder Institute, and others do an amazing job of raising the level of entrepreneurial startups. Admission to the typically three-month programs is highly selective, and they like to work with startup teams at the earliest stages of their development.

For first-time and high-quality entrepreneurs, participation in a top-ranked accelerator program is close to a no-brainer. But the key qualifier here is "top-ranked." With many hundreds (or, by some estimates, thousands) of so-called accelerators popping up around the world, many would be a costly waste of time. So be sure to do your homework before applying!

While the high selectivity of the top accelerators means that they accept only a small handful (five to 10 percent) of applicants, there are other ways that you can benefit from them, even if you are not accepted. Some programs invite the public to one or more of their events or open houses, which is a great way to network with other entrepreneurs. Virtually every program ends with a demo day, to which local angel investors and venture capitalists are invited, and sometimes the general public as well. These are somewhat like a debutante's coming-out party, and the onstage presentations by the startups that have been through the program are often exquisite productions that can serve as role models for your own pitch.

Angel Groups

While membership in angel investor groups is typically limited to investors themselves, angel groups can often be a useful resource for entrepreneurs. Business angels invest in startups for many reasons (chief among them is making money, of course), but at heart they get great satisfaction from assisting entrepreneurs. As a result, many angel groups produce training programs, pitch events, and conferences, all aimed at helping entrepreneurs cut significant time from their learning curves. So be sure to visit the website of your local angel investor group to see what it might be offering.

SCORE

Originally known as the "Service Corps of Retired Executives," SCORE is a nonprofit association dedicated to helping small businesses get off the ground, grow, and achieve their goals through education and mentorship. Because SCORE's work is supported by the U.S. Small Business Administration (SBA), and thanks to a network of over 11,000 volunteers, the association is able to deliver its services at no charge or very low cost. SCORE provides volunteer mentors who share their expertise across 62 industries; free, confidential business counseling in person or via e-mail; free online business tools, templates, and tips; and inexpensive or free business workshops (locally) and webinars (online 24/7). SCORE'S 340+ chapters hold events and workshops locally across the United States and its territories.

Peer Programs for Entrepreneurs

While Meetups and events are good ways to get to know others in the community, they are relatively informal and require little long-term commitment. At the other end of the scale are formal, organized peer groups, where you commit to working with a small group of peer entrepreneurs over a long period of time. The oldest, largest, and most significant of these organizations is the Entrepreneurs' Organization (EO), a global business network of 11,000+ entrepreneurs in 153 chapters and 48 countries. Founded in 1987 by a group of young entrepreneurs, EO enables business owners to learn from each other, leading to greater business success and enriched personal lives. I've been a member of EO for over a decade, and have found it to be one of the most valuable groups to which I belong . . . not to mention that our monthly forum meetings are the one thing in my professional life that I am *never* late for.

The bottom line about engaging with the entrepreneurship ecosystem is that it can add immeasurably to your professional life, and reveal opportunities that you may never have come across otherwise. Precisely because it is so rich and varied, it is possible to fall into the trap of drawing your attention away from your business itself, which must always be your first priority.

PART

II

Launch and Build Your Company

9

Incorporate Your Company for Protection and Investment

As WE'VE SEEN in the first part, there is a lot that you can do (and possibly should do) before your startup IS a startup, including coming up with a name, developing a website, coding a prototype, running market tests, and putting a profile on Gust or other platforms for investors and potential partners to see. You can even begin the process of pulling together cofounders for your venture and establishing the basics of the relationship through a Founders' Compact, such as who will get how much equity. So, if you can do all that, why not just keep on going?

The answer is that while you can do it legally, the effect would be to treat the "startup" exactly as you would be treated as a person.

- You would be personally responsible for all of the business's debts and losses, and, if the company fails, its creditors could come after your personal possessions, including your home.
- Since you can't divide a person, the business also can't be divided. You couldn't have investors or partners, nor could you provide options to any employees.

87

■ As a nonentity, there are a host of other things your business could not do, from getting commercial plates for your car to setting up a 401(k) plan.

To establish the startup as a separate entity (not just "you"), there are several different options. While only one of them makes sense for a high-growth startup like yours (otherwise you wouldn't be reading this book), I would be chastised severely by the Cabal of Startup Book Writers if I didn't at least tell you what the other options are. So, here goes:

Sole Proprietorship   (The company is an entity with its own existence, but you are personally liable for everything from debts to taxes.)

General Partnership   (Similar to a sole proprietorship, except that several people share ownership and liability.)

Limited Liability Company (LLC)   (An independent entity with limited liability, but with no easy way to divide or sell ownership and no way to give options to employees or advisors.)

S Corporation   (A corporation with an independent legal life and limited liability, and with stock, but with all the stock owned by you, and the company treated as invisible when it comes time to file your taxes. This can actually be a good thing, IF the company is losing money and you have no investors and you have other income that you would like to shelter. An S corporation can also be easily turned into a C corporation by filing one form.)

C Corporation   (Bingo! A corporation, with limited liability and divisible stock. What more could a startup want?)

B Corporation   (This is a variant of a C corporation, but designed for businesses that plan to have a social impact by generating public benefits. At this point, the B corporation concept is primarily a marketing ploy, so my suggestion is to avoid it for now. If, ultimately, you feel the need to be a B corporation, to switch is pretty straightforward.)

One factor to consider in deciding whether and when to formalize your business structure is the status of your quest for financial funding. While you will definitely need to be a corporate entity before you can accept cash from any investor or issue stock options to any employees, the specific corporate status of the venture at this stage is less important to investors than its functional status. If all you have is a good idea, you are unlikely to get funding from anyone, even if you are an official corporation with gilt-edged stock certificates.

But if you have a completed product with marketplace traction (such as a million monthly unique visitors with rapidly growing conversion rates to paying customers), you will find investors falling over themselves to meet you, even if you operate as a one-man show from a shack on the beach. I would therefore suggest that you not use "pitching to venture capitalists" as a reason to consider incorporating. If and when you garner real investment interest, proper corporate structuring will be a precondition to any funding.

When should you take the leap and incorporate your business? I suggest that the magic moment is whenever you first have one of the following:

- A partner
- An employee
- An investor
- A customer
- A grant
- A need for a bank account
- Any intellectual property (including trademarks or computer code)
- Any potential liability
- Any assets

Benefits of Incorporation

There are two essential attributes of an incorporated company. The first is that your liability is limited. In plain English, this means that once the company is incorporated, the law considers it to be a separate, freestanding entity that can do most of the things that a real person can do. It can own property, buy and sell things, make a profit, enter into contracts, and so forth. But because "the company" is not the same thing as "the real people who own the company," if the company fails and ends up bankrupt (which, sorry to say, is what happens to more than half of all startups), its debts are not the legal responsibility of its owners.

Instead, the "liability"—the requirement that the company's debts be repaid—is "limited" to the company itself, not the people who own it.

The second essential attribute of a corporation is that its ownership is divided into "shares." That means there can be an unlimited number of "owners" of any given company. For example, there are about 2.5 million different owners of Exxon Mobil Corporation.

By contrast, when a founder creates a company, she owns 100 percent of the stock and has complete control of it. Nothing can take that away from her. Unless, however, she decides that, more important than having 100 percent ownership and control, is having a partner to share the entrepreneurial journey an employee to develop the company's product or an investor to help fund the company's development and growth. In that case, she finds a partner or employee or investor (or multiples of all three) and negotiates the terms of their involvement. Based on what she negotiates, she may or may not give up partial or complete ownership or control of the company. It's all in her hands . . . subject, of course, to the market.

Each of these actions will result in partial ownership of the company changing hands, which is why the company needs to be incorporated and issue shares.

Delaware? But I Don't Live in Delaware!

Having decided that you are going to form an entity, and that it is most likely going to be a C corporation, the next question is where your corporation is going to live (remember, it's an independent entity). Corporations are chartered by each state, so your first thought might be to incorporate in whichever state you happen to be based in. That is logical, but not necessarily the right answer. It turns out that over a million corporations—including virtually all those funded by professional investors—have decided to incorporate in the small state of Delaware, even though the companies and their owners, customers, and employees may never have spent two seconds there. Why do they do it? As the Delaware Secretary of State explains:

> It is not one thing but a number of things. It includes the Delaware General Corporation Law, which is one of the most advanced and flexible corporation statutes in the nation. It includes the Delaware

courts and, in particular, Delaware's highly respected corporations court, the Court of Chancery. It includes the state legislature, which takes seriously its role in keeping the corporation statute and other business laws current. And it includes the Secretary of State's office, which thinks and acts more like one of the corporations it administers than a government bureaucracy.

Incorporating outside of Delaware won't impact your ability to *find* investors, but it will likely be an impediment to *closing* deals with investors—although one that can be overcome without great difficulty. There are many reasons why investors (and corporate lawyers) prefer Delaware, so unless there is some overriding reason to go elsewhere (such as California or Nevada), you should probably start in Delaware. However, if you do not, but then find yourself with an interested investor, you can always re-incorporate in Delaware prior to closing.

Sometimes founders wonder whether registering their new businesses in a well-known tax haven, like the Cayman Islands, is worthwhile. The reasons for registering in a tax haven are complex, constantly changing, and problematic, and the process itself is expensive. I've done it once and would really, really like not to have to do it again.

So, Um, How Do I Incorporate a Company?

Incorporating your new venture is neither difficult nor scary. In fact, there are two ways to get your company up and running in Delaware: the easy way, and the easier way.

Easy

Because Delaware tries to be helpful to small businesses, you can go online to the Delaware Department of State's Division of Corporations, reserve your company name (https://icis.corp.delaware .gov/Ecorp/EntitySearch/NameSearch.aspx), find a registered agent, download the Certificate of Incorporation form (http://corp.delaware .gov/newentit09.shtml), fill it out, and fax it in with your credit card details. Delaware will register your paperwork, incorporate your company, stamp your documents, and return them to you by mail.

Even Easier

But what if you'd like something even easier? There are dozens of companies that have set up shop in Delaware for the express purpose of doing the paperwork for you and acting as your registered agent. The largest are CT Corporation and Corporation Services Company, but my personal favorite is Harvard Business Services, which is the state's largest incorporator and registered agent for startup companies. Simply go to their website (https://www.delawareinc.com), click on the link to "Form a Delaware Corporation," fill everything out online, put in your credit card number, and you're set.

Naming Your Business

As part of the incorporation process, you need to decide what the name of your new company will be. While it would be great if you were able to let your imagination run free, there are important considerations that a smart founder will take into account before deciding on a permanent name for the company.

The Practical Aspects

The two most important principles in selecting a name are to choose one that no one else is using, and for which you can acquire the dot-com URL! Before picking a company name, check its availability with the U.S. Patent and Trademark Office at uspto.gov, and on one of the many URL registration sites, such as GoDaddy.com.

You want to go for ease of spelling and pronunciation, short rather than long, uniqueness where possible, something nonliteral (think Apple, eBay, and Amazon, over International Business Machines), and a name that raises no problematic issues with other languages and cultures.

It can be attractive to communicate a key differentiation in your name. For example: PizzaFast or EasyForm. But there are downsides to this strategy as well.

One reason is that, because of the rapidly changing nature of business, today's competitive advantage can easily become tomorrow's disadvantage . . . or at least irrelevancy.

Think how useful the name Tote.com would be for a shopping site developing a social-sharing universal shopping bag/cart. Pretty cool, huh? But what happens when that business model doesn't work particularly well, leading the company to pivot to a business based on socially sharing images? Wouldn't "Pinterest.com" be a little more useful? (That's what Tote changed its name to when it pivoted, following the New York Angels investment.)

Similarly, "stickybits.com" is ideal for a QR code–tagging site, but doesn't work nearly as well as "turntable.fm" once it becomes a collaborative music-playing site. Another example is "FundingUniverse .com" needing to change to "Lendio.com" when it pivoted from equity to debt.

Of course, you can try to game the system and figure out in advance where you'll be after you pivot and extend your line of business. But then you may end up with customers trying to figure out why a mail-order DVD rental company is called "Netflix.com."

Another problem with literal names is that you will likely not be able to trademark a name that is purely descriptive. So while Cheap-Cars.com might actually be available, you would not be able to protect the brand against anyone else who wanted to use it as well.

Through painful experience, many industry professionals have learned that it usually makes more sense to go generic and ambiguous, allowing your genius marketers to add the meaning to simple, catchy URLs.

That is why, instead of naming your Pez dispenser–trading site "pezheads.com," you'd be better off with "eBay.com." Or instead of using "cheapbooks.com" for your online discount bookseller, a better choice might be the more flexible "Amazon.com." (Sorry, those two names are taken.)

The Legal Aspects

Generally speaking, corporate registration is distinct from trademark registration. Registering your corporate name means only that someone else can't register the same name in the same jurisdiction. Since corporations are registered at the state level in the United States, the fact that I register NewCo Inc. in the state of Delaware means only that others can't do the same thing in the same state . . . but one could register a company called "NewCo Inc." in the state of Maryland, for example.

Trademarks, on the other hand, are federal, and thus distinct from the company's name (you may choose to use the name as your trademark if it is available, but it is not required).

Unfortunately, there are no trademarks that are transnational, so even if you were able to trademark "NewCo" in your own country, there is nothing to stop someone from using the same trademark in any other country . . . unless you go to the trouble and expense of registering it there, which is what large corporations do. (I'm sure that McDonald's, Starbucks, Apple, and Google have registered their marks in every country in the world.)

While simply incorporating a company does not seem particularly tricky (and it isn't), it is everything that you need to do afterward that leads startups down the road to ruin. In the next chapter, I'll discuss why you really do need a lawyer . . . and what that lawyer will do for you.

10

"Lawyer Up" the Right Way

COMPANY FOUNDERS OFTEN wonder what a lawyer contributes to a startup or why they even need a lawyer at all. It may sound obvious, but the most important thing a lawyer brings to the startup table is their knowledge of the law surrounding everything to do with founding, financing, and operating a startup! That doesn't make it any less important.

There are an enormous number of laws that cover the world of business, and exponentially more once you start dealing with fund-raising and financing. More often than not, I've seen startups skimp on legal expenses in the early days only to learn a hard lesson when work has to be done over again and in some cases even jeopardizing the company's existence. The peace of mind that comes from knowing that a good lawyer has your back is extraordinarily liberating. Believe me.

Beyond that fundamental and important function, I've found that other valuable things that a law firm brings to a startup are:

- **Formation/organization documentation and administration:**
  This technical legal function is essential and includes a number

of decision points that can have a real impact on the future of the business. In the last chapter we saw that incorporating your company in Delaware was pretty easy . . . but, in fact, it's everything that comes afterward that can get you into big trouble.

- **Validation and credibility:** While this may not be as important as a law firm will claim, there is truth to it. Because all of the major startup law firms have more potential clients than they can handle, they are choosy about whom they work with, so having a top-tier venture firm as your lawyer provides comfort to investors and reassures others that you are legitimate and should be reasonable to work with.
- **Relationships:** Any good venture lawyer spends most of his or her professional time working with people on both sides of the table, and therefore can make suggestions (and sometimes introductions, if warranted) to investors, advisors, and other companies in the industry.
- **Counsel:** While we call lawyers our corporate "counsel," the truth is that they are not (and probably should not be) your primary source of business advice. But often, any advice from a smart person is better than nothing, and sometimes there aren't other people to turn to.
- **Knowledge of market conditions:** Because negotiating and documenting (colloquially known as "papering") deals is what startup lawyers do, they have more experience than a typical entrepreneur when it comes to market terms, such as valuation, protective provisions, and the like. Assuming your lawyer is a smart, active, experienced deal maker, trust his or her advice when it comes to negotiating terms. (But note those assumptions! An inexperienced lawyer can kill a deal faster than a speeding bullet.)

The bottom-line is that lawyers are a critical part of the startup process, and a good one is worth his or her weight in gold.

How to Choose a Startup Attorney

Attorneys are not interchangeable. Just as there are different types of doctors—pediatricians and pathologists, geriatric specialists and gastroenterologists—lawyers also specialize. Even within business law there are specialties, and in an ideal world you will find a lawyer with serious experience in securities law (that's the part that deals with buying and selling stock). Best of all, you should try to find a (wait for it . . .) **startup lawyer**.

In my experience, there are three distinct groups of lawyers who specialize in startups, and any one of them can work for you if you achieve the right client/counsel relationship.

In the first category are the major national and regional law firms which specialize in corporate, venture, and startup work. These firms have literally hundreds of lawyers, and offices in most of the major business states (New York, California, Texas, Illinois, etc.), and work with companies of all sizes, on all aspects of corporate existence and financing. Among the best known of these firms are:

Bryan Cave	Gunderson Dettmer	O'Melveny & Myers
Choate, Hall & Stewart	Hogans Lovells	Orrick, Herrington &
Cooley	Holland & Knight	Sutcliffe
Covington & Burling	Jones Day	Paul, Weiss
Dentons	K&L Gates	Perkins Coie
DLA Piper	Latham & Watkins	Pillsbury Winthrop
Duane Morris	LeClairRyan	Proskauer Rose
Fenwick & West	Locke Lord	Pryor Cashman
Fish & Richardson	Lowenstein Sandler	Venable
Foley & Lardner	McDermott Will &	White and Williams
Foley Hoag	Emery	Wilkie Farr &
Gibson, Dunn &	Mintz Levin	Gallagher
Crutcher	Morgan, Lewis &	WilmerHale
Goodwin Procter	Bockius	Wilson Sonsini
Greenberg Traurig	Morrison & Foerster	Goodrich & Rosati

In the second category are the hundreds of large national and regional law firms that do not specialize in venture or startups *per se*, but have one or two partners who regularly handle new businesses and financing.

The third category—a relatively recent development—consists of independent lawyers who have struck out on their own (often leaving the venture practices of major firms) to establish one-person practices or small, several-lawyer boutiques focused solely on startups, usually in a particular city or region.

There are pros and cons to each of these (for example, large firms can be insanely expensive, while one-person shops may not have the depth to help with all of your business needs), but they are much less important than the key attribute that all share: They are all lawyers experienced in startups!

Large startup-friendly firms generally have well-defined startup practices. With smaller or less startup-focused firms, be careful who you hire. They should have practices devoted to startups and small businesses, not litigation or big company lawyers dabbling in the startup world.

Also, beyond their technical legal specialty, some startup lawyers have knowledge and affinity for a particular field of business, e.g., biotech, finance, consumer Internet, fashion, or construction.

The third thing I look for in a startup attorney (the first is integrity and the second is professional skill and experience in startup law) is that he or she is a deal *maker*, not a deal *breaker*. As someone who has raised funds from dozens of investors for half a dozen startups, and invested myself in more than 100 startups, I can tell you the heartbreak of watching an overzealous, underexperienced lawyer screw up a deal.

If you are negotiating anything, from an investment round to a strategic contract, you want to be *absolutely sure* that your counsel understands that you want to do the deal, and his or her job is to make that happen (subject, of course, to protecting you). All too often, I see attorneys go out of their way to nitpick, overreach, rewrite, or draw a line in the sand when there is no need to . . . and the result is that the deal dies. Lawyers by nature fuss over nitpicky details the rest of us don't understand. Often they don't understand, either, as some aspects of business law are unquestioned conventions maintained for no reason other than tradition. Your lawyer should have the perspective and experience to know what matters, what motivates you and your investors, and what it takes to close a deal.

The combination of integrity, competence, and deal-closing ability sets apart the great startup lawyers from those who are merely good.

You should choose your counsel on the basis of professional competence, the quality of the working relationship you believe you can create with them, and their billing rate. Even more important than hourly rate is how efficient they are, and whether they will commit to a bottom-line price for a given service. Having done that, you will be asked to sign an engagement letter, which lays out things relating to their professional responsibility, your payment obligations, and so forth. Little, if any, of it is negotiable, so the letter becomes a formality that is executed after you've made your decision and they have accepted you as a client.

Major Legal Matters for Which Your Startup Will Need a Lawyer

Okay, now that you're officially incorporated, there are three primary areas for which you are going to need continuing legal help. Since these are separate specialties, you will likely be dealing with three different lawyers, although ideally they all work for the same law firm and are coordinated by your primary attorney:

Your Corporate/Business Law and Securities Lawyer

Postincorporation legal setup of your company. Getting your C corporation formed in Delaware simply created the entity for you. Now the real work begins. Your startup lawyer will work with you on the following items, which are needed to get your company off the ground:

- Delaware articles of incorporation (needed before you file)
- SS-4 form (application for a federal employer identification number)
- Foreign corporation registration ("foreign" means your home state)
- Local business registration, and any licenses and permits that are applicable
- Action of sole incorporator
- Bylaws
- Organizational action of board
- Suite of stock grants and board action authorizing the same: configuration of a notice, stock purchase agreement, stockholders agreement or equivalent terms built into the stock purchase, spousal consent, 83(b) filings
- Board action authorizing form employment agreements
- Recording of loans and other financial and nonfinancial contributions by founders and initial funders
- 409A valuation review
- Advisors agreement
- Board member agreement

- Indemnification agreement
- Funding agreements, including convertible notes (note and note purchase agreements) and/or equity funding (stock purchase, investors' rights, voting, right of first refusal and cosale agreements, amended articles, various certificates, schedules, and disclosures)
- Various ongoing government reports/filings
- Stock option documents: stock plan, grant notice/agreement, exercise notice/agreement [standard and early exercise, which includes 83(b)], stockholders agreement built in or standalone, spousal consent, regulatory filings (if any) for stock plan
- Ongoing board, shareholder approvals for all of the above
- Terms and conditions, sales agreements, privacy policy, user agreements, etc. as applicable to the business
- Special agreements unique to the business or its industry segment
- Strategic partnerships, development agreements, vendor agreements, etc.
- Various board and shareholder actions, minutes

Your Employment Lawyer

All of the paperwork to recruit, hire, fire, and manage employees.

- Suite of employment agreements (proprietary information agreement and job offer/employment agreement)
- Severance agreements
- Case-by-case advice on special situations involving employment agreements, disputed exits and possible lawsuits, founder entries and departures, and independent contractors
- Human resources forms (antiharassment policies, employee handbooks, etc.)

Your Intellectual Property (IP) Lawyer

Everything to do with information, knowledge, and intangible property.

- Contractor agreements (ongoing, timebased, and special purpose)
- Nondisclosure agreement
- IP assignment agreement

- Patents
- Copyrights/trademarks; advice on names and name conflicts for company, website, application, product or service
- Trade secrets

Any information or data that is generated or controlled by your business is part of your company's IP, which means it needs to be protected and managed. Customer lists, contracts with suppliers, software code, plans for future products—these and other forms of information can all qualify as IP with a definite financial value that your lawyers can help you protect.

The costs of patent processing—technically called "patent prosecution"—will depend on whether you are simply seeking to do a preliminary placeholder "provisional" application (which might run somewhere around $2,500–$5,000), or a full-blown patent application, which will almost certainly (if done correctly) cost tens of thousands of dollars.

Some entrepreneurs have an exaggerated concept of the practical short-term value of a patent. Merely having a patent—much less filing for a patent—does not in itself provide protection against a competitor producing a product or service that basically duplicates your company's offering. There are a number of real-world reasons why this is so.

First of all, the patent process takes a long time—typically years (think 5 to 10 years). Until the patent actually issues (assuming that it does—and many, many patent applications are rejected), you have no protection. Even after it issues—and even if someone is directly infringing on the patent—if you went all the way to a full legal challenge, it might cost you $1 million or more in legal fees.

As a result, merely filing a patent in the near term will not significantly affect anyone's decision to compete with you. This does not mean that a patent is valueless, or that you shouldn't bother to obtain patent protection for any genuinely novel invention you or your employees create. You should do so, and be prepared to defend your patents vigorously. They may provide validation to investors and peers, particularly in fields like biotech where patents are a matter of course for growing companies. But do not assume that owning a patent gives you an automatic, unassailable claim on the economic value that your idea generates.

Budgeting for Legal Expenses

The legal costs for a startup are a combination of one-time, ongoing, required, and optional expenses. Here is a rough guide to what you should expect it to cost, based on the rates that might be charged by a high-end solo practitioner or small boutique. A top-tier firm in a major market is going to be about twice the cost in every category. Firms in less expensive markets, and second-tier smaller firms, are somewhere in between, say 30–50 percent more than these figures.

Formation: $2,500–$5,000. This involves a law firm doing everything necessary to establish your venture legally as a company, including filing a certificate of incorporation with the state and then drafting your corporate bylaws, setting up an option plan, providing form legal documents for hiring employees and contractors, and all the other items noted above. In some cases, particularly for startups being launched by known serial entrepreneurs or companies that have come through accelerator programs, law firms may be willing to defer payment until after the first round of financing is completed (although you will eventually pay for it).

Pre–Seed Consulting/General: $5,000. From the time that your company is formed until you raise a fair amount of funding with your first real investor, it is likely that you will be calling your lawyer periodically for advice—to draft contractor or employment agreements, file for a trademark, and so on. The average legal billing rate for a decent lawyer in the United States is about $500/hour, and you can figure on roughly 10 hours of legal work before you get any investment.

Seed Convertible Note Documentation: $2,500–$5,000. Once you have your first dollar nibbling at your hook (perhaps from friends or family, or a local angel investor, or even an accelerator program), the terms upon which they will provide funding must be negotiated. The easiest and cheapest way to do this is with what is known as convertible debt, but even then, the act of drafting and negotiating the documentation will take your attorney at least 5–10 hours.

Series Seed Preferred Round Documentation: $7,500–$15,000. Assuming that you use the money from your initial funder to gain traction and become interesting to a larger investor, the next stop on your startup path will be a serious round (perhaps $500K–$2M) from a seed stage venture fund, an angel group, or a collection of professional in-dividual angel investors. Because these are, professional investors, they will insist on investing in convertible preferred stock, albeit a stripped-down, simplified version. This will cost you another 10–20 hours of your lawyer's time.

Investors' Series Seed Counsel: $2,500–$7,500.   The bad news is that not only do you have to pay your lawyer to help you close this round, but you also have to pay the investor's lawyer, so that will almost double your legal costs. Yikes. (You may, however, be able to negotiate with the investor for a cap on this number.)

Post–Seed Consulting/General: $1,000–$2,000/Month.   With great power comes great responsibility, and with a million dollars of investor cash in the bank comes the need to be sure that everything is done correctly and legally in your operations. Whether it's sitting in on board meetings and taking notes, or answering trademark or patent questions or dealing with employment law, you are likely to be spending 2–4 hours a month talking to your lawyer . . . all of which gets billed, of course.

Series A Venture Documentation: $15,000–$30,000.   After your Series Seed round, if everything works out, you'll be ready to move into the big leagues, and that means a traditional venture capital investor putting in $3M–$5M, or more. This will happen just like the previous round, except that now it is likely you will be using the full model le-gal documents from the National Venture Capital Association. These are much longer than the simplified ones used previously, and require more work, more review, more time . . . and the same time from the investor's attorney. The wide range here represents the difference be-tween a standard deal with one investor, and a complex deal with mul-tiple investors.

Post–Series A Consulting/General: $5,000–$10,000/Month.   You will be using your lawyers on an increasingly regular basis as your business becomes more complex, as you have more employees, more investors . . . more of everything.

Mergers & Acquisitions: $50,000–$150,000.   At the end of the day, you've hit the ball out of the park and your company has an acqui-sition offer from a larger company. Since this is the end of the line for your company as an independent entity (and for your investors completely), there is much scrutiny and are many small points that need to get considered and "lawyered up" on the way to the altar. I threw a wild dart at the numbers here, but, depending on the circumstances, it could be a bit lower . . . or much higher.

When and How to Change Your Law Firm

There may come a time when you are dissatisfied with the service you receive from your law firm, and it is not uncommon for a young firm to try two or three lawyers before one clicks. When that time comes, don't think in terms of "firing" your law firm. That approach is only appropriate when there has been malfeasance or real incompetence. Instead, think of it as "changing law firms," a normal practice in the business world.

Before it gets there, if you are dissatisfied in any way about your service, have a talk with the lawyer you are working with, or the partner in charge of your relationship if that's a different person. Tell them about your issue, whether it's responsiveness, open communication, quality of work, or meeting billing and delivery expectations—which are the most common complaints. Ask what they can do to help. That's what they're there for. If they won't help, or don't improve, or if you've just outgrown them or found a more cost-effective firm, it's perfectly reasonable to move on. Good lawyers are on the lookout for clients that switch firms based on unrealistic expectations, or to avoid paying bills, but switching firms once or twice for a good reason in the course of a startup is perfectly reasonable and normal.

Consider what it's done for you so far, and what the deal is. How did you start out documenting the engagement? Verbally? In writing? You will likely have signed an engagement letter, so pull it out and read it. What does it say? Finally, let me suggest that you quietly start interviewing lawyers to whom you might want to switch, and discuss two matters with them. (1) what arrangement they're willing to make with you, and (2) their advice about how to switch firms. This thing happens all the time, and there is a standard practice for sending your client files from one firm to another. Remember, your files and any work products are yours, a law firm can charge you for copying, but cannot refuse to give them back even if you are behind on the bill.

11

Recruit Your Boards of Directors and Advisors

ONCE YOUR COMPANY is incorporated, you are legally required to have a board of directors. Its official purpose is to represent the rights and viewpoints of shareholders—you, as well as your fellow company owners. But the board of directors should also serve a number of purposes that can fuel and sustain your company's growth and long-term success.

Understanding the Composition of the Board

A company's board of directors is technically elected by the company's shareholders, so before a startup receives outside funding, the board is "elected" by, and usually consists of, the founders (for a tiny company with one or two founders, "the board" may exist in name only).

Once a company receives its initial seed, angel, or venture funding, there are now other owners of the company in addition to the founders. There are specific rules for determining who gets to make what decisions, because, although "ownership" at its core level implies "control," it is possible to separate the two. Once your venture is incorporated, the ownership of the company is divided into millions of shares of common stock, and the fundamental concept is that each share gets one vote.

All of the shareholders then get together to vote for a board of directors to represent them in running the company. The board of directors hires a chief executive officer (CEO), who is charged with running the company on a day-to-day basis. The CEO then hires (directly or through subordinates) and controls all other employees in the company.

What gets tricky is that all of a company's shareholders can get together and voluntarily agree to sign a shareholders agreement in which they agree to cast their votes in a certain way. So for a startup company that has taken in an investment from angel investors or venture capitalists who might own, in total say, 20 percent of the company's shares, the shareholders agreement might provide that the company will have a board of directors consisting of three people, and, regardless of how many shares anyone has, everyone agrees to vote for one director nominated by the company's founders, one director nominated by the investors, and one "outside" director on whom everyone can agree. In this case, although the founder still owns 80 percent of the company, the investors have an equal voice when it comes to control.

In a larger startup, perhaps after one or two investment rounds have taken place, the board might be expanded to five people, with two directors chosen by the common stock holders (the founders), two by the investors (for example, by the directors of venture capital funds that might have invested in the business, or by the most important angel investor, if any), and one independent director agreed to by everyone.

If, at this point, the company has a nonfounder CEO, that position might get a board seat (with one for the founders). If there's only one major investor, they may choose to fill one of their two seats with an industry expert.

Typically, the common seats will be filled by the founder(s); the investor seats by the lead angel (for an angel deal) or the venture capital partner and/or an associate (for a venture-led deal); and the independent seat(s) by someone experienced, knowledgeable, and acceptable to all parties.

The Role of the Chairman of the Board

Many people new to the business world find it easy to confuse the role of the chairman of the board with that of the company's CEO.

Traditionally, the chairman of the board is the senior person on the company's board of directors. This may be an early lead investor or, rarely, an independent director who is well known or has particular industry clout. The chairman is elected by the other members of the board, and usually neither is an employee of the company nor works full-time on company business. The board as a whole (but not the chairman individually) is responsible for the company's overall strategy and major strategic decisions, as well as hiring (and firing) the CEO. The chairman of the board will typically serve exofficio on all board committees (including the executive committee), run all board meetings, and consult frequently with the CEO. While the chairman has the same vote as any other director, there is an implied seniority and gravitas to the chairman's role.

The CEO, in contrast, is the chief executive officer of the company. He or she is the highest-ranking full-time employee of the company to whom all other employees ultimately report. The CEO, in turn, reports directly to the full board of directors. In most cases, the CEO prepares the company's operating plan and projected budget with the guidance of the board. This is then presented to the board for approval. Similarly, the CEO handles all hiring, firing, and proposed employee option grants (which are then ratified by the board).

The one exception to this structure is in the case of an executive chairman, which is a full-time, compensated, operating employee role that directly manages the CEO (although, depending on the particular company and people involved, both might instead directly report to the board).

Because all power in a company ultimately stems from the board of directors which represents the interests of all shareholders, the board determines how much power it delegates to the chairman and the CEO. For a chairman or CEO to get more relative power, she needs to hold sway over the other members of the board, either technically (because she has the right to appoint board members, according to the shareholders agreement) or unofficially (because the other members will take her side in the case of conflicts).

I caution, however, that having a company where the chairman and CEO are at odds with each other is a toxic situation from which no good can ever come. It is much better for the party with the weaker hand to move on to another organization.

Keys to Assembling a Great Board of Directors

There is a saying in the not-for-profit world that your board members should be able to deliver one or more of the following: wealth, work, or wisdom. In my experience, the same qualities also apply to for-profit boards:

Wealth—as in investors who can write checks and help with fundraising in future rounds;

Work—as in directors with specific skills who can be helpful in recruiting, business development, customer introductions, exit analyses, and so on; and finally,

Wisdom—in the form of smart, experienced mentors who can provide sage advice to the CEO from an objective perspective.

In an ideal world, all of your board members would be able to contribute in all three areas. In the real world, however, you hope, but settle for the best you can get . . . which can be challenging for a new startup. Because board members in a startup are not going to be compensated with cash, getting one or more great people to give voluntarily of their precious time is a tall order. What you should NOT do, however, is to be cavalier about your board. Don't put any of your management team on the board (except for a cofounder); don't put someone you don't trust absolutely on the board; and don't put your mother or your best friend on it. Instead, think about someone with business experience who has been advising or mentoring you along the way. Typically, the initial board is in place for a short period of time only. Once you accept outside investment, the shareholders agreement (as discussed above) will almost certainly specify exactly who will be on the board—at which point the initial extra director(s) should be thanked for their service, and perhaps moved to a separate advisory board.

When it comes to compensation, it is unheard of for any board members of preprofitable startups to receive cash salaries or stipends. While founders, company employees, and representatives of venture capital funds receive no compensation for their board service, it is not unusual for outside directors—such as an independent director jointly selected by the founders and investors—to receive stock options (in the range of 0.5 to 2 percent), typically vesting over two to four years.

The edge case is when an angel investor occupies a board seat. There are no hard-and-fast rules, but typically, if the angel is the primary investor in the round and already has a significant equity stake, there would not be an additional amount allocated for board service. If, on the other hand, the angel has only a small bit of equity, and is on the board representing a larger group of investors, then he or she might be treated like an independent director, with a point or two of options on a vesting schedule.

Maximizing the Value Created by Your Company's Board

To get the most out of your board, you should follow best practices in your approach. Brad Feld and Mahendra Ramsinghani have written the definitive book on the subject, and it is worthwhile reading.[*] Here are some suggestions to get you started:

- Set up a regular schedule for board meetings appropriate for the stage of your company and composition of the board. In an early stage funded company with rapid growth and changes and many interested parties, might have its board meet once a month. A mature company with relatively stable revenues and management team, might have its board meet semi-annually. In my experience with early stage ventures, four to six meetings a year (one every two or three months) works best.
- The CEO should send a full information package to all board members several days in advance of the meeting. It should include current month-, quarter-, and year-to-date financial reports; updates on key performance indicators (KPIs); and the slides to be presented at the meeting.
- Have a standard agenda for the meeting distributed in advance and followed firmly. I'd suggest devoting the first quarter of the meeting to the CEO's review of the previously distributed management

---

[*]*Startup Boards: Getting the Most Out of Your Board of Directors*, John Wiley & Sons, 2014.

reports, the second quarter to a more in-depth presentation to the board by a different management team member, and the final half of the meeting to a full, interactive discussion of strategic topics which require board input.

■ The meeting nominally should be run by the board chairman, although in many cases he or she will defer to the CEO for administrative purposes. At the end of every meeting, there should be a few minutes set aside for an executive session, during which the CEO and any management team members are asked to leave the room. That will provide the outside directors (the investors and independent members) an opportunity to discuss potential management issues without having to demand a secret session.

■ Finally, after every meeting, draft board minutes should be distributed to all members for review. Minutes should include only the names of the members in attendance and the specifics of any resolutions that were passed or actions that were taken—nothing else!

The Role of a Board of Advisors

Often, a startup founder will find that there are people whose advice, contacts, and/or knowledge might be valuable to the company, but who are not appropriate for, or interested in joining, the board of directors. These might include influential industry experts, people with valuable networks, wise advisors, or highly visible people who are willing to lend their names to validate the company. These people can be recruited to serve the company under the rubric of the board of advisors.

Unlike the board of directors, the board of advisors has no legal role or responsibilities and is typically much more informal. It may never meet in person, although I would suggest that bringing it together once a year for a company update and to meet one another is a good idea. In my experience, advisors usually serve the company through one-on-one relationships with the CEO, who might call them individually as frequently as weekly, or as rarely as annually. They can refer customers, leverage their social media influence, provide mentoring or counseling to the CEO, or provide insights into the company's markets. Advisors would generally be compensated with options at perhaps half the level of board members.

Startup Mentors for Your Entrepreneurial Journey

Wikipedia's definition of *mentorship* is:

> "a relationship in which a more experienced or more knowledgeable person helps to guide a less experienced or less knowledgeable person. . . . It is a learning and development partnership between someone with vast experience and someone who wants to learn."

The problem is that the term has become overused and debased, for the simple reason that the majority of people have never had a real mentor. A true mentorship relationship takes years to develop, is between two people who have worked closely together for a long time, and can last a lifetime. Most people go through life without ever experiencing this, and those who are lucky enough to find one rarely find one twice. Instead, the term "mentor" as it is commonly used in business circles refers to someone who functions as an occasional advisor.

The challenge in finding a true mentor is that there is a mismatch of your needs and those of a potential mentor. I strongly believe in giving back, teaching, and sharing my experiences with others, and I receive multiple requests each week from new entrepreneurs asking me to mentor them. The problem is that of all the resources that I possess, the one that is in shortest supply is time. If I were to serve as a mentor for all of the deserving entrepreneurs who ask me to do so, I would have no time to eat or sleep, let alone run my own entrepreneurial company or invest in other startups.

The paradox is that the people you want as mentors are exactly the same people who don't have the time to serve in that role because they're doing the things that make them good mentors in the first place. The best that experienced people can do is try to figure out ways to "scale" their mentoring so as to help the largest number of potential mentees.

Instead of embarking on a fruitless journey to find a startup mentor, I strongly suggest that you devote your energy to soaking up all of the publicly available "mass mentoring" you can find: Read the books in the Startup Reading List in Appendix A; follow the blogs of industry experts; read answers to thousands of startup founder questions on Quora; and attend any of the hundreds of public lectures and events on startup topics. Then, do the best job you can at whatever project or startup you're undertaking.

Do that, and the odds are good that in the course of your activities without forcing the issue or explicitly asking for mentorship, you will find that, as the old Eastern maxim says, "When the student is ready, the guru appears."

12

Select an Accountant and an Accounting System

KEEPING TRACK OF THE MONEY coming in and out of your startup is simultaneously a boring, painful chore most entrepreneurs would rather avoid . . . and a scary, reality-forcing discipline that most entrepreneurs would rather ignore. Which are, of course, two of the chief reasons that it has to be done right from the beginning. More startups fail because they run out of capital than for almost any other reason; unless you manage your money correctly, you are setting yourself up to go over the proverbial cliff.

In this chapter, I'll give you the basics you need to know about business finance, advice on how to find the right accountant, and pointers to cost-effective online accounting systems that will make your life easier.

Business Finance 101

Let's start with some fundamental terms and concepts.

Profit and How It Is Measured

Regardless of how big or small a company is or how it is structured, it has one or more owners who own the company's stock.

Some, all, or none of those owners may work for the company. But it is crucial to understand that *ownership* of a company is a completely separate thing from *working* for a company.

The sum of all the money received from sales of products or services (known as *gross revenues*) minus the sum of all money spent on earning that revenue (*total expenses*) = *net income* . . . another way of saying *profit*.

Your business's net income can also be expressed as a percentage of gross revenues. The resulting percentage is referred to as your business's *profit margin*, and the higher it is, the better. If, for example, in a particular year your business has gross revenues of $10 million and net income of $500,000, your profit margin would be $500,000 divided by $10 million, or five percent.

Generally accepted accounting principles, tax laws, and other regulations include precise definitions of the relevant terms; their application can be quite complicated. For now, let's focus on the basic formula for profitability:

Gross revenues – total expenses = net income

In most cases, a portion of the net income is set aside for various business purposes, such as to buy new equipment, invest in expanded marketing, or reserved in anticipation of possible emergency needs. The remainder of the net income may then be distributed among all of the owners of the business according to their respective ownership shares.

A person who works for a company while also owning part or all of the business gets two different payments: a salary paid by the company to compensate them for the work he or she is doing, and a dividend remitted by the company representing their share of the profits.

If you are engaged in launching a company, either by yourself or with a team of cofounders, it's important to keep these two roles distinct, along with the two streams of income they may ultimately produce for you.

Basic Processes of Accounting and Bookkeeping

The tool that is used to keep track of all of the company's financial transactions—virtually always in electronic form—is called the *general ledger*. The process of maintaining the general ledger by recording all financial transactions is referred to as *bookkeeping*, and handling this work in a clear, accurate, and timely fashion is important for any business, large or small.

The general ledger reflects five categories of items: *assets, liabilities, owners' equity, revenue,* and *expenses*. Every entry has an impact in two places in the general ledger (hence the term double-entry bookkeeping). For example, when you sell a product, the money you receive will be entered as a positive addition to the income category of the ledger. The same amount will be subtracted from the asset category, which is where the value of the goods in your company's inventory is recorded. For example, when you sell a product, the money you receive will be entered as an increase to the revenue category of the ledger. However, the same amount will be entered as a decrease in the asset category, which is where the value of the goods in your company's inventory is recorded. This recording of the flow of value from one part of the general ledger to another, that is inherent in every financial transaction, is what maintains the balance between what the business owns and what it owes to the entities that fund it. Every competent bookkeeper or accountant understands how the process works and can ensure that your business maintains its books correctly. Working with an online or computer accounting software package will also help you develop a feeling for how the double-entry bookkeeping system works and what its impact is on your business.

The data in the general ledger is used to generate a number of important financial documents, including the *income statement*, the *balance sheet*, and the *cash flow statement*. Stick with me in this chapter, because those three documents will be needed again and again, in multiple contexts, for as long as you are involved with the business.

The **income statement** is a document that lists your business's revenues and expenses for a given period of time. Most businesses prepare monthly income statements, which enable the managers of the company to track how its finances develop in the short term, enabling course corrections as necessary. Monthly income statements are then rolled into annual statements that reflect how the company performs for an entire year. Because the income statement reflects revenues and expenses, it yields a profit (or loss) figure that is one important measure of the health of the business. Thus, it may also be called the *profit and loss statement*.

The **balance sheet** shows the assets and liabilities of the business at a given moment in time. It is usually prepared on a regular basis—for example, as of the first day of every month—so that comparisons can be made easily. The business's total assets minus its liabilities equals its *net worth*—that is, the value of the business at that moment in time. Net worth may fluctuate, but over the long term it should grow, showing that the company is becoming more valuable over time.

The **cash flow statement** shows how money flows into and out of the business during a particular period of time—typically one month. It lists the amounts and sources of income (such as sales of products or services, or income from investments) and the amounts and nature of expenses (such as the cost of operating the business, tax payments, and so on). Although this may sound suspiciously like the income statement, it's important to understand the difference. The income statement deals with theoretical profits and losses, but the cash flow statement deals with real money. For example, if you close a million-dollar deal to sell some goods to Walmart, as soon as you ship them the products and send an invoice, you have completed the deal, and that million dollars goes into the income statement. But the fact that Walmart pays Net 90 means that you won't actually get the money for over three months! In the meantime, you can't pay your employees in Walmart promises . . . which is why the first rule of startups is "Cash is king!" The cash flow statement reflects the hard cash realities that can make or break your business.

Budgeting

Your budget is a financial plan for the near future, indicating your anticipated income and expenses for a specified period of time (most often a year). The purpose of creating a budget is to provide a tool for monitoring and controlling your expenses and keeping them closely aligned with revenues.

When you create your budget, try to project your income and expenses for the coming year as accurately as possible. Identify specific categories of income and expenses as precisely as possible. Then, break down the budget according to monthly increments.

The monthly budget figures give you a baseline against which your monthly income statement and its various component parts can be compared. Discrepancies can provide an early warning signal about costs that may be spiraling out of control or revenues that fall short of expectations. It's rare that a company's performance tracks the budgeted numbers precisely (it never happens—ever); but the value of budgeting lies in the power it gives you to make changes in your business activities as needed during the year, thereby enabling you to fix small problems before they become big ones.

Managing Cash Flow

Cash flow refers to the change in the amount of money available to your business between the beginning of a given time period and the end. If the amount of cash available increases during the period— which could be a month, a quarter, or a year—then the business is said to have *positive cash flow*. If the amount decreases, it has *negative cash flow*.

Cash flow should be considered separately from profitability, because of the crucial element of timing, as we saw in the Walmart example. Gaps of this kind often produce a negative cash flow. If the negative cash flow becomes too great, there's a danger that the business will run out of cash and be unable to meet payroll or other expenses. In a worse case, the company may be forced to go out of business.

Effective budgeting can help you avoid a serious negative cash flow problem. Anticipate periods when revenues are likely to decline, and plan to reduce or delay expenses accordingly. Try to find ways to make your revenue streams more consistent—for example, by conducting seasonal sales to encourage buying during periods when customers would otherwise be scarce or inactive. You may also be able to even out your expense pattern from month to month—for example, by requesting a level billing plan from your utility provider so that seasonal spikes in energy costs don't drain your bank account.

Paying Yourself

We've noted the importance of distinguishing between the two roles an individual may have in relation to a business—one as an owner and one as an employee. If you are working for your startup business as CEO or in some other capacity, you will need and want to include a salary for yourself in the annual budgeting process. Determining an appropriate salary requires careful consideration.

Do your research before deciding what salary you wish to draw from your business, and remember that, in the long run, your personal financial situation will be best served by owning (or sharing ownership in) a highly profitable, sustainable, and growing company.

In practice, for high-growth businesses that are not yet profitable—and are being funded by outside investors, such as friends and family or business angels—the expectation is that founders will draw very low salaries. You are not expected to work for free, but since any money going to you is NOT going to fund other business expenses, you should expect to receive perhaps a quarter or half of what the market rate might be for your role.

How (and Why) to Hire a Good Accountant

As long as your venture is in the prestart stage, during which you or your cofounder may be personally coding the product while working out of your homes, there won't be a lot of money changing hands, and you can put accounting issues on the back burner. But at just about the time that you feel the need to incorporate your business, you should start acting like a real company and take control of your finances. That "should" becomes a "must" the second you take in your first investment dollar, hire your first employee, sign your first lease, or sell your first product.

While keeping track of the first few sales and expenses of the company sounds like something you can do yourself with an inexpensive online website, in practice you will find that the details quickly begin to metastasize. Without help, there is no question that you are going to end up in trouble some way, somehow. I have an MBA in finance, but I assure you that I wouldn't consider setting up a startup without consulting with a good accountant.

There are several separate financial-related functions that have to be done for your company, whether you want to do them or not. Some you can (in theory) do yourself, some are best handled by a part-time or full-time employee, some can be handled by a "drop-in" financial consultant, but some just have to be done by a certified public

accountant. In sequence, here is what you need to do, and who should
do it:

1. Your first order of business is to consult with a real accountant
   to review this list and set up a plan. Most accounting firms are
   eager for new business and will likely not charge you for this first
   meeting or at least will charge only a nominal amount. The goal
   is to have them work with you to set up a "chart of accounts" that
   is appropriate for the business you are building, and to have them
   instruct you on what they will need you to have done when they
   come back into the picture later. They will advise you on what
   software to use and may be able to identify people to fill the other
   roles you need.
2. With your accounts set up and a plan in hand, you need to start
   keeping track of all cash flow into and out of the business, including invoices, purchasing, and check writing. You need to
   set up and manage your bank account and payment processors
   (more about that in Chapter 14), and regularly reconcile the
   monthly bank statements to make sure that income and expenses
   are recorded accurately. All of this is called bookkeeping and is
   something that starts now and not stop until the company is no
   longer in existence. While this is not rocket science—as a high-
   growth founder you are perfectly capable of entering the data into
   a simple online program—in practice, I find that 95 percent of
   my portfolio company founders bring in someone else to do it.
   For a pure startup, this can be as simple as engaging a freelancer
   (perhaps someone recommended by your accountant) to come in
   once a month, take all the financial receipts from the shoebox
   into which you have thrown them, and enter them correctly in
   your system, reconciling the bank statements along the way. As
   the company grows, the monthly visits should become weekly. By
   the time you've raised your first seed round, you may find that you
   have enough work to keep a full-time bookkeeper busy on your
   own payroll.

   (One caution: Beware of relying on a one-person internal
   accounting department without carefully defined and consistent checks and balances. Giving one person the power to dis-
   burse funds and balance the books is an invitation to disaster.

Making fraud and embezzlement easy creates temptation that may weaken the integrity of an otherwise honest and reliable individual.)

3. With the underlying information accurately captured, you eventually need to make sense of it by having someone transform the raw data into the financial statements discussed earlier, as well as maintain your future financial projections. This work is generally beyond the pay grade of your bookkeeper, but also something that is not within your personal skill set, and would be overkill to pay your accountant to do. In larger companies, this would be handled by the chief financial officer (CFO), but at this point you're likely too small to be able to afford a full-time one. Luckily, a new class of "drop-in CFOs" has arisen: experienced financial professionals with CFO-level experience, who handle multiple clients on a time-sharing basis. You will likely engage one of these folks to serve as an adjunct part of your management team until such time as your company has grown large enough to require a full-time CFO.

Among the tasks that this person will undertake are:

- Prepare monthly, quarterly, and annual financial reports.
- Work with you to manage your financial projections.
- Prepare financial documents for potential investors.
- Offer you and your leadership team financial advice and guidance.

Finally, some things simply must be done by your accountants. (Remember them?) These include:

- Preparing your corporate tax returns and dealing with the Internal Revenue Service as needed and
- Preparing reviews or audits of your financial statements if requested or required by potential investors.

Choosing and Using Online Accounting Tools

Modern computerized accounting tools make routine bookkeeping and financial accounting processes quick, convenient, and accurate. The original game changer was the QuickBooks software program released by Intuit in the mid-1990s. With the rise of the Internet, a number of new entrants produced inexpensive cloud-hosted solutions that quickly gained market share.

Today, there are half a dozen strong solutions that can easily handle a startup company's basic needs, and grow along with the company to provide institutional-grade accounting system.[*]

One of the more powerful, yet easy-to-use, cloud-based solutions—and my recommendation for most startups—is the suite of online tools from Xero, a New Zealand–based company.[†] Like most of the other online accounting tools, Xero is available in several forms with varied pricing and offers features that can greatly streamline your accounting, including:

- Handling routine banking transactions via a direct electronic link to your bank(s)
- Updating and managing your books, entering income and expense data as you provide it
- Connecting your data electronically to the accountant of your choice, making it easy for your professional advisor to keep track of your business's finances
- Providing customized invoicing systems to make billing your clients easy and efficient
- Managing and producing payroll-related documents, such as W2 and 1099 forms
- Cutting payroll checks and/or handling direct-deposit payments to employee bank accounts
- Exporting your financial data to the tax software system of your choice, making the filing of tax returns easier and more accurate

---

[*]Learn about these software tools by visiting their websites at:

QuickBooks.intuit.com

Sage.com/us/sage-50-accounting

Concur.com

AccountEdge.com

Waveapps.com

[†]www.xero.com/us.

- ■ Offering the Xero Touch mobile app, which allows you to provide your employees access to appropriate financial tools using their smartphones

Xero software also serves as a platform for over 400 additional features offered via apps by a wide array of outside companies, many of them free or easily affordable. The chances are good that almost any financial management tool you can imagine is available for use with Xero.

13

Establish and Manage Your Credit Profile

ONE OF THE MOST crucial resources a startup has is the money that it will use to pay for products and services, and invest in its growth . . . not to mention pay the founder a living wage. Unfortunately, the nature of the beast is that startups typically begin with no cash at all, so one of the first orders of business after you've passed the theoretical stage is to find at least a minimal amount of funding. In the next part, we'll discuss equity fund-raising, and how you will put in your own capital, hit up your friends and family, seek out angel investors, and perhaps try to land a venture capitalist. But in this chapter, we'll start with the obvious question "How can I borrow money to fund my startup?"

Answer: You can't. At all. Why? Because banks and other lenders are not in the business of investing or taking risks. They are, instead, in the business of renting money. Just as for a car rental company the number one thing it cares about is getting the car back in one piece at the end of the rental, with banks, the thing they care most about is getting their money back at the end of the loan. Unfortunately, startup businesses are historically very, very bad risks, and a majority of them fail completely. That's why you won't be able to get a loan.

123

But.

While no one is going to lend you cash money, there is a small to moderate chance that a vendor, supplier, or service might be willing to advance you credit, even if it's only to let you charge on a credit card until the end of the month. But these people are also concerned about your startup's ability to pay your bills, so before advancing you any credit, the first thing they are going to do is review your history (such as it is) to see if you might be worth taking a risk on. That review is known as a "credit check," and typically starts with them reviewing your credit profile . . . which is the history of your previous interactions with other lenders and people who have advanced you credit. The cleaner and better your history, the better your credit score . . . a number that corresponds to how likely you are to pay your bills without trouble.

Having a positive credit profile is important for virtually any small business. A high credit score will make it easier for you to borrow money when needed, allow you to establish a line of credit that can help you navigate short-term cash flow problems, and reduce the cost of borrowing by making you eligible for lower interest rates and reduced fees. But how do you develop and maintain a good credit rating, especially for a brand-new startup? It's challenging, but it's doable.

Basics of Business Credit

More than half of all small business owners use personal credit as a source of part of the capital needed to start and run their businesses. In some cases, the founder simply uses a personal credit card to buy goods and services needed by the company. In other cases, he or she takes out a personal bank loan or establishes a personal line of credit, often secured by home equity or some other personal asset.

This approach to financing your business may be your only option, but it carries risks and disadvantages. One problem is the cost of credit: You will usually pay a higher interest rate on a personal credit card than would be available with a business credit account. Another is that personal credit cards aren't designed to help with business cash flow issues. If you can get one, a rotating line of credit is a better way to manage short- to medium-term business debt than letting a large balance accumulate on a personal credit card. What's more, a business downturn could leave you with personal debt you might not be able to manage, hurting not just your business credit rating, but also your personal credit score. You don't want business setbacks to cost you your family home or other personal assets.

If you find that your only option to move your business forward is to rely on personal credit during the early stages of launching and growing your business (and if you've got informed consent from your spouse or significant other), then you must take careful steps to minimize the risks involved:

- Keep the sums of money you borrow to support your business relatively small and manageable.
- Pay off the amounts you borrow as quickly as possible.
- Avoid amassing significant levels of debt, which lead to costly interest charges.
- Keep close tabs on your personal credit rating, making sure that the business debt you incur isn't causing damage to your personal financial status.

Given the downsides of financing your startup business through personal borrowing, at some point, early in the growth of the business, try to establish a business credit account separate from your personal credit account. This is relatively simple, although your credit is likely to be limited in the early days. For example, you can obtain one or more business credit cards, or you may be able to obtain a bank line of credit secured by the assets of your business. When you do this, you will begin the process of building a business credit profile that will stay with your company as it grows.

Starting Your Credit Profile with a D-U-N-S Number

Dun & Bradstreet (D&B), founded in 1841, is the leading organization that monitors, records, updates, and disseminates credit information regarding companies large and small. If you have been in business for some time, your company may already have a business credit profile with D&B, whether you know it or not.

If your business isn't already active in the D&B database, you can start establishing a business credit profile by obtaining a D-U-N-S number.* D-U-N-S stands for Data Universal Numbering System, a program operated by D&B that provides a way of identifying businesses and ensuring that another company's bad credit will not get mixed up with yours . . . and vice versa. Upon request, D&B will provide your company with a unique, nine-digit D-U-N-S number. These identifiers are used around the world and serve as a handy, unmistakable form of business identification analogous to the use of Social Security numbers to identify individuals.

Participating in and using the D-U-N-S system has a number of advantages for young businesses. By providing a single identifying number for every company in the world, the D-U-N-S can help simplify and consolidate your internal record-keeping systems. Thus, if you're engaged in business-to-business commerce with a growing list of client companies, you can organize your data around D-U-N-S numbers, which provide a clear, simple way of tracking businesses that is less subject to confusion or error than relying on company names. Having a company's D-U-N-S number makes it easy to obtain accurate and up-to-date information about that company, which is readily available from D&B itself, as well as from other sources. It also makes some business processes simpler and faster—for example, an SSL certificate (which is a special code used on web servers to make online financial transactions secured) can be obtained more quickly if you have a D-U-N-S number.

Finally, having a D-U-N-S number is mandatory for a number of things your startup may want to do, from joining the Apple Developer program so that you can upload an app to the Apple App Store, to selling your product through Walmart, to qualifying for a loan from the Small Business Administration (SBA) or applying for work as a federal government contractor.

Getting a D-U-N-S number is not very difficult, and the process is free of charge.† The steps include:

---

*Contact D&B customer service by calling 1-866-785-0430, or by visiting http://iupdate .dnb.com/iUpdate/mainlaunchpage.htm.
†Get started at http://www.dnb.com/get-a-duns-number.html.

- Gathering the information needed for the application: your company's legal name; the name, address, and main phone number of your business headquarters; whether or not your business is home based; any other names under which you may do business; the name and title of the individual who will be your main D-U-N-S contact; the legal structure of the business; the year in which the business was founded; and the number of employees in the business.
- Verifying your identity and obtaining a username and password. To do this, you will answer a series of questions based on geographic and demographic information.
- Completing the D-U-N-S number application form, which generally takes just a few minutes. You should receive your company's D-U-N-S number free of charge within 30 days. An expedited process is available, which generates a D-U-N-S number within five days for a fee.

D-U-N-S numbers are so standardized that you can obtain one even if you only operate outside the United States. Currently, there are about 225 million businesses with D-U-N-S numbers operating in some 90 countries around the world.

Building and Maintaining a Good Credit Profile

Once you have a D-U-N-S number, your business will begin to accumulate data about its financial interactions, all of which will shape your company's credit profile. Banks, vendors, potential investors, would-be employees, and even customers can—and will—check your credit profile when they are deciding whether to do business with you. The impact on your company's finances can be substantial, especially when you borrow money or seek a credit line increase.

According to the Small Business Administration, "Since most loan decisions below $100k are automated, the business credit file will often dictate the amount and terms of a loan. For businesses with poor credit ratings, top national banks may increase credit card interest rates on average from 9 to 18 percent and loan interest rates on average from 8 to 12 percent." The difference between a good credit profile and a poor one can literally cost your company tens of thousands of dollars per year—or more.

The first step in maintaining a positive credit profile is understanding how the profile is assembled and how you can track its contents.

There are three major credit reporting agencies—Experian, Equifax, and TransUnion. You may already be familiar with them from the world of personal credit, since these are the same three agencies that track, monitor, and grade the credit worthiness of individuals. However, rather than using the familiar individual credit rating scale, with a high score of 850, business credit ratings range from 0 to 100, with a score of 80 to 100 indicating that a company has a low risk of defaulting on a payment due. In addition, Dun & Bradstreet tracks the credit history of businesses and produces its own business credit rating (also on the 0 to 100 scale), often referred to as a D&B score.

D&B and each of the three credit agencies use different algorithms to calculate your company's credit score. Thus, your score from each of the three services may be slightly different. However, the kinds of data they all use are roughly similar. They include payment and banking data from company suppliers; information about any suits, liens, and judgments against your company; data drawn from business registrations, incorporations, and bankruptcy filings; information in your corporate financial reports; and other data that may be available. Data that is more than seven years old is supposed to drop off your credit report and stop affecting your score.*

What can you do to make sure that your business credit profile is as positive as possible? Many of the steps that apply to your personal credit score apply to business credit as well. Consistently paying your bills on time—including payments due on loans or credit card accounts—will enhance your credit score. A pattern of late payments will reduce your credit score. So will failure to pay a bill, any legal judgments against you, and, of course, any bankruptcy proceeding you've gone through.

You may wonder whether and how your personal credit report and your business credit report affect one another. Technically, the two are separate, but they may have an impact on each other. The Fair Credit Reporting Act (FCRA) is the 1970 federal law that governs the

---

*For more on the business credit scoring practices of the "big three" agencies, visit http://www.nerdwallet.com/blog/credit-cards/business-credit-score-basics.

handling of data about personal and business finances, enforced mainly by the Federal Trade Commission. According to the FCRA, lenders such as banks may review an individual's personal credit history when considering a business lending proposition.

Why and How to Keep Tabs on Your Credit Report

False information does crop up on credit reports, both through simple error (such as confusion between two businesses with similar names, which is one good reason to know your D-U-N-S number) and fraud. In fact, the SBA estimates that between 15 and 30 percent of all business credit losses are caused by fraudulent activity. The dangers posed by fraud, hacking, and identity theft are one reason why it is important for you to keep tabs on your credit report.

The FCRA includes provisions designed to help you force the deletion of erroneous information from a credit profile by reporting the error to the appropriate agency. However, it may take a few months for the correction to kick in. So, if you spot any incorrect information on your credit report—for example, an erroneous claim that you failed to pay a bill on time, or a false report about a lawsuit that never happened—call attention to it promptly. The more quickly you act, the smaller the likelihood that the error will impact your business finances.

There are a number of companies that provide services that make it easier to monitor and deal with changes in your credit profile. These services not only help you ensure that your credit score remains high but can alert you when false information has been recorded, thereby helping you prevent fraud and identity theft.

Credit agencies themselves are one source of such services. For example, Dun & Bradstreet offers services that send you automatic alerts when your D&B score or credit rating changes, tell you how often your credit report has been accessed, provide guidance on steps you can take to improve your credit score, and allow you to benchmark your credit data against the profiles of one or more comparable peer companies. These services are available at various levels, starting with a basic freemium model and increasing in complexity and sophistication in return for commensurate monthly fees.

Similarly, Experian offers a paid monitoring service called Business Credit Advantage that provides instant e-mail alerts regarding changes to your credit score, credit inquiries, collection filings, and other relevant activities around your credit report. Business Credit Monitor for Small Business from Equifax offers comparable services. Check out the websites of these bureaus and compare their offerings to determine which service is most appropriate for your business.*

---

* http://www.experian.com/small-business/services.jsp;
http://www.equifax.com/business/business-credit-reports-small-business.

14

Open Bank, Credit Card, and Merchant Accounts

You've probably been using banks for many years as an ordinary consumer. But choosing and using a bank in your role as the founder of a startup business presents a number of new challenges.

Working with Your Bank

The most basic type of bank account for your startup is a **business checking account**. In some ways, this is similar to a personal checking account, in that both have monthly fees that may be waived under certain circumstances, typically by meeting a minimum balance requirement. Both charge fees for specific services such as overdrafts. However, most business accounts limit the number of free transactions—including checks, deposits, and withdrawals—that you can perform each month, and pay interest at lower rates than interest-bearing personal accounts—in many cases, they pay no interest at all.

Where a business checking account is used primarily to manage your funds and pay your vendors, a **merchant account** is used primarily to accept credit card payments from customers. Until recently, this was the *only* way for a business to take credit cards. However, the last few years have seen the emergence of specialized payment processing companies which can streamline the process for small businesses, especially those operating online. While there is still a role for bank-offered merchant accounts (particularly for companies with a high volume of credit card transactions), you will find that it makes more sense—at least initially—to handle your card transactions through one of the new payment processors we'll talk about later in this chapter.

Another change over the past decade (which probably seems like forever to most young founders) has been the advent of **online and mobile banking**, which make many business-oriented financial services available around the clock from any location, on computers, tablets, and smartphones. For example, many business-oriented banks offer business customers the ability to access their accounts and services—including cash management, foreign exchange, asset management, international banking, and more—at any time. With some banks you can set alerts to notify you when certain kinds of transactions occur, and automatically download transactions into accounting software systems, such as Xero, QuickBooks, and Quicken.

Just as technology has made it easier for *you* to bank anywhere, any time, it has also made it easier for hackers to attack your accounts in the same way. As a result, there is a never-ending battle between the forces of good and evil, and it is up to you to work with your bank to **protect your accounts** from being misappropriated. The most obvious thing you can do is be extremely cautious about *phishing* attacks. These take the form of official-looking e-mails that purport to come from your bank and ask you to enter or change your password or put in other sensitive information. Your bank will never ask you to do something like this! If you have any concern whatsoever about an e-mail or other communication from your bank, go directly to the bank's website by typing in its web address in your browser (do **not** click on a link in the e-mail), and verify the request with the bank's legitimate online system.

Because it is possible for someone to steal or guess your password, or otherwise try to impersonate you, many banks now offer (or, for larger accounts, insist on) special technical security measures to ensure that they are dealing only with legitimate clients. Some of these approaches include:

- Only accepting online log-ins if you are coming from a known IP address at your office or home
- Requiring the entry of a special code generated by a tiny device that you carry with you at all times, called a *token*
- Sending a special code to your mobile phone that you must enter into the bank's online system whenever you try to log-in.

Ask your bank about its security features, and work with it to figure out which are most appropriate for your circumstance.

Kinds of Financial Credit and How to Use Them Wisely

One of the most important services provided by banks is credit—making money available through borrowing to finance your company's ongoing operations as well as its growth. There are several forms of bank credit, each with specific advantages, disadvantages, and recommended uses. They include:

Business Credit Cards.   You will want to obtain one or more credit cards for you and your employees to use in handling daily business expenses. Be aware, however, that choosing a credit card for your startup may involve different factors from choosing a credit card for personal use.

When considering a business credit card, be sure to check the interest rate charged on cash advances and unpaid balances (usually expressed as an annual percentage rate, or APR). The APR will vary widely from one card to another. Look for a card with a low annual fee, one whose benefits and reward offerings fit your business type and working style, and one with record-keeping systems that will make your accounting processes simple.

American Express, for example, offers a range of credit cards under its OPEN program designed expressly for small businesses. The Amex reward program can provide you with points or cash back based on your credit card spending you do, as well as significant discounts on a variety of business services.* In addition, because Amex cards have no preset spending limit, they can be used as a source of revolving credit when needed.

---

*https://www.americanexpress.com/us/small-business.

Personal Loans.   Many startup owners use their personal credit as a source of funding for the business. There's no need to explain the nature of your business to the bank or to justify its likely profitability, since you are borrowing funds not in your role as business owner, but simply as an individual consumer. Of course, the stronger your personal credit rating and the better your personal borrowing history, the easier it will be to get access to personal credit and the more affordable the interest and other charges are likely to be.

Personal loans frequently used to finance business startups include credit card borrowing, home equity loans, home equity lines of credit, and personal installment loans. Each has its advantages and disadvantages. Credit card debt is often costly, having a higher interest rate than most other forms of borrowing. Interest on a home equity loan is often tax deductible (your accountant can confirm your eligibility for this benefit). However, the amount of money accessible through home equity borrowing is, naturally, limited to the amount of equity in your home. If you are already carrying a large mortgage on your home, the sums available may be small.

Remember the big(!) downside to funding your startup with personal loans: Even though your business may be incorporated, home equity and personal installment borrowing carry the risk that you may lose your home or other personal assets used as collateral (such as a car, a boat, or stock holdings) if you default on the loan.

Business Term Loans.   In most cases, it is hard—if not impossible—for a startup to obtain a business loan from a bank. The prospects of most startups are simply too risky to meet the lending criteria that most banks follow. However, as your business grows and establishes a track record of consistent revenues and profits, bank borrowing for specific purposes (such as to finance the buying of new equipment or expansion into new markets) may become easier. Having a long-term relationship with a single bank that provides a variety of services—all of which help make your company a source of revenue and profit to the bank itself—will enhance your chances of being considered creditworthy. You will also need to submit a sound business plan and a solid financial history. Even with these positive business attributes, you will be expected to guarantee the business loan personally, which can put your personal and family assets at risk should you default on the loan.

Revolving Line of Credit. This form of credit gives you access to a prelimited amount of financing that you can access without the need for additional approval. Depending on the nature of the credit account, you may request a cash transfer by calling the bank, or you may be able to access your credit by writing a check against the account. Your business will be charged interest on the amounts you actually access, and in most cases monthly payments, including principal and interest, will be automatically deducted from your checking account. Interest rates generally fluctuate over time depending on economic conditions.

A revolving line of credit usually gives you access to a moderate amount of capital, typically in the range of $50,000 to $100,000 for an early stage company. This form of credit is especially suitable for dealing with periodic variations in your business's cash flow. For example, if you run a seasonal business, accessing a line of credit can be a simple way to meet your expenses during the slack periods. Be sure to repay the sums you borrow as soon as your increased cash flow permits so that you don't face onerous interest charges and fees on large, persistent amounts of debt.

SBA-Backed Loans. The federal government operates a number of programs designed to help small businesses get access to credit through local lending institutions.* The programs supported by the Small Business Administration include:

- The 7(a) Loan Program, which helps startups and existing small businesses that might not otherwise qualify for credit obtain loans from banks and other lending institutions.
- The Microloan Program, which provides small, short-term loans to small businesses through community-based nonprofit lenders.
- The Certified Development Company 504 Loan Program, which encourages economic development by providing long-term loans to help small businesses buy equipment or expand their operations.

The SBA also runs lending programs that target businesses with special needs—for example, companies that have been injured through

_____
*https://www.sba.gov/content/sba-loans.

a disaster and companies that are seeking to develop or expand their operations as exporters of U.S.-made products into overseas markets. Ask the bank where you do business about the kinds of SBA financing for which you may qualify.

Venture Debt.   This is a particular form of lending done by only a few banks that specialize in dealing with high-growth startups. Because most unprofitable early stage companies will not be able to qualify for the business loans, lines of credit, and even SBA-backed loans described above, it is likely that your early funding will come from equity investments by friends and family, angel investors, and possibly venture capitalists (VCs). In unusual cases, even though you are raising equity funds, your startup may have an opportunity to greatly increase its value in a short time if you have even more money available to you—for example, to lock up an exclusive with a major partner by prepaying royalties or to expand your production capacity rapidly to fulfill a huge product order from a major retailer. That's where *venture debt* comes in.

Venture debt is a high-risk loan to an unprofitable but rapidly growing startup. Because of the risk, these loans carry high interest rates, short repayment time frames, and equity kickers that incentivize banks to make the loans. They are generally only available for *less* than the amount you've just raised from your VCs . . . who will be required to subordinate their repayment to the bank. Venture debt should only be considered in circumstances where the short-term value to the company greatly outweighs the high cost and risk of the loan.

Receiving Credit Card Payments

If you are going to be in business, your customers are going to pay you for something, and that means you need a way to get the money from your customers' wallets into your bank account. The most cumbersome method is for them to mail you checks or give you cash, which you must walk over to your bank. Somewhat easier is for them to give you the *numbers* from their checks, which you can use to make an "electronic check" that can be deposited online through your bank's automated clearing house (ACH) process. For large amounts, the usual way to move money is through a bank-to-bank wire transfer, which is efficient but costly and complicated. For everything else, the common method to receive payment for your services is through a credit or debit card transaction.

You can begin accepting credit card payments through a merchant account with your bank. However, since banks generally resell credit card-processing services of other companies, they may have expensive pricing and inconsistent customer service.

Your best bet in handling these payments is to have an account with a payment processor that integrates with your website and will allow you to receive payments from any credit or debit card in the world. There are three main players in the field, each of which processes billions of dollars in transactions every year. But because each is optimized for a slightly different purpose, you should compare their focus and pick the one that best suits your situation.

The biggest of the three is **Braintree**, which is owned by PayPal.[*] This service can handle virtually any payment vehicle on the planet, from credit cards to PayPal to Venmo to Bitcoin. It is very powerful, has scaled pricing that drops as your volume increases, and is good for companies with in-house programming capabilities.

The most startup-oriented of the three is **Stripe**, which provides flat rate pricing, simple tools for integration into your website, and good customer service.[†]

The simplest and most mobile-friendly is **Square**, which is best if you plan to sell products in person and accept physical credit cards, or do not have a programmer on staff.[††] While all three services offer point-of-sale credit card readers, Square's is a free, slick, tiny device that plugs into your mobile phone's headphone jack. It also has a small, battery-powered, Bluetooth-connected reader that can accept the new chip-and-PIN cards, as well as the contactless Apple Pay and Android Pay systems.

---

[*] https://www.braintreepayments.com.

[†] https://stripe.com.

[††] https://squareup.com.

15

Choosing Your Key Technologies, Platforms, and Vendors

THIS IS A CHAPTER that would not have been included in any business book as recently as a decade ago but one that is indispensable today. The exponential growth of technology since the introduction of the Internet has fundamentally redefined the way in which businesses operate, and the primary beneficiary is . . . you.

In years past, it would have taken a huge amount of time and money and significant number of people to set up the basic infrastructure systems that a high-growth company needs to operate. Today, you can sit at your keyboard and, in a few hours at virtually no cost, set up a complete office full of tools and services that are as effective as those of a Fortune 100 company. Because these are all services delivered through the Internet, you can start in your bedroom and seamlessly transition to a coworking space, a dedicated office, and a mega-million-dollar business campus as your company grows, without missing a beat. Even better, the services work across geographies and time zones, allowing you to build a completely virtual and distributed company. The result is to make working with a colleague a thousand miles away as easy as working with someone at the next desk.

Because technology is continually advancing, and because an essential feature of Software as a Service (SaaS) is that it can be continuously updated without you needing to do anything, it is likely that by the time you read this book there will be a new set of tools to make your business startup even easier. That said, I will give you the general categories of tools to use, the best options in each category as of mid-2016, and my personal pick within the category. While switching from one SaaS platform to another is not the end of the world, I suggest that you standardize one choice from each category across your whole organization . . . whether that organization is just you, or a team of 100 based in a dozen countries.

Hardware

The first choice you make is your hardware platform. In a world that has moved online, this is less of an issue than it used to be, but your life will be substantially easier if you and your work colleagues all use interchangeable equipment. The choices are well known: the market-leading (by numbers) Windows/Android hybrid ecosystem, with desktop/laptop computers running Microsoft's Windows and phones/tablets running Google's Android operating system; or the market-leading (by value) Apple ecosystem, with desktop/laptop computers running MacOS and phones/tablets running iOS. Which one you choose is a matter of personal preference, but my choice (and, in my personal experience, the majority choice of U.S.-based tech startups) is the world of Apple. That is because, with a single manufacturer controlling both the hardware and operating systems, the integrated experience is more seamless, more secure, and more stable.

Office Suite

The next significant choice you make is the software for your basic business operations, from writing reports and proposals to producing spreadsheets and presentations. Again you have a wealth of choices from the same players, each of whom offers a complete suite of integrated tools and cloud services to connect them. The traditional, dominant player in this category has long been Microsoft with its Microsoft Office suite, including Word for word processing, Excel for spreadsheets, PowerPoint for presentations, and Outlook for e-mail.

But as Apple began its run to become the world's most valuable company, it decided to take on Microsoft with Pages for word processing, Numbers for spreadsheets, Keynote for presentations, and Mail for e-mail . . . and to bundle them free with every computer, notebook, tablet, and phone. Not to be left in the dust, Google, which began life as a search engine, took to the cloud with a vengeance and produced the first suite of office tools that were completely online: Google Apps. This includes Docs for word processing, Sheets for spreadsheets, Slides for presentations, and Gmail for e-mail.

In this three-way face-off, the least widely accepted player is Apple, whose software has never achieved the penetration that its hardware has. Microsoft's offerings are still used by the (very) large majority of traditional businesses, but Google's suite—in no small part because it is free—has made rapid inroads with newer, smaller businesses.

If I were starting from scratch today, I would probably look to the future and standardize on Google. However, as an old warhorse I confess that personally I use a combination of Microsoft's Word and Excel for word processing and spreadsheets, Apple's Keynote for presentations, and Google's Gmail for e-mail. While this combination is not seamless, there is enough interoperability among the three platforms that I manage to function effectively.

Cloud Hosting

When I founded my first Internet-based company in the 1990s, our software ran on big computers—known as servers—that were located in a special room in our office with air conditioners to keep them cool. By the end of the dot-com boom in 2000, we had moved those computers to a "colocation facility," a large building that held and maintained the Internet servers for many different companies. By the time I founded Gust in the mid-2000s, there was no question whatsoever: Of course we wouldn't have our own servers. Instead, all of our software and websites would be hosted in the cloud, running on servers owned by someone else. We would not know, or care, where the machines were physically located, and we wouldn't even care what kind of machines they actually were. All we had to know was that, when we needed computing power, we just had to request it from our vendor and it would magically appear. It meant, too, that we relied on our vendor to do the management, maintenance, and security operations that would otherwise be prohibitively expensive for us, and to use its immense scale and redundancy to operate at a service level far better than we could achieve on our own.

This idea of amorphous cloud hosting was pioneered by Amazon in 2002, when it realized that it could take the powerful facilities it had built to service its own e-commerce business and leverage that infrastructure into providing services for other companies through Amazon web Services. Since then, as the cost of computing hardware has dropped exponentially as its power has increased exponentially, the cloud has become a prime battleground, as five behemoths compete to host every Internet offering in the world.

Because the specific offerings, features, pricing, and competitive advantages among the five change almost daily, and because different offerings are appropriate for different types of services and coding styles, my advice is that, when you are ready to select a cloud hosting vendor, you have your technology expert compare all five based on your specific needs. Given the intense, almost cutthroat level of competition among vendors, you are likely to find that each will be pleased to make you a special offer of free or discounted services to set up on its platform. The value of the offer depends to some extent on how hot they believe your startup may become, so the cloud providers have special marketing teams that work with accelerators, incubators, law firms, angel groups, and venture capital funds to identify and entice startups with high potential for growth.

The first and largest (by a factor of 10) cloud provider, and the one that has historically been the industry leader in features, functionality, and ease of use, is Amazon Web Services. Its combination of Elastic Compute Cloud (EC2), Simple Storage Service (S3), and other services make it the service standard to beat. But over the past five years, competition from very serious players has be come strong, and you should check out its major competitors before deciding on your cloud host. They are Microsoft Azure, Google Compute Engine, IBM Soft-Layer, and Rackspace.

Other Platform Choices

The first three platform choices require the biggest commitment and have the highest switching costs. After these come a host of other tools that will give your startup the power of a big company and the efficiency of a well-oiled machine. You may not have to implement all of them immediately, but if, within a year or so, you haven't found that you really *do* need one solution from each category you are not on your way to scaling up to be a high-growth company, or you are in serious denial about the impact that technology-based tools can have on business. In each category, I note my current best choice with an asterisk.

Website

For businesses that do not require large, custom-coded Internet applications that are deployed on cloud-hosted platforms, there are many vendors that provide powerful, easy-to-use tools for quickly and inexpensively designing and deploying custom websites. It is remarkable how much you can do without having to be—or hire—a designer, programmer, or computer expert. These platforms give you the power to set up complete e-commerce–enabled web stores, photo galleries, blogs, media properties, and more.

Best options: SquareSpace*, WordPress, Weebly, Wufoo, Wix

Surveys

Whether you need to create a simple poll of existing customers, conduct an in-depth market research survey, plan an event, or collect data from employees, these services give you the tools to design a survey, send it out to targets, collect answers, and analyze and report on results. All offer free basic plans, and more expensive ones that include advanced features, such as supplying focus groups for market surveys.

Best options: SurveyMonkey*, Google Forms, SurveyGizmo, Zoomerang

Customer Relationship Management (CRM)

The first pioneer of Software as a Service (SaaS) was Salesforce.com, which revolutionized the world of business sales teams and the industry of software distribution. Following in its footsteps, customer relationship management systems organize the entire sales process and keep track of past, current, and prospective customers. With comprehensive reporting, sales pipeline generation, and a nearly infinite variety of add-ons and additional features, CRM systems serve as the backbone of a company's revenue generation activities.

Best options: Pipedrive*, ZoHo, Salesforce, SugarCRM, Highrise

Human Resources

For a newly minted startup that consists of just you—or you and a co-founder—you will likely be able to handle by yourself the paperwork related to your employment with the company. But as soon as you have more than a handful of employees, you will find that keeping track of everyone's health insurance, benefits, and other paperwork is a painful activity. Luckily, a spate of platforms have come online to take that trouble off your hands. Most of them will not only give you easy tools to manage the paperwork but will also connect you to inexpensive benefit providers.

Best options: Zenefits*, Justworks, Insperity, Workday, TriNet

File Storage

While it used to cost thousands of dollars to purchase physical disk drives to hold all of your data, today, data storage in the cloud is virtually free, and competition has moved to the areas of features, interconnectivity, and ease of use. The major ecosystem players incorporate full cloud-based file storage into their offerings (Google Drive, Microsoft OneDrive, Apple iCloud), and you will probably be best off sticking with the one that comes as part of—and integrates seamlessly with—your office solution suite. However, there are other stand-alone services as well.

Best options: Dropbox*, Box, IDrive

Team Communications

As your team grows, it is increasingly important to have effective communications systems in place so that nothing gets lost between the cracks. This is important if your team works side by side in a single office. It is critical if your team is virtual, dispersed, or often on the move. Unlike e-mail, services like Slack and Yammer are used for short, effortless, real-time, text communication. It's just like turning your head to speak to the person at the next desk. For remote, virtual teams that need to function as a single operation, a new offering from Sococo gives the uncanny impression of everyone being in the same physical office by combining avatars, text chat, videoconferencing, and more (it's really slick . . .).

Best options: Slack*, Sococo*, Yammer

Project Management

Running a startup means keeping track of dozens of different balls in the air at any given time. Chief among these is the development and deployment of the company's main product or service, often referred to as project management. In the old days in the twentieth century, project management meant planning everything at the beginning, and keeping track of large charts showing "waterfalls" of steps that needed to be done in sequence. In the twenty-first century, that process has been largely supplanted by the lean development approach discussed in Chapters 2 and 6, in which everything is fluid, many tasks occur in parallel, and priorities change weekly or even daily. To manage development and projects in this changing environment—especially when many people are working together—it is essential to use a system to keep track of what is happening, and to manage the company's priorities.

Best options: Trello*, Basecamp, Asana, Pivotal Tracker

Teleconferencing

When you consider that the first time anyone saw the Queen of England on television was in 1957, it is remarkable that less than 60 years later, multiparty, real-time, high-definition, mobile video-conferencing is so ubiquitous that it is a free service. Regardless of the specific industry in which your company operates, you need to have a way to instantly talk to and share screens with one or more people inexpensively and in real time. While the lines are becoming blurred, two general types of conferencing are audio teleconferencing (the ubiquitous conference call) and video teleconferencing (including webinars, presentations, and screen sharing).

Best options for audio calls: UberConference*, FreeConference

Best options for video calls: join.me*, Skype*, Google Hangouts*, FaceTime, GoToMeeting, WebEx

Customer Support

As your business grows, so too will your customer base—and no matter how easy to use or self-service your product or service is, you will invariably have customers who require support, report bugs, or have questions. Customer support platforms provide powerful tools to manage the process from report to resolution.

Best options: Zendesk*, Get Satisfaction, Freshdesk

E-signatures

With the passage of the Electronic Signatures in Global and National Commerce Act (ESIGN) in 2000, the U.S. government officially recognized the legality of digital signatures on digital documents. The days of mailing or faxing paperwork for physical signatures are rapidly fading into the past and you will want to establish an account with an e-signature provider to make your life easier as you negotiate and execute documents.

Best options: EchoSign*, DocuSign*, HelloSign, CudaSign

Marketing

Whether or not your business is completely online, it is likely that the majority of your sales leads will be developed online, and the first point of contact will be through e-mail. Once you have your first customers, you will want to maximize their lifetime value to the company by keeping in touch with them and delivering sales messaging on a regular basis. While this can be done manually for a few (or few dozen) contacts, it is impractical once your mailing list includes thousands or millions of names. When that time comes (if not before), you will need a special mailing service to handle and track your e-mail campaigns, ensure that your messages don't get caught in spam filters, and integrate with all of your other sales and marketing programs and platforms.

Best options: MailChimp*, HubSpot, SendGrid

Social Media Management

Social media, which includes platforms like Facebook, Twitter, and LinkedIn, is an effective way for your startup to get more traffic and generate new leads. Having a presence on all the major networks is a necessity for any business, whether online, off-line, or a combination of the two. You therefore need to have a presence online and to monitor that presence in a way that will keep it relevant but not become a full-time job for you. You can accomplish this feat by working smart as well as hard, using marketing software, dashboards, and publishing tools to enhance your social media savvy.

Best options for social media: Twitter*, Facebook*, LinkedIn*, Google+, Quora

Best options for social media management: Hootsuite*, Buffer, SocialFlow, Sprout Social

16

Measure Your Business
with Data Analytics

WHEN YOUR STARTUP is small, it is easy to gauge its health. From your vantage point as the company's leader—and perhaps its only employee—you can readily track the arrival and departure of customers, the growth or decline of revenues, and changes in profitability as costs rise or fall. But as your company grows and its complexity increases, measuring the success of the business becomes more difficult. It is important to develop a well-thought-out set of metrics, or measurement tools, and to apply them consistently.

In Chapter 12 I discussed the basics of financial accounting, which provides a crucial set of metrics that every business founder needs to understand. Now we're going to extend our metrics tracking with some of the measurement tools and techniques that you will use in the second phase of the lean startup cycle: Measure. These are designed to provide methods so you can quickly and easily monitor the changing levels of success experienced by your startup as you build and iterate on your product.

Use Your MVP to Establish Baseline Metrics and Begin Experimental Improvements

Creating a minimum viable product (MVP) is the best way to test the validity of your business plan with real-world customers. By offering the MVP to customers through sales and marketing channels like those you plan to use when your business is fully operational, you can determine whether there is a real market for your product—and whether you need to retool your offering to serve a genuine customer need.

You can use your initial offering of the MVP to establish baseline metrics for your business. For example, suppose your product is a software as a service that will be sold through online subscriptions. When you offer your MVP to an initial group of customer prospects, results will include click-through rates for your advertising message, sign-up rates, trial membership rates, conversion rates, annual subscription rates, lifetime value rates for each customer, and the cost of sales and marketing activities per customer created. These baseline metrics are a valuable starting point you can use to measure the success or failure of future modifications to your product offering and marketing strategy.

The baseline metrics generated by your first offering of the MVP will probably be worse than the financial projections you sketched in your initial business plan. It is discouraging—but it's common even normal. Having established this as a place to start, you can work to improve your growth model by developing alternative hypotheses that define changes with potential to improve results, then testing those hypotheses in sequence to see which are valid and which to eliminate.

These alternate hypotheses may relate to improvements in the product itself. For example, through customer interviews, surveys, focus groups, or brainstorming among members of your business team, you might conclude that your product can be made more attractive by simplifying it. This idea can serve as a working hypothesis for you to test through an experiment with a more basic version of your MVP. If the metrics generated in this experiment are an improvement over the baseline metrics, you can conclude that the hypothesis is probably correct. You may want to create further hypotheses about improvements in the product and further experiments.

Over time, a series of short, simple, rapidly iterated experiments will help to refine your growth model until it is effective, producing metrics that match or exceed those in your original business plan. Note that it's important to test *one and only one* hypothesis in each experiment. If you conduct a market experiment that features both an improved product design and a redesigned website, it will be impossible to draw a clear conclusion about a cause-and-effect relationship from the results achieved, since you won't know which change was responsible for the increased or decreased metrics.

Many startup founders find that split test experiments (also known as A/B tests) provide useful insights into customer needs and preferences. In a split test experiment you divide a prospective customer pool into two different, randomly selected groups. Then you offer different versions of the product to the two groups of customers at the same time, or offer the two groups the same product using differing marketing strategies or advertising messages. Different behaviors by the two groups of customers enable you to draw inferences about the attractiveness of the two product versions or marketing approaches.

Experimental product offerings can be combined with survey and feedback tools to provide additional information about customer reactions to your MVP. For example, the Net Promoter Score (NPS) is a tool developed by Satmetrix that can be used to analyze customer concern about a problem or enthusiasm for a particular solution. In this system, customers are asked to respond to a single question—"How likely is it that you would recommend our company to a friend or colleague?"—choosing answers from a 0–10 scale, 10 being "extremely likely" and 0 is "not at all likely."

- **Promoters** (score 9–10) are loyal enthusiasts who will keep buying and refer others, fueling growth.
- **Passives** (score 7–8) are satisfied but unenthusiastic customers who are vulnerable to competitive offerings.
- **Detractors** (score 0–6) are unhappy customers who can damage your brand and impede growth through negative word-of-mouth.

Subtracting the percentage of detractors from the percentage of promoters yields the NPS, which can range from a low of −100 (if every customer is a detractor) to a high of 100 (if every customer is a promoter). Many companies actually have a negative NPS, but the top growth brands with loyal customers, such as Amazon and Zappos, operate in the range of 50–80.

Your NPS is a metric that can be tested through varying iterations of your product design, marketing strategy, and other changes to your business model. The more your metrics improve, the stronger your business model becomes.

How to Make Sure That the Metrics You Gather and Analyze Are Meaningful

The nature of your business will determine which metrics to use in analyzing the growth rate of your business. Among the most popular and important metrics that startup managers find valuable to track across all business categories are customer counts, number of repeat purchases, and sales revenues. But more granular data related to a particular business model may be equally important. If you are building a business for which selling advertising represents an important revenue source, then metrics related to the number of individuals who visit your website or download your media content—as well as their demographic characteristics—are crucial, since advertisers will be interested in buying the eyeballs of large numbers of prospective customers with specific qualities (high incomes, for instance).

Intelligently designing the metrics and the reporting systems on which you'll rely are important. As Eric Ries explains, all the metrics that you rely upon should be actionable, accessible, and auditable.*

- An *actionable* metric is one that demonstrates a clear cause-and-effect relationship. Your metrics are actionable when you can separate the impact of various factors on your startup's rate of growth. By contrast, when the data you gather and analyze reflects the effects of two or more factors—for example, changes in product design, marketing strategy, and communications message—it is difficult to determine which factor is responsible for a change in

---

*Described in *The Lean Startup*, Chapter 7.

growth rate. Making smart decisions about future actions based on the data is nearly hopeless.

- An *accessible* metric is one that is simple, clear, people based, and available to everyone in the organization. In many organizations, access to data is restricted to a few top managers. However, a well-run startup makes most or all data available to all employees so that analysis, insight, and learning occur throughout the company. The presentation of data is also important: You must make sure that your metrics are presented in a written or visual form whose meaning can be grasped easily. One frequent approach to disseminating metrics is to use management dashboards. These are special web pages constantly refreshed with live data, providing an easy, one-glance overview of a company's most important metrics.

The dashboard in Figure 16.1 was generated by the software-as-a-service platform Geckoboard.com, which can pull in information from many dozens of different sources and display them in an easily accessible manner.

Figure 16.1   Management Dashboard

- An *auditable* metric is one that is credible and susceptible to checking through customer interactions. Don't rely on your programmers to develop metrics by themselves; instead, members of your product management, marketing, and service teams should shape the metrics and see that they reflect the information that really matters. You should spot-check the metrics that are reported to you through live interactions with customers. All too often, flaws in the design or reporting of metrics mean that the data presented to managers is inaccurate and therefore misleading. Discovering and correcting such errors must happen quickly to avoid taking your company down the wrong path.

Cohort analysis is important technique to apply to the analysis of your company metrics in order to ensure that they are actionable, accessible, and auditable. This refers to the practice of studying the behavior of separate groups of customers who come into contact with your product at various times rather than lumping all customers together in a cumulative set of statistics. Cohort analysis enables you to distinguish the impact of changes in your business model on your results. It is especially important during the startup phase, when you are conducting experiments to refine your business model to make it more responsive to customer needs and preferences.

The fundamental method of performing cohort analysis is to view all customers who make contact with you during a particular time period—say, a certain month of the year—as a single pool. You track the relevant metrics for this pool of customers throughout their history with the company, from the initial contact (by clicking on your website URL) through any purchasing activity and down to additional interactions (such as repeat purchases). This history is often referred to as the customer life cycle. Quantitative results from the life cycles of particular cohorts—for instance, the May 2016 cohort—can then be compared with the results for the preceding and following cohorts. Changes from one cohort to the next will reflect improvement—or deterioration—in the business model.

The results of cohort analysis are often more meaningful than those reflected in cumulative data, which lumps together customers encountered under widely differing circumstances. Cohort analysis can enable you to pinpoint specific product, marketing, sales, and messaging strategies that have been effective—for example, a particular social media campaign, advertising blitz, public relations coup, or promotional offer that yielded much-greater-than-average results.

Following these principles when analyzing your company metrics will enable you to avoid relying on vanity metrics. These are numbers that give a rosy picture of company growth, even when the actual performance is lagging.

Gross metrics—in which customer numbers, sales data, revenues, and other figures are accumulated month over month—are likely to fall into the "vanity" category. By their nature, such cumulative data inevitably increases over time, often creating curves that produce an impressive image on a graph or table. Unfortunately, these escalating curves disguise the fact that successive groups of customers are not responding more favorably to your product or its marketing; in fact, the changes you introduce to your business model may have no effect—or even a negative impact—on customer response.

Cohort analysis helps you avoid the trap of believing the false image produced by vanity metrics by making it easy to see how customer response to your business model evolves. Don't just gloss lightly over this warning! Entrepreneurs are an optimistic lot, and self-delusion is fundamental to our psychological makeup. We don't like to be disappointed or to disappoint others. We therefore have an innate tendency to hold fast to good news on the theory of confirmation bias. Just as looking at yourself naked in the mirror is a better way to help you lose weight, so too is understanding the real metrics surrounding your customers' behavior is a better way to the truth.

Finally, as you develop your metrics, define the growth milestones you hope to achieve and the metrics for achieving them in advance rather than after the fact. This practice will ensure that the targets you reach are meaningful rather than plucked from the air to create an illusory feeling of success. Defining the metrics you hope to achieve before beginning a particular experiment will prevent target slippage and improve the rigor of your analysis.

Tools for Analytics

One positive aspect of the increasing move of startups into the online world is that everything can be tracked, measured, and recorded online . . . everything. If you wanted, you could record every interaction of every customer with your online product, including how long they stay on each page, what their click path is through your site, and even where on the screen their eyes are looking during their time on each page! Because we can generate such data, however, doesn't mean that it would be particularly useful to us as a management tool.

Fortunately, a wide range of online tools have been developed to allow you to track, organize, and make sense of the important things that are happening on your website. Here are some of the most useful that I've found:

Google Analytics is a free service for small businesses that has become the standard way of tracking website interactions with users. By adding a few simple lines of code to each web page, you can easily capture and report on customer acquisition, benchmarking, conversion, performance, cohort analyses, and more (see Figure 16.2).

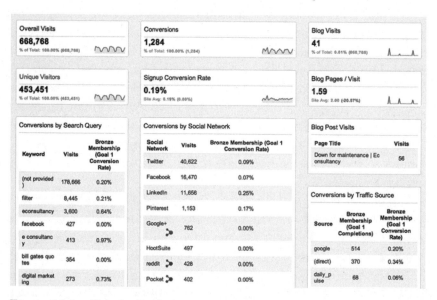

Figure 16.2   Google Analytics

Chartbeat is a business dashboard that shows you a summary of success. You can track concurrent visitor counts, compare web traffic against Twitter chatter, analyze how people find your site— say, by searching Google or clicking a link on Facebook—and see a history of web traffic at a glance. To use Chartbeat, simply insert a small code snippet into the header and footer of each web page (see Figure 16.3).

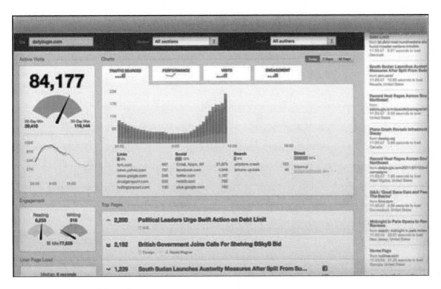

Figure 16.3   Chartbeat

Kissmetrics is a comprehensive and easy-to-use analytics platform designed to optimize your marketing and conversion rates (see Figure 16.4).

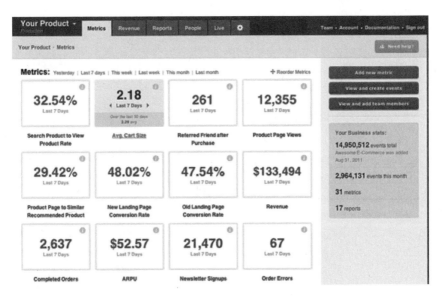

Figure 16.4   **Kissmetrics**

Mixpanel gives you tools for tracking user engagement across your product and following individual users and their specific actions, as well as doing detailed conversion analyses of your sales funnel (see Figure 16.5).

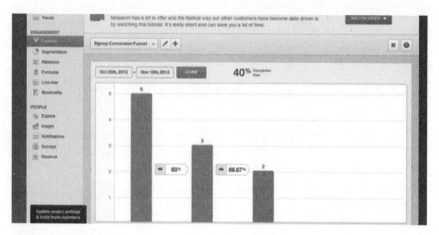

Figure 16.5   Mixpanel

Indicative is a newer analytics platform specializing in the customer journey (see Figure 16.6). For most businesses, that journey

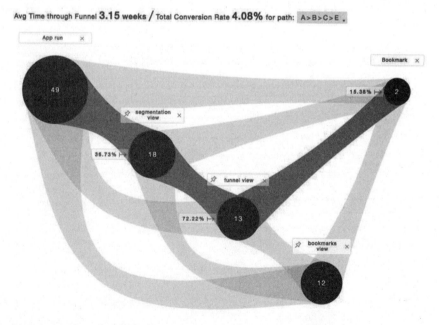

Figure 16.6 Indicative

has become exponentially more complex, with many digital and physical touch points. In any engagement or conversion process, there are many paths to take and steps that may be skipped—users may even backtrack and repeat steps. Traditional analytics tools do not fully capture the complex nature of this interaction and flowcharts of every interaction quickly become illegible. *Indicative* allows you to model complex, nonlinear user flows and to drill into every step of the customer journey to identify issues and opportunities for improvement.

Key Growth Issues to Study with Lean Analytics

As you've seen, the main purpose of lean analytics for the startup business is to help you define the most effective strategies and tactics for achieving a high rate of growth of customer numbers, sales revenues, and profitability. To do this you will probably want to conduct experiments to test the appeal of various product designs, marketing strategies, and sales approaches. In addition, you should consider conducting experiments on other factors that may affect your growth rate, including:

- **Product pricing**: The best way to test customer response to different pricing strategies is through actual marketplace experiments—especially through split testing of alternative prices for the same product. You may be surprised by the responses you receive. It is not unheard-of for a product to attract more customers when the price is higher, since a higher price is often associated with enhanced quality.
- **Channel effectiveness**: Depending on the nature of your product and its likely customer base, varying channels for reaching customers may produce widely differing sales results. For example, entrepreneurs Gabriel Weinberg and Justin Mares, in their great book *Traction: A Startup Guide to Getting Customers*, identify 19 vdifferent "traction channels" by which customers can be acquired.[*] You may discover that a channel you considered

---

[*] Gabriel Weinberg and Justin Mares, *Traction: A Startup Guide to Getting Customers* (S-curves Publishing), 2014.

irrelevant turns out to be your most powerful customer acquisition tool.

- **The customer decision process**: Every product is sold through a unique customer decision process, beginning with discovery of the product in a particular online or off-line venue and involving a series of interactions that culminate in a decision to buy (or not to buy). One important and useful piece of marketplace knowledge you can develop is a detailed map of the customer decision process for your product, identifying such parameters as: How will most customers become aware of the product? What messaging factors will determine their initial degree of interest in the product? What questions will customers ask about the product? Whose opinions about the product will customers value? How will friends, family members, work colleagues, and others impact customer decisions about your product? How will customers test your product's quality? What kinds of triggers in the product offering will lead to a purchase decision? You can—and should—develop hypotheses about each of these elements in the decision process and test those hypotheses through experiments. The results will enable you to fine-tune your product offering and your marketing strategy to maximize their customer appeal.

Remember that it's not enough to monitor the growth of your customer base and sales revenues over time. You also need to keep tabs on the amount of money you spend to attract prospects and turn them into customers. This includes such expenses as the costs of designing and maintaining a website, the personnel costs for marketing and sales employees, costs for advertising and the purchasing of mailing lists, and so on. As part of the lean analytics process, you should track the total cost of acquiring a customer through the various marketing and sales channels you test. Some channels are far more efficient and cost-effective than others.

You can combine this information with demographic data to determine the plausible scalability of your business. It's great to identify a large population segment with characteristics that match those of the customers who are attracted to your product. But your business will only be able to grow to scale rapidly and profitably if you acquire large numbers of those potential customers through channels and marketing methods that are affordable.

17

Round out Your Team with Employees and Freelancers

THINK ABOUT THE NUMBER of distinct job titles/responsibilities that are needed by McDonald's Corporation. With 1.8 million employees in 112 countries, my guess is that they have hundreds—if not over a thousand—separate roles to be filled. These range from the CEO to a counter person in the Wichita downtown drive-through; from a director of human resources to a U.S. quality systems/food safety manager specializing in potato and oil products.

By contrast, consider a hot dog vendor on a street corner. The fact is that virtually all of those same roles are required . . . it's just that they're all filled by the same person. The counter person making your hot dog happens to be the CEO of the company, who manages his own health insurance and, by the way, is responsible for ensuring that his potato knishes are safe to eat.

Similarly, in a startup, there are an infinite number of roles that can be filled, but all are filled by a limited number of people who are multitasking. For example, in the canonical "hacker/hustler" startup team, the former may combine every role from chief technology officer

(CTO) to junior assistant regression tester in the quality assurance department, and the latter, every role from CEO to night shift call center operator in the customer service department.

What this means is that a startup will take all the help it can afford, shedding whatever burden is possible from the shoulders of the founder(s), who are the default incumbents in every other role. New hires will be prioritized to take on the most urgently needed activities, the specific positions being a function of (1) the unique business of the startup, and (2) the unique skill sets of the founder(s).

As an example, if the tech founder happens to be a superb product designer as well as a skilled coder, the earliest hires are likely to be in the area of sales and marketing. But if the tech founder is primarily a hard-core hacker, the most urgent need may be for a visual designer.

Along the same lines, if the business founder is primarily finance oriented, the first hires might be salespeople. But if she is a consummate salesperson, then the initial hire may be an operations person to handle ordering and fulfillment.

Note that lack of a design function integrated into the fabric of every startup is one of the most challenging issues in the startup world—in large part because good design is somewhat intangible and tends to get lost in day-to-day priorities. If your startup is not able to dedicate an early key role to user experience and interface design, at least make sure that someone on your founding team has design as an integral part of his or her portfolio.

Only you can know for sure when it is appropriate to add to your team. One caution: many more startups have gotten in trouble from over hiring than underhiring. As entrepreneurs, we are genetically programmed to be optimistic and to see our companies as the successful operations we know they are going to be. It is therefore tempting to hire up in advance of a big order or product adoption . . . I've been guilty of doing this in virtually every company I've ever founded. But long experience has taught me to heed Ben Franklin's advice that "a penny saved is a penny earned." I've learned that exercising the discipline of keeping a tight team—even if you have funding to spend—more often than not is your best course of action.

Recruiting and Hiring Employees

As an entrepreneurial founder who has been building startup teams for decades, I have made every mistake in the book when it comes to hiring. What helped me figure out what I was doing wrong was a seminal guide called *How to Think About Hiring*, by Lex Sisney, a serial entrepreneur who became the guru of effective organizational design with his classic book *Organizational Physics*. I cannot recommend these books highly enough, particularly once your startup moves from "trying to figure it out" to "now we have to really grow."

What follows, included with Lex's permission, is a taste of his approach to hiring. It is based on his observations of how the best sports teams manage their recruiting:

> "Consistently great teams don't scout and hire for talent. They scout and hire for talent that is a supreme fit for their system. They always think about building a team with a strong collective identity at a fair price instead of just collecting individual talent at any price."

The New Hire Draft Board

Taking a page from the sports recruiting playbook, Lex suggests that you have a "draft board," as shown in Figure 17.1, that allows you to think clearly and accurately about whom to hire and why (and whom not to hire and why), and where the value of a particular candidate lies.

If you had such a system, you could place all prospective new hires on the draft board and see if they're a fit or not, what the trade-offs are for each candidate, and how candidates compare to existing staff. In a word, the draft board brings clarity.

Like most great things in life, this draft board is both simple and powerful. It groups an organization's current staff and/or potential job candidates into one of four quadrants:

The **Team Leaders** in quadrant 1 demonstrate high skills and are a good fit for this position or role. They have shared vision and values, and they demand fair compensation (defined as at or below market rates for your industry and corporate life cycle stage) for this position.

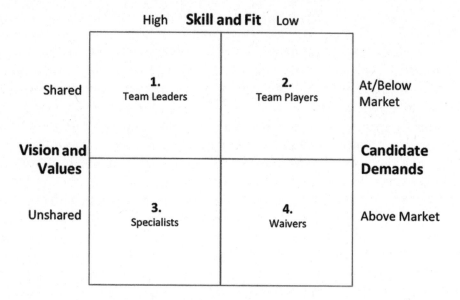

Figure 17.1   New Hire Draft Board

They could get more money elsewhere, but they choose to take less because they value being part of the team and the opportunity involved in a role that is well-suited to their strengths and interests.

Team leaders define the way of your organization. Think of your team leaders as stars, starters, or captains. You want to reward and retain them for as long as possible. Give them ownership opportunities, career paths, and autonomy, and support them as role models for the rest of the company.

The **Team Players** in quadrant 2 don't have the same technical skills, fit, or experience as team leaders, but they share the same desired vision and values, and don't cost an arm and a leg relative to market price.

Team players are essential to your success, and you definitely want them around. It's hard to find people who share the same vision and values, and embody the way of your organization. If they have the raw talent, it's much easier to develop their technical capabilities over time to become team leaders—if not, to remain as valuable team players. As they develop their capabilities, a role in the organization may open up that is a very strong fit for their style. Think of your team players as your role players or bench. You need to coach them to develop technical proficiency and groom them into the right roles while celebrating them as key contributors to the team's success.

The **Specialists** in quadrant 3 have high technical skills and are a strong style fit for the job, but they do not share the same vision and value and/or may be expensive compared to market rates.

Specialists are viewed as highly capable experts who don't fit into the desired organizational culture. While Specialists can get the job done, but great organizations rely on them sparingly and never place them in core leadership positions because they don't share the desired vision and values. Think of specialists as mercenaries or free agents who get paid well to perform a specific function. If you do choose to use them to fill in some talent gaps, keep them on the periphery of the organizational core and pay them cash on the barrelhead for a job well done. Avoid putting them in leadership positions, but allow them to express their high level of skills outside of the leadership core.

The **Waivers** in quadrant 4 do not have the skills and fit and do not buy into the desired vision and values. Or, they simply demand too much compensation beyond market rates for a company of your size and industry.*

Waivers are the people whom you try to avoid hiring in the first place. The easiest time to make a "waiver" is before they even get hired! If, in the interviewing process, you notice the signals of a quadrant 4, it's straightforward: DO NOT HIRE.

This framework provides a strong foundation as you consider who's on your team now and whom you want on your team in the future.

- You need a strong core of team leaders who are extremely talented at what they do, are a great fit for your system, share the desired vision and values, and will work at a fair price relative to market rates.
- You need a deep bench of team players who aren't yet as talented as the starters (or lack the same level of job fit), but buy into the desired organizational culture, and do so at fair market price.
- You want to avoid using specialists who, if placed in a leadership position, can quickly turn the organizational culture toxic or tip

---

*The term "waivers" comes from a labor management procedure of the U.S. National Football League, in which a team that no longer wants to keep a particular player can waive its right to the player's contract and allow other teams to hire him.

the payroll balance by demanding exorbitant fees to be part of the core team.

■ You must avoid hiring and retaining waivers, who don't have the skills, aren't a fit, don't buy into the vision and values, or make it too expensive in time, energy, and/or money to keep around.

When you are in hiring mode, ask yourself questions like: Are you seeking a team leader for a critical leadership position? Or will you accept a specialist for this position because it is outside the company core and you need a high level of technical skill and role fit to get the job done? Are you in the market for a Team Player, but prepared to expand the scope to a Team Leader if you stumble across the right candidate? Or is this a Team Player hire because that's all that's really required for this role?

Note that this is only a small taste of Lex's system, which is based on matching styles, personalities, and skills to an organization's needs. You can read much more about it on his comprehensive blog, OrganizationalPhysics.com, which includes such cool things as the World's Fastest Personality Test, a free, 15-second test to help you understand the basics of someone's personality style (including your own).

Using Employment Contracts

As you build your team, it is important that everyone sign an employment agreement on his or her way in the door. This goes for you and your cofounder(s) as well. The specifics can be tweaked (although in general they are pretty standard), but the basic points should include salary and benefits details, confidentiality, intellectual property assignments, and employment at will. Depending on the circumstances and whether there is equity involved, the documents may also include option grants and vesting schedules, noncompete/nonsolicit provisions, job responsibilities and reporting, and severance provisions.

All of this sounds daunting, but it is extremely common and will be part of every corporate setup package if you use a lawyer to incorporate. It can also be handled through an online self-service legal site or through your benefit provider.

That said, I strongly recommend using an experienced startup lawyer for this process. An attorney helps ensure that the terms you're asking for are reasonable. If there is a specific area of concern for your business, a knowledgeable lawyer can guide you through the process of explicitly discussing the issue and negotiating a fair contract clause up front.

Doing this at the beginning will save you enormous headaches down the road (because you will ultimately need it anyway, and doing it retroactively can be 10 times as expensive) and go a long way toward inoculating you against problems caused by misunderstandings (intentional or otherwise).

Building a Corporate Culture That Is Authentic, Universal, and Consistent

As your company grows from you and a handful of employees to a larger group, it becomes increasingly difficult—and increasingly important— to find ways to ensure that the spirit of camaraderie, dedication, and creativity that mark the earliest days of a startup continue to infuse the daily operations of the business. This is the realm of what business experts call corporate culture, and entire books (including Lex's!) have been written about the challenge of creating and maintaining a corporate culture that attracts the best people and encourages them to perform their best.

I've tackled and observed this task from many perspectives. My conclusion is that for a company to survive and thrive, its culture needs to be **authentic, universal,** and **consistent.**

Let's take those traits one at a time:

Authentic

Based on my 30+ years of experience in business, I don't believe that it is possible over the long run to sustain an invented culture. I've never seen success from a company bringing in a culture consultant or a marketing firm to tell employees what they should believe or how they should act. Culture in an organization starts from the top down and is remarkably penetrating. If the founder/CEO is a jerk, employees end up modeling behavior on what they see in practice. It's a case of "Your actions shout so loudly I can't hear what you're saying."

Universal

Although culture and values start at the top, for them to be maintained throughout the organization, they need buy-in from all the people who count—whether they are senior managers or quietly influential peer leaders. And because it's virtually impossible to buy into a value in which you don't believe, major hiring decisions are critical when it comes to culture.

Consistent

For me, consistency as a matter of business leadership means a close-to-zero-tolerance policy for behavior that violates our cultural values. When I say that I don't lie—and we say that Gust doesn't lie— we mean it. If I were to discover that someone on the team did lie, either internally or externally, that person would be terminated on the spot. Because We. Just. Don't. Do. That.

A company's culture has to be real, stemming from the authentic values of the person (or the people) at the top. You then need to be sure, when hiring senior management and staff, that team members share the same culture when they come in. Then you need to be 100 percent consistent, with no wiggle room—reinforcing the things that are important to the company.

Work/Life Balance and a Supportive Corporate Culture

The question of work/life balance is tricky and in the real world there are always going to be trade-offs. A great corporate culture can go a long way toward resolving the imbalance.

Every real entrepreneur will tell you without reservation that there simply is no such thing as work/life balance for an entrepreneur, and that is something one must accept if one chooses this path in life. We are on duty 24/7/365, paying for the privilege, often receiving neither thanks nor economic rewards, and our families suffer because of it. Anyone who tells you otherwise is not a real entrepreneur . . . or is lying.

At the other end of the spectrum, working a unionized, highly structured, nine-to-five job in a large corporation or for a public sector employer with excellent negotiated benefits, the equation is literally reversed. Your job, in that case, is something on which you spend 35 of your 168 hours each week, to generate the economic ability to fund a life with your family, as well as vacations, hobbies, and other interests.

Everything else lies somewhere in between. No ordinary person should be expected to put in entrepreneurial hours. By the same token, few sustainable, growing businesses in 2016 will be able to succeed with a nine-to-five, by-the-clock workforce.

The challenge is that working in a startup is much closer to the former end of the spectrum than it is to the latter. No startup that I know of can survive with people working leisurely four-day weeks, punching out at 5:00 PM to be home for an early dinner, and taking 20 holiday and 25 vacation days annually. That's just not the way a startup works, and everyone on your team should know that before joining.

Real high-growth startups are fundamentally incapable of providing what many people mean when they say "work/life balance." But for those who choose to work in this world, it is possible (although difficult) to live in a fulfilling, challenging, viable environment.

The Outsourcing Alternative

When you are starting out and don't have the funds to pay full-time employees, or when you need to increase your company capabilities to meet the demands of growth, hiring more employees isn't the only option. Instead, there is an exploding world of freelance workers available who can do virtually anything and everything a full-time employee could. In today's world, this is known as the "gig economy," and as a lean startup you may be able to benefit from the flexibility of freelancers and the lower cost of skilled workers in other areas.

Two of the largest freelance sites of the early 2000s recently merged into a giant, cloud-based platform that is the current pinnacle of work on demand. Upwork.com, formed by the merger of ODesk and Elance in 2015, has over 10 million freelance workers registered on its site who have been used by over 4 million businesses to commission over $3 billion in work. That is a LOT of work, all done by people who don't work full-time for the companies that hired them.

The kind of work a freelancer can do is limited only by your imagination, provided that it can be done on a computer. The top categories for which startups and other companies hire freelancers on Upwork are technology, administrative support, writing and translation, design and multimedia, mobile development, sales and marketing, and finance and legal.

In fact, many startups get their minimum viable product by using freelancers and only then begin hiring full-time employees after they either are generating revenues or have raised investment capital.

Here are some suggestions from Darrell Jones of Upwork for attracting the best freelancers and making the relationship work:

Communicate with Your Freelancers.

Communication is everything, especially when your freelancer is remote. Remember that the person isn't there daily to absorb the nuances of your project, so you need to define your needs and expectations from the start. Use concrete examples when possible in your project description. Unclear communication is almost always to blame when a project doesn't go as expected.

Stay on Top of Projects.

It's imperative to stay involved with projects that are longer term or have multiple milestones to ensure things stay on track. The slightest derailment (say, an improper but accepted milestone) can leave your freelancer spending countless hours developing work that is not what you're looking for.

Pay on Time, and Pay a Fair Price.

You want great work, and you want a great pool of freelancers who are excited to work on new projects with you. It's essential to pay fair rates based on the work involved and experience level needed. Take a look around the site to get a sense of the marketplace and the going rates.

Consider Using Milestones on Projects.

If you have a bigger project, think about hiring on a fixed-price basis and breaking the project into several smaller milestones. That way, you can put money into escrow and release funds as each milestone is met. Another benefit is that you only have to fund the next milestone—not the entire job.

Hire Intelligently.

Before you make the final hiring decision, be sure to vet freelancers. View feedback and reviews from other clients before reaching out to prospective candidates. The interview is a critical part of the process, where you can get to know the candidates and their work styles to determine who might be the best fit. You can also look at job factors from previous projects to see how pleased other clients have been with the freelancers you are considering.

With these suggestions in mind, you should have a better understanding of what it takes to be a professional and top-notch client with whom freelancers enjoy working. That's the basis of solid and long-standing relationships, and something you'll reap benefits from as you build your startup.

18

Establish a Stock Option Plan to Incentivize Your Team

ONE OF THE MAJOR attractions for most employees who are considering working for a startup (rather than a long-established company) is the chance of receiving equity—thus becoming a partial owner of the company—as part of their compensation. If the company goes on to be very successful, there's a chance that their equity share may make them extremely rich. So getting in on the ground floor of a promising business is attractive to a degree that the salary alone rarely justifies.

If you are an entrepreneur on the verge of hiring your first employees for a new startup business, you should consider establishing a plan that will enable you to provide equity participation for the key people you want to attract. This might be optional for a traditional company, but you are starting a scalable, high-growth business—and in today's market, that means that an employee stock option plan is mandatory.

As I've suggested several times in this book, begin by talking to a lawyer who is familiar with setting up startups rather than try to handle things yourself. When the company is first registered (since only you and your cofounders are owners of the business) you don't need to set aside shares for anyone else. That happens only when either (1) you start hiring employees who will receive options instead of shares, or (2) you take your first equity investment (such as in a Series Seed or Series A convertible preferred stock financing) from outside investors.

At this point, the company establishes what is known as an option pool, consisting of a block of shares of common stock that are reserved for use when employees or others eventually exercise their options. An option is precisely what it sounds like—a piece of paper giving the holder the option of purchasing a share of stock. The company must ensure that it will always have those shares available.

In contrast, when investors come along, they are directly purchasing shares of stock from the company, and as part of the process the company will authorize and issue new shares (which will, of course, have the effect of diluting the ownership stake of anyone who already has shares).

There are two things to note:

- Although the option pool for employee grants will likely be established at the time of your first investment and will cover options to be granted in the future, the full amount of the option pool (typically 10 to 20 percent of the company's ownership) will be deducted before the investors calculate the company's valuation. While this doesn't seem fair from an entrepreneur's perspective, there are valid reasons for it (your entreaties to do it any other way will be about as effective as a dog howling at the moon).
- Although your option plan may not kick in until after you begin hiring employees or take i n your first investment, I would highly suggest that, from the very beginning, you establish founder reverse vesting with your partners. This is something that gets an undeserved bad rap among entrepreneurs, but without it you are asking for trouble. Think about it: Three people cofound a startup with equal shares, they have a hit, raise a million bucks in angel or venture money, and the next day one of the partners says, "Hey, it was fun, but I'm outta here—and oh, by the way, I'm keeping my one-third ownership of the company, which I'm sure you guys will make really valuable. Thanks!"

In the tech startup industry, the near-universal practice is for every-one in the company—from the CEO to the receptionist—to participate in the option plan with identical terms. Having only certain employees chosen to participate is a recipe for internal cultural problems.

The only difference among employees is the number of options each person is granted . . . and, except for the C-suite group, which might have option plans that are individualized, the number is almost always determined by the level of the role. For example, an entry-level employee might receive options for 5,000 shares; a manager, 10,000; a director, 20,000; and so on.

Note that because any method of handling "antidilution protec-tion" has the effect of helping the equity holder—who is being pro-tected at the cost of someone else—this provision is hotly negotiated and *always* only for the benefit of investors at a cost to the founders and employees. In the real world, it is completely unheard-of for founders or employees to get prophylactic antidilution protection because the golden rule of early stage investing is: "The investor with the gold makes the rules."

That said, there are certain circumstances where management (but virtually never founders or rank-and-file employees) may have the negotiating leverage to get some protection for themselves. This usually happens when the company is facing tough times and the value of management's original options have decreased to the point that the equity no longer serves as an incentive for their staying with the com-pany. In that case, faced with a potential exodus of crucial manage-ment personnel needed to keep the company going, investors might approve a onetime management option grant to effectively protect some of the team's equity, or, if the company is positioned for sale, promise them a management "carveout" from the proceeds of the sale. This means that management gets a stated piece of the cash up front, before the investors.

More common is the practice of "evergreening" employee options, in which employees are given one or more additional option grants once their original grants have fully (or partially) vested. That keeps the carrot ahead of the employees, with a continuing incentive for re-maining with the company. Otherwise, once all the options are vested after four years, theoretically there is no additional equity benefit to employees in sticking around.

Managing Your Option Plan and Cap Table

Your initial cap table starts with the incorporator of the company own-ing 100 percent of the equity; your startup lawyer will take care of the legal work involved with establishing your company's option plan. That's the easy part. The problem is that the minute you start hiring employees, giving advisors equity, or raising money from investors, things start getting complicated very fast.

Luckily, there are several companies that offer comprehensive, cloud-based services to manage your cap table and your option plan in a simple, easy-to-use way. These programs tie in to your legal agreements, can be reviewed by your lawyer and accountant, and provide accounts to your option holders and investors so that they can manage their own holdings (see Figure 18.1).

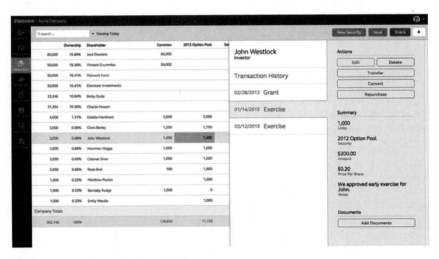

Figure 18.1   Sample Cap Table

As employees are hired, funds are raised, and options are vested, the programs track all of the interactions and automatically update the company's master cap table and the individual accounts of the option holders and investors (see Figure 18.2). Because they hold all of the information about all of the equity holders and their various rights and preferences, each of these sites also offers advanced modeling of the outcomes (known as the liquidation waterfall and discussed in

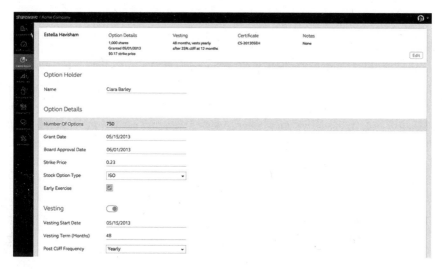

Figure 18.2   Sample Stock Option Account Statement

Chapter 25) when it comes time to distribute the proceeds, whether in a good case (a rich acquisition) or a bad one (a bankruptcy liquidation) (see Figure 18.3).

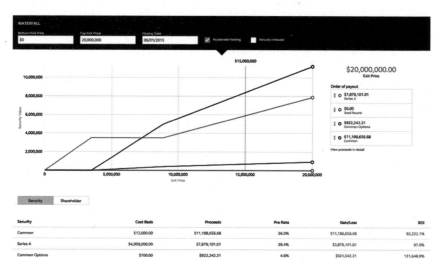

Figure 18.3   Sample Waterfall Analysis

Among the online cap table/option management programs are offerings from Gust, Capshare, eShares, Ipreo, and Solium.

409(a) Valuations and the Meaning of "Fair Market Value"

The essence of a stock option is that the company gives a contract to the employee (the stock option grant) that says the employee is allowed to purchase X number of shares of the company at their fair market value today. If you think about that for a minute, you'll realize that, according to this definition, a stock option isn't worth anything today. And that's a good thing! What makes it good is that, because it has no value, when you give it to the employee there is nothing changing hands that can be taxed. Instead, the employee waits until the company's stock price is higher than today (remember, you're a high-growth startup) and then exercises the option to buy the stock in the future at today's low price.

Just as getting the *investment* valuation right is critical when raising money from angels or venture capitalists, it turns out that the *fair market* valuation of your company for option purposes is a completely different valuation that you need to be aware of as well.

"Wait a minute!" I hear you cry. "Isn't that fraud?! How can the same business have two different valuations?? Isn't the fair market value the same number at which I just raised money in the, umm, fair market?!?"

Those are perfectly valid questions, but it turns out that there is a perfectly logical answer, one with which your lawyer, your accountant, and the IRS will all be comfortable. That's because the options your employees are getting are options on common stock, whereas the stock your investors are purchasing is convertible preferred stock. Remember that the investors' stock gets paid back first in all cases and typically comes with a host of protective provisions and controls that the common stock doesn't have. In addition, the negotiated investment valuation that you and the investors agreed upon was primarily a way of dividing up the future value that you both think the company may eventually reach. But the IRS is cold-eyed, is pessimistic, and doesn't care about futures. So if your company doesn't have revenues yet (let alone profits), it doesn't care if you and your investors are cockeyed optimists about some mythical future IPO.

The good news is that while the IRS's view of your startup's value may be depressing ("$5 million for a company that hasn't shipped a product yet?! *Snort*"), it actually benefits you and your employees. It allows you to issue options priced at a low number without tax consequences so that when you DO make it big, the values of everyone's options will be greatly increased. Otherwise, you'd be in the position of granting options at a high price (so there would be less of an increase), or at a low price, but making the recipient pay taxes today on the difference.

This special valuation process for options is described in Section 409(a) of the tax code, which requires that, in most cases, it be done by an outside valuation firm. There are half a dozen specialist firms that set up to process these types of valuation analyses rapidly and economically, which is important, because the IRS requires that the latest 409(a) valuation be done within the past six months any time you issue options. Among the leading ones are Gust Equity Management, Silicon Valley Bank, Scalar, Teknos, and Aranca.

A recent development in option valuations is the rapid integration of cap table management platforms with 409(a) valuation platforms. This provides great efficiencies and economies of scale and has seen the cost of the required routine 409(a) valuations drop from around $10,000 per report to $2,500, or even less (although the cost of a valuation increases with the complexity of a company's equity structure).

PART

III

Raise Funds; Collaborate with Investors; Plan for Your Exit

19

Understand the Funding Process and What Investors Want to See

SOME VERY SMALL BUSINESSES—particularly those that offer the professional or personal services of a single individual—can be launched and grown with little other than human time and talent. But most businesses require some money before they can be started— to pay for software, buy tools or equipment, lease office space, or pay for the time worked by employees or outside contractors. Since most entrepreneurs are not independently wealthy, and since, as we saw in Chapter 13, banks won't lend money to startups, it is often necessary to raise funds by exchanging an ownership interest (equity) for money. The people who are willing to make that exchange are investors, and their interests, motivations, and capabilities cover a wide range, both in the amount of money they can provide and the stage your company needs to have reached before they invest.

How Much Money Can I Raise, and from Whom?

The amount of money you can raise from a particular investor varies depending upon whether you're talking about a family friend, an individual angel investor, an organized angel group, or a professional venture capital fund (VC). To scale things, the average individual investment in a given company by business angels who regularly invest in early stage ventures in the United States is roughly $25,000. Outside of major tech centers, you might find individuals participating in the $5K–$10K range, although there are high-net worth individuals who can, and do, invest upward of $1 million in one chunk in early stage deals.

The average amount invested by organized angel groups these days is in the range of $250K–$750K, which is roughly the same range as the so-called super angels or seed funds, who are more correctly described as micro VCs.

Traditional venture capital firms have historically started their Series A investments in the $3M–$5M range, with follow-ons in later rounds going up to tens of millions of dollars. However, with the rapidly decreasing cost of starting up a business and pressure at the low end from angels and seed funds, many VCs are dropping down and, either directly or through special-purpose funds, making smaller investments.

Putting it all together, in VERY rough ranges, it looks like this:

From $0–$25,000 you will likely be investing your own cash from your own pocket; otherwise no one else will be comfortable investing at all. This money stays in and is part of what makes up your founder's equity (along with your work and your intellectual property).

From $25,000–$150,000 you will likely be rounding up friends and family to put in the first outside cash on top of yours. This will usually be recorded as a straight sale of common stock, or as a convertible note that converts into the same security as the next professional round, but at a discount (which is actually better for everyone). I'll discuss the mechanics of these investments in Chapter 22.

From $150,000–$1.5M you are in business angel territory, either by lucking into one really rich and generous angel or (more likely) pulling together a bunch of individuals (at $10,000–$100,000 each) or one or more organized angel groups, or one or more micro-VCs (super angels) or seed funds. They will invest either in the form of a convertible note (with a cap on valuation), or else in a Series Seed or Series A convertible preferred stock round, using similar documentation to that used by larger venture capital funds (which we'll cover in Chapter 22).

From +/– $1.5M up to about $10M you are looking at early stage venture capital funds, which uses something like the National Venture Capital Association's Model Series A documents. They will make their first investment about half of what they're prepared to put in, with the rest coming in one or more follow-on rounds if you execute your plan successfully.

North of, say, $10M–$20M, you'd be getting money from a later stage venture capital fund whose paperwork will be similar to the earlier VCs. They will put in larger amounts of cash, but your valuation will be much higher, so they may end up with a smaller stake than the earlier investors (who would likely continue to invest in each round to maintain their percentage ownership).

Although this is the canonical progression, keep in mind that the number of companies that get all the way through it is very, very small. A majority of companies started in the United States begin and end with the first stage: the founders' own money. The number of companies able to get outside funding then begins to drop by orders of magnitude: the percentages (very rough) are that 25 percent of startups will get friends and family money; 2.5 percent will get angel money; 0.25 percent will get early stage VC money; and perhaps 0.025 percent will make it to later stage VCs.

The Investment Process and the Funding Round

Investments in high-growth businesses are often described in terms of a series of *funding rounds*. Technically, a funding round means a company accepts one or more investments from one or more investors on similar terms within a certain period of time. This could cover many different things, such as:

■ Your parents lending you money to cover your expenses while you code your product

- 25 individual angel investors funding a startup on a convertible note
- Two angel groups investing money in Series Seed preferred stock purchase
- A single venture capital fund putting in the full amount as a Series A convertible preferred investment

In all these cases, the fundamental requirement is that the company and the investor agree on the amount being invested, and the terms. These items are included in what is known as a term sheet. What the terms end up being, and how a company and investor(s) arrive at that term sheet, may differ widely.

In an ideal world, an entrepreneur bootstraps a startup, gets traction in the marketplace, and is noticed; a smart investor calls the company and says, "Hey, I think you're doing great things. I'd like to invest a million dollars in exchange for 10 percent of your common stock." The entrepreneur agrees; the lawyers quickly draw up the documents; the investor sends over a check; and the deal is done.

To say this is a rare occurrence would be to overstate wildly the likelihood of it happening.

What does usually happen? First, a company gets started and gets some traction. (These days, it is difficult to nearly impossible to get funded without having an operating company and a product that is near completion.) Then the founder talks to as many investors as he can find, ideally introduced to them by mutual acquaintances. This is known as "starting a round."

With luck, at least one of the investors will make a funding offer by presenting a term sheet. If they offer the full amount the entrepreneur thinks he needs, and the terms are acceptable (perhaps after some negotiation), the paperwork is signed, the money wired, and the round closed.

However, if the investor is willing to put in some, but not all, of the money needed, and both sides agree on the term sheet, the company has a round in progress with a lead investor. At that point, the entrepreneur (assisted in some cases by the lead investor) goes to other investors with the term sheet from the lead to try to fill out the round. Other investors will be invited to put in money on the same terms as the lead investor (thus, being part of the same round).

In some cases, the term sheet provides that the round will be closed (that is, stop taking in new investments and have the investors transfer in their money) by a certain date, regardless of whether other investors join. Typically, however, the term sheet provides for a minimum amount to be raised before anyone, including the lead investor, actually transfers the money. It may also provide for a maximum amount, beyond which no additional investors will be allowed to join. In either case, since the terms of the round have already been negotiated and agreed upon by the company and the lead investor, the decision for the following investors is much simpler, a take-it-or-leave-it choice based on the signed term sheet (and therefore much easier to get).

The challenge is that getting that lead investor is the toughest thing in the startup world, because someone needs to take the first step, similar to getting the first pickle out of a tightly packed pickle jar.

The ideal lead investor will have the following characteristics:

- "Smart money," which means they know the startup business and the particular domain of the company, and can be helpful in many ways going forward
- A strong commitment to the company, so they will devote time and effort to the company during and after the fund-raising round
- A significant amount of money they are willing to invest (typically, at least 25–50 percent of the target raise)
- Deep pockets (that is, more cash reserved for follow-on rounds)
- A network of other investors to whom they can introduce the company
- Good personal chemistry with the entrepreneur

However, because it is so difficult to get that lead investor, entrepreneurs often have no choice but to try shortcuts. One is to draw up a term sheet themselves, setting a valuation, terms, and target amount. They then try to function as their own lead investor by presenting their term sheet to potential investors, getting quickly to the easy take-it-or-leave-it decision and skipping the tough step-up-and-lead decision.

Unfortunately, this is often problematic, because an entrepreneur "negotiating" that self-proposed term sheet with himself will not end up with the same term sheet that a smart, tough lead investor would have negotiated. And because (1) the pseudo–term sheet will be less investor friendly than a real one and because (2) there will be no smart, committed, deep-pocketed, well-networked investor providing validation, support, and a good chunk of funding for the round, the resulting easy take-it-or-leave-it choice is turned into an even easier "leave it."

What Are Investors Looking For?

Having spent many decades on both sides of the startup investment table, I realize that founders and investors can look at the same company and see very different things. The visionary, optimistic entrepreneur sees a world of possibility (with a few potential road bumps along the way), while the pragmatic, rational investor sees a company that may or may not have the skills and resources to survive and thrive (with the potential of turning into a home run, if everything works out perfectly).

The smart founder looking to raise an investment for a startup will develop the habit of examining his or her own business from an investor's perspective. The sooner you study your company objectively as an investment possibility, the sooner you can work to improve its prospects by making changes to enhance its attractiveness to those who have the capital you need.

Here's what smart investors are looking for in your startup:

Strength of the Management Team

The entrepreneur or business founder is key to the success of any new venture. Any smart investor will start examining a possible investment by evaluating the founder's *business experience* (that is, his history as a—hopefully successful—business manager and leader), his *domain experience* (his history in the specific industry where the startup is located), and his *skill set* (his abilities in the activities that will be central to the startup's success).

Almost as important is the *founder's flexibility*—referring not just to the founder's willingness to pivot when necessary, but also the personal characteristics that make the entrepreneur easy to work with. One key issue is whether the founder will be willing to step away from the CEO role if it becomes apparent in the future that this would be the best thing for the company. As an entrepreneur, you will want to think hard about this question even before you talk with investors, since it's an issue that often arises in the life of a growing company.

In addition, investors will carefully evaluate the *completeness* of the management team. If the CEO is Superman and able to do everything in all areas, this might not be crucial, but in most cases investors consider it important to know what skills the company already has in-house and which need to be hired.

Size of the Business Opportunity

This refers primarily to the market size for the company's product or service, including the scope of the overall industry market and the specific amount of money that customers are already spending each year on substitute products for the one that your company will offer. If all the possible customers in the world are spending only $20 million or $30 million today for similar products or services, it is hard for you to claim that your company will produce a monster hit down the road. Smart investors look for market segments where people are already spending many hundreds of millions—ideally, billions—of dollars, with a growing field of potential customers.

One way of measuring the size of the business opportunity—especially among angel investors—is by evaluating the startup's potential for revenue within five years. There is nothing inherently wrong with a long-payoff venture, such as building a nuclear power plant. However, angel investors (as opposed to venture capital or private equity funds) do not usually have very deep pockets. This means that large-scale, capital-intensive ventures that will take a decade or more to generate profits are usually not appropriate for angel funding. The question becomes how quickly your company can start and scale its revenues and how likely those revenues are to be realized within a reasonable time frame (say, five years, beyond which time frame no one can project).

In addition, investors will consider the strength of the competition the business will face. They are looking for the Goldilocks answer: not too much, not too little, but just the right amount. In an ideal world, your company will be enter a space not already over crowded with entrenched, well-funded competitors. On the other hand, if it truly has no competitors that will be a warning sign to a savvy angel investor. Why are there no competitors? By definition, that means no one currently thinks that what the company is doing is worth paying for!

Product or Service

If the product or service is something generic that everybody will want because it can do everything, your company may be doomed to failure. Investors look for a clear, focused, and distinct definition of what specific need there is for it and precisely who will be the market.

Next, investors will want to know how your specific product fits the market need that has been identified—and more important, why? Investors prefer to invest in "painkillers" that solve an existing problem rather than "vitamins" that are better/faster/cheaper.

The smart investor wants to know about the path to product acceptance. Is this a solution where people immediately will know what it is, why it's of value to them, and how they can use it?

Finally, investors are interested in understanding the barriers to entry. How hard is your product or service to copy? Who is likely to do it? Sure, Google or Apple probably could knock it off, but is your product likely to face stiff competition in the near term? If so, how does your company emerge as winner? When speaking with investors, have sound, believable answers to these questions.

Type of Industry

If the industry you are entering is based on rapidly advancing and highly cost-effective information technology, that will be a plus in the eyes of investors, because a small investment can help a company go a long distance. So would a business-to-business venture or even a consumer-facing startup that is highly scalable (that is, susceptible to easy and rapid growth). A traditional business that demands a lot of cash up front but doesn't provide investors with leverage may be viewed by investors as problematic.

Sales Channels

How will your product actually get into the hands of customers? Have your proposed methods for selling, marketing, and promoting the product been tested and implemented, or do they exist only in theory?

Stage of Business

Is your business just an idea? A runaway smash hit with happy, paying, repeat customers? Or something in the middle? Different investors prefer to invest at different stages: a seed investor will not make a Series B investment, nor will a late stage VC fund a seed round.

Quality of Business Plan and Presentation

While the correlation between the quality of your business plan and its presentation and the prospects for your business isn't perfect, it is more accurate than most entrepreneurs would like to think. If you have a clean, comprehensive business plan, presented in a cohesive, persuasive way, the odds are good that you have a better-than-average chance of succeeding. Conversely, a confusing plan presented in an unappealing way suggests a business that is likely to struggle.

Yes, Virginia, There May Actually Be Some Free Money.

Although most startups are funded by their founders, their friends and families, or early stage investors, the full funding picture includes one additional source of capital that might be available for you.

The closest thing to free money for a company is when the government gives it cash and doesn't expect it back. Governments at virtually all levels, in virtually all countries, provide grants to small companies, to support entrepreneurial development.

In the United States, the Small Business Innovation Research (SBIR) program, established in 1982, encourages domestic small businesses to engage in federal research/research and development (R/R&D) that has the potential for commercialization.* The theory,

---

*https://www.sbir.gov.

according to the Small Business Administration, is that "by including qualified small businesses in the nation's R&D arena, high-tech innovation is stimulated and the United States gains entrepreneurial spirit as it meets its specific research and development needs." Each year, federal agencies with outside R&D budgets that exceed $100 million are required to allocate 2.5 percent of such budgets to these grants.

As of this writing, 11 federal agencies participate in the program. SBIR enables small businesses to explore their technological potential and provides the incentive to profit from its commercialization. Through the end of 2013, over 140,000 awards were made totaling more than $38.44 billion, and over 2,400 companies that received grants went on to receive venture capital financing. The program's goals are fourfold:

- Stimulate technological innovation
- Meet federal research and development needs
- Foster and encourage participation in innovation and entrepreneurship by socially and economically disadvantaged persons
- Increase private sector commercialization of innovations derived from federal research and development funding

The SBIR program issues grants to companies in two phases. The objective of Phase I, which offers grants up to $150,000, is to establish the technical merit, feasibility, and commercial potential of the proposed R/R&D efforts, and to determine how well the company can deliver on its promises. Phase II grants of up to $1M are intended to continue the R/R&D efforts, and funding is based on the results achieved in Phase I and the scientific and technical merit and commercial potential of the project proposed in Phase II.

A second federal program, run parallel with SBIR, is the Small Business Technology Transfer (STTR) program for technology transfer grants. The two programs are similar, except that STTR projects must be done in conjunction with a university, and the program allows the principal investigator not to work full-time at the company (a requirement of SBIR grants).

Each agency administers its own program, designating general research and development topics in its solicitations. They accept proposals from small businesses (which to them means "under 500 people"), and awards are made on a competitive basis. What's interesting (and not widely known) is that the award rate is roughly 25 percent . . . which means that a company with a viable proposal is 10× as likely to be able to get an SBIR grant as it is to get angel funding (discussed below) and 100× as likely as to get venture funding!

Every state and many local governments have economic development agencies dedicated to assisting new and established businesses to start, grow, and succeed. Services provided by these agencies include startup advice, training and resources, business location and site selection assistance, employee recruitment and training assistance, and financial assistance. Including loans, grants, tax-exempt bonds, and—in many instances—state-funded seed and venture capital funds, these agencies expend a great deal of money and effort to help new businesses get off the ground.

Okay, now that you have a broad-brush understanding of the early stage investment process and funding sources, let's examine ways to find those elusive investors and get them excited about your venture.

20

Nurture Your Investor Pipeline

BEFORE YOU LOOK for investors, it is important to understand some basic facts about the world of entrepreneurial finance:

1. There are many more entrepreneurs than there are investors, with the result that only one company out of every 400 that seeks venture funding actually receives it (even in the less formal angel world, the odds are still no better than one in 40).
2. Therefore, the competition, from an entrepreneur's standpoint, is very tough. In order to be competitive, a startup company needs to have everything in place, from its product to its team to market traction, before it is ready to seek funding.
3. Given this imbalance, most angel investors and venture capitalists (VCs) are reactive rather than proactive. They spend less time seeking out new deals than they do responding to inbound deal flow. As an example, a typical VC might see 500 opportunities cross his desk every year; for larger, more prominent ones, the number could be closer to 2,000.

4. For this reason, angels and VCs use whatever heuristics they can in order to triage the deal flow. One of the primary ones is the referral source. This means that by far the most effective way to reach a would-be investor is to be introduced by someone who knows both of you and thinks that you would be a good match.

For all these reasons, an entrepreneur should recognize that there is no magic bullet for fund-raising. No matter what you might have heard or read in the blogosphere, there is no quick, easy, guaranteed way to attract money from investors. However, there are tools and techniques that will increase your chances, and in the rest of this chapter I'll present some of them.

When to Connect with Investors

My view on the right ways to interface with potential investors before starting a funding round has changed over time, as the pace and level of activity in the startup world has begun to hyperaccelerate. It is desirable for you as an entrepreneur to be able to approach an investor with whom you've had at least a nodding relationship, because a personal connection immediately differentiates you from an over-the-transom funding request; and you are more likely to get an answer.

So if you are acquainted with—or even have a friend-of-a-friend acquaintanceship with—one or more active investors in startup businesses, it would seem to make sense to approach those investors, describe your business, and ask whether they would be willing to get together occasionally to talk about how your company's growth is proceeding. This is a modest suggestion, one that could lead to positive results for both parties one day—and it's exactly what I recommended to many startup founders in the past.

On the other hand, if I were to respond affirmatively to this kind of request by every company that might start a funding round, I would be the world's most dysfunctional investor (and entrepreneur, and husband, and father, and human being). To illustrate the math, let's say that there are 1,000 companies a year who pitch me somehow (a reasonable guess of the right magnitude). To convert this into the number with whom I would meet if I were to get together occasionally with all of the likely candidates, we'd have to multiply by three to take into account the ones that won't eventually get to pitch me. And then we'd have to multiply that number by three because "occasionally" implies more than once. That would mean that each year I'd be getting together with entrepreneurs 9,000 times . . . which, when divided into the 250 workdays available, means that I would need to have 36 get-togethers every single day. (Hint: that won't work.)

Given these realities, I think the best approach is a compromise. Be actively involved in your local startup community. Go to tech Meetups and hackathons; attend startup conferences and other events where you can engage with both entrepreneurs and potential investors. But hold off on trying to set up meetings with investors until you are fully ready to pitch. That means having all of your ducks in order; your product in the market (or at least your prototype done); all (or at least the key people) of your team together; your financial plan carefully thought through; your investor pitch finished, refined, and rehearsed; and all of your materials pulled together in one place.

Today, *any time* you talk to an angel or VC, the assumption is that you are pitching, and that will be the way your approach is received. Therefore, I believe it is harder to overcome an initial negative reaction to a not-yet-ready pitch than it would be if his or her first exposure to you is when you are all dressed up and ready to go.

This view runs counter to the traditional wisdom of the venture world (and what I used to recommend myself, and what you'll hear from a number of investors to this day). But I've observed that the nature of time and the volume and pace of business change every day, and it's important to adjust your strategy to the market as you find it.

How to Connect with Investors

Once you have identified a particular investor (whether angel or VC) who you think (after doing your research) would be appropriate for your venture, your goal is to get introduced him or her.

Professional Networks

This is where the explosion in online networking is your friend. Through professional networking sites like LinkedIn, the odds are good that you will be able to find someone who knows both of you or knows someone who can connect the two of you. In my case, for example—counting both the people who are part of my personal network and the people connected to those people—there are over 20 million potential founders who can reach me through a recommendation from either one or two people between us. Most professional investors are willing to respond to a cold call from an entrepreneur to whom they are linked by a mutual acquaintance (or two).

Angel Groups

The exception to the "Don't cold-call" approach is when a group of angel investors band together and put out the welcome mat for submissions. An angel group of this type typically receives many inquiries from entrepreneurs—often dozens or more each month—and most groups have a multistep process through which they review all opportunities. The first step is a prescreening by the group's staff (if it has one), followed by a screening committee of investor members, followed by a presentation at the group's monthly or quarterly meeting. If you hope to have your startup considered for funding by the members of such an angel group, expect to follow the screening protocol established by the group.

In a development that will ease your outreach burden, the majority of organized angel groups around the world have standardized on Gust as the international online platform for accepting submissions. It is somewhat like the common application for U.S. college admissions: You create a single comprehensive investor relations profile which you can then share with any angel group you think might be a good match.

Pitch Competitions

These public forums are another way to make connections with investors. In a pitch competition, entrepreneurs make presentations to an audience of potential investors. They vary in usefulness, and you should think carefully about selecting the competitions that make sense for you. The bottom line, as you might expect, is the value of the time and money you must invest in the process.

At one end is the opportunity to participate in a business plan competition run by an accredited angel group or a not-for-profit organization, such as a business school or regional economic development association. These are usually free or may require a small registration of $100 or so. They can be excellent ways to hone your pitching skills, get feedback from real investors, and meet others in the startup ecosystem.

At the other extreme, if you're looking at paying $15,000 to make a five-minute pitch at something that bills itself as a venture capital summit, but is attended by no real investors or press (or perhaps only low-level associates attending in order to enjoy a free lunch), then that makes no sense at all and is pretty close to a scam.

Things get squishy in the middle ground, where you're asked to pay a hefty fee (anything over $500) to pitch at an event where you don't know the makeup or quality of the audience. In 80 percent of these cases, knowledgeable insiders would advise you not to waste your money. But there are just enough in the remaining 20 percent that it probably makes sense for you to do some homework on potential pitch competitions. Check them out by asking people who should know— local VCs, mentors, and other entrepreneurs.

Connecting through Intermediaries

You may be approached by a broker or "finder" who offers to serve as an intermediary, providing connections to potential investors for a fee.

Professional early stage investors, including angels, angel group members, seed fund managers, and VCs, tend to be averse to participating in brokered funding rounds. There are many reasons for this, but early stage investors typically want all their cash going into the company, not out the door to an intermediary. They also have extensive personal networks for deal sourcing that make them proactive rather than reactive.

The situation is different, however, in private equity—even at the low end—where brokers are the norm, not the exception. And there are certain groups of investors, such as family offices or "casual" angels, who are more reactive in considering opportunities.

In general, my suggestion is that if your company is looking for true seed capita from "smart money," you would be well advised not to use an intermediary.

When to Tell an Investor "Thanks but no Thanks"

For 97.5 percent of aspiring entrepreneurs, the issue of when and how to turn down funding isn't a problem, because they never get offered it in the first place. For the other 2.5 percent, it can be agonizing, because it seems to violate the first rule of entrepreneurship: Take money whenever it's offered!

In reality, however, there can be sound reasons for passing up an offer of financing.

The first, and most important, is who the investment is from. It is impossible to overemphasize the value of "smart money" and "good money" over "dumb money" and "evil money." You should do at *least* as much diligence on your potential investors as they are doing on you. You should check references (speak with as many of their portfolio CEOs as you can, cold-calling them preferably) and read everything written about them—and that they have written. Have long talks with them about what they are looking for in the relationship, what your respective ideas are when it comes to exits and long-term management of the enterprise, and how much dry powder they are keeping for future follow-on investments. Above all, look for unimpeachable integrity and strong personal chemistry so that you will both feel comfortable when tough decisions need to be made.

Virtually every investor and serial entrepreneur I know will take smart, good money over evil or dumb money any day of the week, even if the valuations differ by 10 times (or more). Trust me, I've been there, done that, and gotten the T-shirt.

There can be other reasons to say no to a venture capitalist or other investor. They include:

Strategic Issues. When faced with a choice between a financial (venture) investor and a strategic (corporate) investor, entrepreneurs will often find that the strategic player appears to have a seductive offer: a higher valuation for the company (which means less dilution for the entrepreneur), industry expertise, access to large markets, and support with distribution, development, and marketing.

This may be true, but there is something important to remember: while a financial investor is motivated solely to increase the company's economic value (usually a good thing for the entrepreneur), a strategic investor by definition has some other agenda (that's the strategy they're following!). This can sometimes mean that the entrepreneur finds himself or herself forced (or at least urged) to move the company's product path in a certain direction, enter into exclusive contracts with the investor, or even concentrate marketing in certain cities or among certain demographics. I was recently involved in a tragic case where one of my portfolio companies was effectively forced into bankruptcy by a strategic investor who had previously appeared to be a white knight. The problem was not so much one of evil intent, but instead a complete unfamiliarity with the challenges that face early stage startups.

Operational Issues. You can often get an idea of what the long-term relationship will be from the way investors deal with you during the courtship phase of the relationship. Did it take 10 meetings to get them to commit? Did they ask to see reams of documentation during the process? Did they want to sit down individually with each of your senior managers and dive deep into detailed spreadsheets and forecasts? Did their process take up so much of your time that it had an impact on your ability to run the company?

If you are an experienced CEO in a lean, fast-moving business, if you have multiple options, and if you believe that a particular investor may ultimately be more trouble than he or she is worth, that is a legitimate reason to walk away from the money on offer.

Control-Related Issues. With few exceptions, every time you exchange money for equity, you transfer a few more shareholder votes from you to someone else.

For most high-growth startups, this is a clear choice made by the entrepreneur in exchange for the funding necessary to grow the business. But if you have the option of taking in money or not, and, like Lucifer, you would prefer to "reign in hell than serve in heaven," then turning down available funding might be a choice you would make.

Economic Issues. Finally, the decision to take in funding or not often comes down to a cost/benefit analysis, also known as risk vs. reward, or, in its bald and honest expression, fear vs. greed. Taking in funding means agreeing to part with a share of all the good things that will happen with the venture, in exchange for protecting yourself from failing by running out of money.

If you are the rare entrepreneur who can successfully bootstrap your business to profitability, you may have the opportunity to turn down funding in order to keep the rewards for yourself. Alternatively, you may be able to delay taking in funding until farther down the road. By then, if the business has already achieved a high enough valuation, the smaller economic dilution of your equity may be worth taking a penny-pinching, lean startup approach during your early months and years of operation.

The Materials You Will Need to Pitch an Investor

Since angel and venture investing (other than through Title III funding platforms, which I will discuss in Chapter 21) is limited to accredited investors, the transactions are exempt from the registration requirements for publicly traded stocks. If your company is seeking funds from angels, you will be exempt from having to provide the detailed information book (known as a private placement memorandum) that would be required in certain circumstances if you were raising funds from any people who were not accredited.

As a result, there are no legal rules determining what—if anything—you need to provide to a prospective angel investor. At the same time, there is no requirement for the angel to decide to invest in your business.

For this reason, and because of the risky nature of early stage investing, it is typical for a company founder to give a prospective investor anything and everything he or she asks for. In my role as an investor, I can assure you that if any entrepreneur refused to give me anything I wanted (such as a cap table, customer lists, projected financials, and so on), there is no way that I would be investing.

While there is an almost infinite amount of information that an investor can legitimately ask for when doing due diligence on a company, the following materials represent the basics that you should be prepared to provide as an entrepreneur seeking the interest of potential funders:

Written Documents

- A one-page overview/teaser.
- A two- to three-page executive summary.

- A slide deck specifically designed to be handed out.
- A thoughtful, comprehensive business plan—either a carefully prepared and annotated Business Model Canvas that you prepared in Chapter 1 or a more traditional 10-page+ written plan that will be the output of the lean plan methodology you employed in Chapter 2.
- A finished (or prototype) marketing brochure.

For a Live Presentation

- A 5-minute quick pitch
- A 15- to 20-minute angel/VC PowerPoint/Keynote pitch
- A sub–15-minute organized product/site demonstration

Online

- A functional public website for the company
- A short video pitch
- A dedicated, controlled-access investor relations website

Summary Financials

- Past financial information to date
- Financial projections for three to four years going forward after funding
- Operating budget, projected revenue, and amount of capital to be raised

Naturally, the financial projections you provide will involve a high degree of uncertainty—even guesswork—and experienced investors will understand this. But the more plausible and well-thought-out your financial forecasts are, the more believable your overall business plan will appear . . . and the more likely it is that investors will have the confidence to back you with their hard-earned cash.

The Pitch Deck

Of all the items in the preceding list, the one with which you and your prospective investors are likely to spend the most time is the infamous pitch deck. While it can come in different forms, the most common is a computer-based slide presentation created with Microsoft's PowerPoint presentation program. Other tools that are frequently used are Apple Keynote, Google Slides, Adobe Acrobat, and Prezi, an interactive presentation program that is available in online and offline versions. One new arrival that has been designed specifically for fund-raising pitches is SlideMagic.com, a cloud-hosted application with simple template slides that give you everything you need for a classic, professional fund-raising presentation.

There are many excellent books on how to deliver a great funding pitch. They include *Presentation Zen* by Garr Reynolds, *Slide:ology* by Nancy Duarte, and *Presenting to Win* by Jerry Weissman. For those who want a short, free crash course in How to Pitch a VC, I direct you to my Technology, Entertainment, Design (TED) Talk on the subject, which by now has been viewed nearly a million times: http://www.ted.com/talks/david_s_rose_on_pitching_to_vcs.

21

Crowdfunding and Online Platforms

YOU'VE PROBABLY HEARD about raising money online through some of the best-known crowdfunding platforms—sites like Kickstarter, Indiegogo, RocketHub, ArtistShare, and Sellaband—and you might have wondered whether this approach could be used to fund startup companies. Under the crowdfunding model, supporters of a project contribute funds to support something they believe in and receive rewards or perks in exchange.

The key thing to understand is that in traditional online crowdfunding as it existed in the United States from 2003 until 2014, supporters are not in any way purchasing ownership in the company or project, nor will they receive any benefit from the success of the project other than the promised product or thank you gift.

Another activity using online platforms that is sometimes confused with crowdfunding is peer-to-peer lending. Like crowdfunding, peer-to-peer lending is not a form of equity investment, since the lenders do not acquire an ownership interest (and thus a share of the profits and losses) in a company. Instead, they are simply lending money to a person at a fixed interest rate.

As these strictures make clear, an entrepreneur cannot use Kickstarter or other traditional crowdfunding sites to raise equity capital for a business. However, this limitation has recently changed.

The JOBS Act

On April 5, 2012, the Jumpstart Our Business Startups Act was signed into law by President Barack Obama. Known as the JOBS Act of 2012, this landmark legislation has three major components.

The first, Title I, makes it easier for companies to stay private for a longer period of time and to go public at a later date when the time is right. The provisions of Title I went into effect immediately upon the president's signature and had a significant impact on later stage private companies, but little effect on startups.

The second component, Title II, makes it possible for the first time for startups to let everyone know that they are seeking funding—which opens the floodgates for online equity fund-raising. Companies are still restricted to taking investments only from accredited investors (people with over $1 million in assets, not including the value of their home, or with over $200,000 in annual income [$300,000 in annual income if they file jointly with their spouse]), but now they don't have to do it behind closed doors in angel groups. Title II went into effect on September 23, 2013, and has already had a major impact on startup financing by making it possible for companies to seek funding openly on Internet-based platforms.

Finally, Title III, which took over four years to go into full effect on May 15, 2016, for the first time allows people who are not accredited investors to legally participate in startup funding though a new category of carefully regulated online platforms.

Accredited Investor Funding Platforms

There are hundreds of websites that purport to connect founders with funders. But since, as you have seen in the preceding chapters, raising money for a startup is hard, there's a big difference between claiming to provide funding and actually providing it.

There at least a dozen legitimate, serious sites that can be helpful for an entrepreneur during the fund-raising process. It is important that you look at them with your eyes open, however, because there is no such thing as a free lunch. In fact, the selectivity of the online platforms is as high as that of angel groups and individual investors. A minuscule percentage of companies are accepted for listing on the platforms in the first place, and not all of them succeed in raising money. With that in mind, let's run through some of the major online funding platforms as of mid-2016. The first group operate under Title II of the JOBS Act, and only accredited investors may participate in their funding rounds:

AngelList (https://angel.co) was one of the early online matching services for angels and startups. While any company can claim its profile and be listed on the platform (as we learned in Chapter 7), in order to raise money online you need to have already found an investor willing to fund your venture. That investor leads a syndicate, which is a group of other investors who look to the syndicate leader to make the initial investment decision, handle the due diligence investigation, and negotiate the terms of the round. In exchange for that work, the syndicate lead and the platform together receive a "carried interest" of up to 25 percent from the other investors, as well as administrative fees.

SeedInvest (https://www.seedinvest.com) is another early leader in the field, but works on a different model. You apply directly to the platform to be accepted for listing, and, if you meet its selective criteria (it accepts fewer than one percent of companies that apply), it will circulate information about you to its more than 15,000 accredited angel investors, who decide individually whether to invest. This platform does not take a carried interest, but instead charges 7.5 percent of the amount raised, plus 5 percent warrant coverage (which has value only if the value of the company appreciates in the future).

FundersClub (https://fundersclub.com) is similar to SeedInvest in that it makes the decision directly whether to list a startup and is similar to AngelList in that it takes a 20 percent carried interest and 10 percent administrative fee from its investors. It, too, is highly selective, accepting fewer than two percent of companies that apply.

CircleUp (https://circleup.com) is a platform designed for post-seed companies. Unlike the others, which work with startups in any category, this platform has a specific industry focus: It accepts only U.S. consumer products companies, typically ones that have more than $1 million in revenue for the current fiscal year and a tangible product or retail outlet. Like SeedInvest, CircleUp is a registered broker/dealer and charges a commission of 5 to 10 percent of cash raised through the platform.

OurCrowd (https://www.ourcrowd.com) is an online platform that is a cross with a traditional venture capital fund. Like a VC fund, OurCrowd sources its own investments (you can't apply directly) and puts its own funds into the company as the lead investor. It syndicates the balance through its online platform to its group of accredited investors and is compensated with a carried interest and management fee, like a traditional fund.

The online funding industry is still young, and all of these platforms, models, and prices are still very much in flux. The platforms described above have each facilitated over $100 million in investments and have roughly similar-sized investor bases and selective criteria.

The oldest and largest online platform connecting startups and investors is Gust, which has been used by over 350,000 startups in 190 countries to connect with over 50,000 accredited investors in over 750 investment organizations, supporting and tracking over $1 billion in investments. Since as the founder of Gust I'm biased with regard to this particular platform, I will leave the discussion of it to a separate section at the end of this book, which you may choose to read or ignore.

Before you consider engaging with an online platform, you should spend time thinking through all of the issues surrounding your startup, (as we discussed in Chapters 1 and 2.) You should then put serious effort into crafting your profile. After all, you're trying to convince an investor to give you hundreds of thousands—or even millions—of dollars to execute your vision. Isn't that worth investing at least hours, or even days, of smart, hard work?

In listing your venture on an open platform like Gust or AngelList, or applying to one of the selective platforms listed above, take full advantage of the tools the platform offers to tell your startup's story, as I explained in Chapter 7. I am constantly flummoxed by the number of startups that create a profile or send in an application with a few lines of text, incomplete data, a host of misspellings, and other errors.

Because of the fund-raising nature of these sites, most online profiles consist of two parts: a public profile and a private one. The goal of the former is to get you maximum exposure; the latter, to provide all the information that investors need to move a relationship to the next step. Your public profile should include everything nonconfidential about your business that might attract the interest of potential investors, while your private profile should contain complete, accurate information about details of the business that will lead investors to request an in-person meeting with you.

With profiles that will be viewed online by a large number of potential investors, the vast majority of effective ones have something in common: a killer video. I can't emphasize enough how important videos are when you are attempting to mass market your startup. Virtually every successful, large campaign on Kickstarter has had a great video introducing it, and that approach has transferred to the equity funding platforms. This does not mean sitting in front of your webcam while you read a prepared speech. While that is probably better than no video at all, the most successful campaigns have videos of the type that would cost \$5,000–\$10,000 if you had to pay a professional to create them.* The good news, however, is that technology has advanced so rapidly that the tools to produce a great video are already at your fingertips (bundled with your computer, included with your smartphone, or available online) at virtually no cost. All you have to do is be willing to put in the hard work to use them.

Nonaccredited Investor Crowdfunding Platforms

As important as Title II online funding platforms have become over the past few years, the publication of this book coincides with the official implementation of Title III of the JOBS Act. For the first time, the "crowd"—that is, people who are not accredited investors—will be allowed to invest in private companies, such as your startup. In order not to do away with all the security regulations of the past 80 years, the JOBS Act places strict limits on how much companies can raise this way and how much people will be able to invest in total each year if they are not accredited investors.

---

* https://www.americanexpress.com/us/small-business/openforum/articles/lights-camera-action-creating-online-videos-to-market-your-business.

For a company to take advantage of Title III crowdfunding, it may raise no more than $1 million in a 12-month period and must run its campaign through a registered broker/dealer or a special new funding portal set up and approved specifically for Title III crowdfunding (that is, not one of the platforms described above). It then must file a Form C with the SEC, covering what it will use the money for, the amount of the raise, the price, a description of the business, the names and history of directors and officers, any owners of 20 percent or more, company debt, related offerings, a detailed list of risks, restrictions on transfer of stock, financials, and a number of other business specifics.

Unlike rewards-based crowdfunding or equity funding to accredited investors under Title II, there are strict limitations on advertising and promoting a Title III fund-raising campaign. All a company can do is point to the official offering on the platform—so don't expect to see banner ads and mass e-mails promoting a startup crowdfunding campaign.

Finally, keep in mind that if you take the Title III path, while it opens up a new world of potential funders, it also comes with irrevocable side effects. These include the requirement that the company's financial statements be prepared under generally accepted accounting principles (GAAP)—which may require additional work—and the company file annual public statements with the SEC. If the raised amount is between $100K and $500K, the statements will have to be reviewed by a public accountant. If the raised amount is between $500K and $1M, they will need to be audited by a public accountant. These are not trivial requirements and may give some startups second thoughts about going the Title III route.

On the other side of the table, Title III puts significant restrictions on investors as well. Specifically, for crowd investors whose annual income or net worth is less than $100,000, then in any 12-month period they can invest no more than 5 percent of his or her net worth or 5 percent of his or her annual income (whichever is greater) in total, across ALL companies in which he or she is investing. For those with income or net worth over $100,000, the limit is the lesser of 10 percent of net worth or income. Because of these requirements for companies and investors, as well as the requirements for the platforms themselves, it is unclear how much of an impact the JOBS Act will have on startup fund-raising.

Blended Funding Platforms

One interesting new development is the appearance of blended platforms. These are online funding platforms that offer *both* Title II and Title III fund-raising, each in compliance with appropriate regulations. These may provide promising startups with a seamless path to raising funds from a combination of sources. A company could start with initial funds from friends and family, continue to small amounts from the unaccredited crowd under Title III, move up to aggregated investments from small dollar investors under Title II, and finally raise a large round with major investments from professional angels, venture capital funds, or institutional investors.

22

Survive the Term Sheet Negotiation and Investor Due Diligence

IN CHAPTER 19, we noted that one of the principal roles of the lead investor was to negotiate the terms of an investment with the founder of the startup. In theory, the terms could be "Here's a million dollars to use; if the company becomes a big success, please give it back to us." Unfortunately, that's not the way it works.

The Different Types of Equity Investments

When a corporation is established, its ownership is divided into pieces called shares of *common stock*, as discussed in Chapter 9. That's what you as a founder have, which is why it's also known as founders' stock.

There is a different kind of stock that investors can choose to purchase, called *preferred stock*. While the name makes it seem preferable to common stock, preferred is not inherently better; it's just different. Here's why:

When the time comes to turn the value of the company into cash (during an exit), that cash may be more or less than the value that you and the investors agreed the company was worth at the time of

215

the original investment. That is where the difference between the two types of stock is critical.

Preferred stock is paid out *first* before any common stock is paid—but it gets back *only* the amount that was paid for it (plus perhaps some dividends, which for this purpose act like interest). In contrast, common stock gets paid out only *after* all the preferred has been satisfied—but it gets its proportionate share of *all* the remaining value.

What this means is that, if you were an investor, you would want to own common stock if the company turns out to be a smashing success (because you share in the upside), but you would want to own preferred stock if the company is sold at a loss (because then you have a chance to get your money back before the founder sees a penny). What investors in startups buy is actually a hybrid type, called *convertible preferred stock*, which lets them have their cake and eat it, too.

The primary feature of convertible preferred stock is that in an "up" scenario it converts into common stock, and everyone is happy.

If a "down" scenario occurs, it works differently: The first money that comes in goes to pay off the cash that the investors put in. Anything leftover goes to the holders of common stock. The effect of this is to adjust retroactively the nominal value assigned to the founders' contribution.

At a basic level, the purpose of different classes of ownership in startup companies is to ensure a match between risk and reward for founders and investors coming in at different times under different sets of conditions. Because the common and convertible preferred stocks are separate types of shares, the company's charter and other documents can (and usually will) be amended to give different rights and privileges to the different types of stock . . . typically in the form of protective provisions for the investors.

I've included a sample convertible preferred stock term sheet in Appendix D, with detailed annotations that explain what each provision means, and why you should care about it.

Note Financing

Selling stock is not the only way you can raise money from investors; you can also borrow money to help get the company off the ground.

The Note . . .

The key difference is that borrowing money results in a fixed payback to the investor regardless of whether good or bad things happen, while selling equity makes the investor a partner, and his or her payback becomes variable: anything from $0 (if the company goes under) to billions of dollars (if the company ends up worth a lot of money).

Debt has its advantages to a lender—primarily, the certainty of return—and advantages to the borrower—primarily, not having to share any upside in value as the company grows. But startup investors aren't interested in ordinary debt with its attendant low returns. Instead, they want to own an equity share of the company (and therefore its upside potential), which is why they're willing to take the risk of dealing with a startup in the first place.

However, to avoid the cost and complexity of documenting an equity round (which is much more complicated than simple debt) while still providing investors with the enticement of being able to participate in the upside of equity ownership, it is not uncommon these days for startup funders to loan a startup seed money through a hybrid investment vehicle known as a *convertible note* (where "note" is the technical term used to describe the document that sets forth the terms of the loan).

Is Convertible . . .

A convertible note carries the promise that, at some future point, the angel will be able to convert what started out as a loan into the equivalent of cash and use that money to buy stock in the company. This can be useful, quick, and less expensive for the company and the investor, but it creates complications. Here's why:

If the investor is putting $100,000 into your startup in the form of a loan the only thing you need to discuss is the interest rate that the company will pay to the investor for using his or her money until it gets paid back. On the other hand, if the investor is putting $100,000 into the startup in the form of equity, you need to decide what percentage of the company's ownership the investor will end up with in exchange for the investment. To figure that out, we use the following math equation:

$$[\text{Amount being invested}] \div [\text{company value}]$$
$$= [\text{percent investor ownership}]$$

Since we can calculate any one of the three terms if we know the remaining two—and since we already know how much the investor is putting in ($100,000)—in order to figure out what the ownership percentage will be after the investment, you and the investor simply need to agree on what the company valuation is (or will be) at the time he or she purchases his or her shares of stock. You would negotiate a valuation figure you are both willing to live with. Then he or she would give you the money today, you'd give him or her the appropriate percentage of the company's stock, and you'd be all set.

But that's not what you're doing when you raise funds using a convertible note. Instead, you are borrowing the money today with the understanding that the investor will be able to convert that money into its equivalent in stock someday.

Because that conversion will happen at some point in the future (while you're getting the money today), you need to figure out a few things *today*, before the investor will give you the money. Specifically, you need to decide (1) *when* in the future the debt will convert to equity and (2) *how* the valuation of the company will be determined at that point.

The answer to both questions turns out to be the same: You and the seed investor will wait until a larger, more experienced investor— such as a venture capital fund—agrees to buy equity in the company. At that point, the debt will convert into equity (which answers question 1), and you will use as the valuation whatever the new investor is using (which answers question 2).

And Discounted . . .

So far, so good. But you're not quite done. The fact is that the angel investor was willing to invest in your startup at a time when that other investor was not, and you (hopefully) used the investment to make the company more valuable (and therefore got a high valuation from the other investor). Although it would be better for you, it really doesn't seem fair that your first investor should bear the early stage risk yet get the same reward as a later stage investor.

You solve this problem by agreeing that the first investor will get a discount on whatever valuation the other investor sets, which is why we call this a *discounted* convertible note. The discount is typically set at anywhere from 10 to 30 percent of the next round pricing.

And Capped.

Okay, that's better. But although that sounds fair, it really isn't (or at least serious investors don't think it is). That's because the more successful you are at using the original seed money to increase your startup's value, the higher the valuation the second investor will have to pay. Pretty soon, the little discount the first investor is getting doesn't seem so fair after all. For instance, if the big investor would have valued your startup in its early days at $1 million, but is willing to invest in your now-much-more-successful company at a valuation of $5 million, that means you were able to increase the company's value by 500 percent using the original investor's seed money.

If the convertible note says that it will convert at a 20 percent discount to that $5 million (if you do the math, $4 million), the investor would seem to have made a bad deal. Why? Because he ends up paying for your company's stock based on a $4 million valuation, instead of the $1 million it was worth in its early days when he made the risky investment.

The industry has solved this problem by saying, "Okay, because the angel is investing early, he'll get the 20 percent discount on whatever valuation the next guy invests at. But to be sure that things don't get out of hand, we will also say that, regardless of whatever valuation the next investor gives, in no case will the valuation at which the angel's original debt converts ever be higher than $1 million." That figure is known as the "cap," because it establishes the highest price at which the debt can convert to equity. And that is why this form of debt investment is called a "discounted convertible note with a cap."

Changing Forms of Startup Financing

Over the past 20 years, the structure for seed/angel deals has shifted from common stock (in the mid-1990s) to convertible notes (late 1990s through early 2000s) to full Series A convertible preferred (mid-2000s) to convertible notes with a cap (late 2000s) to Series Seed convertible preferred or similar (present). This shows the increasing sophistication of investors and founders, the increasing experience and publicity surrounding the advantages/disadvantages of various options, and the increasing availability of model documents and online generators for different choices.

SAFE Funding

In late 2013, Y Combinator, the leading accelerator program, unveiled a type of investment structure called a Simple Agreement for Future Equity (SAFE). SAFEs have some of the good features of convertible notes, but, because they are not actually a form of debt, they avoid some of the problems. Y Combinator has open-sourced the documents and published them at http://ycombinator.com/safe. In recent years, SAFEs have found a niche in very early investments at low dollar amounts in pure startup companies, particularly in cases where seed investors are willing to wait until an expected future round for their protections. In practice, that has meant chiefly for hot deals (such as those from Y Combinator, where the company can dictate terms because it has more investor interest than it can take) or friends and family rounds (where simplicity is paramount). To date, SAFEs have not been adopted by angel groups or financially focused angels who are proactively leading investment rounds.

Term Sheets and Closings

All investments in a company are made according to detailed legal documents that specify everything about the relationships between the various parties, the terms of the value exchange, and the rights and responsibilities of everyone involved. The paperwork can range from three to five pages for a simple, nonconvertible note to 120 pages or more for a full convertible preferred stock round. Because these are legal documents, both you and the investor(s) have your own lawyers, who work together to develop the agreements signed by the principals.

The collection of documents that constitute the investment agreement are summarized in a much shorter document known as the term sheet (anywhere from one to half a dozen pages, depending on the type of investment). Think of the term sheet as a shorthand way of documenting an agreement in principle that takes many pages of legalese to implement. It deals specifically with all of the major points of the relationships, and thus allows both sides to determine quickly whether they want to enter into a deal.

A term sheet is usually (although not always) drafted by the investor and presented to you with a defined date by which it needs to be accepted. If you sign and return it within that period, the deal is in motion, and the lawyers for each side go back and forth on the documents that will be signed at the closing. Alternatively, you may respond by declining the terms as presented, but indicate that you would be receptive to a deal at a higher valuation, or with a larger investment, or something else. In that case, the ball is back in the court of the investor, who may simply walk away or come back with a revised term sheet.

The period between when an investor presents a signed term sheet to you and the expiration date of the offer is critical for everyone. Since you are not bound by anything in the term sheet until you sign it, you are free to do whatever you want with it, including taking it to other potential investors and saying, in effect, "Look! Here is a signed term sheet that I've been given by Tom. Dick, would you be interested in matching or beating it? Just so you know, I'm also speaking with Harry, who has expressed interest as well."

While it would not happen in exactly that way, I guarantee you that the Holy Grail of fund-raising (from a founder's perspective) is having more than one term sheet from which to choose. And since market competition is a main driver in early stage finance, one term sheet often brings others from potential investors who were sitting on the fence.

Because of the possibility (if not likelihood) of their term sheet being shopped around by you to other investors and used as a stalking horse, investors try to make the consideration time as short as possible. In most cases, an interested investor will have several conversations with you to figure out the range of terms you are likely to accept. They may also send over an unsigned draft of the sheet that is not binding on them, to get feedback. After the real term sheet is delivered with a signature, you usually have one to three days to accept or decline the offer.

Once you have signed the term sheet, it is binding—not just legally (for at least some parts of it), but also ethically. If either party backs out of a signed term sheet without a good reason, word will get around, and the action will have long-term repercussions, including a stain on your—or the investor's—reputation.

After both parties have signed, the lawyers work on the full documentation for the round. One lawyer (usually specified in the term sheet) will be responsible for the base drafting, with the other making comments, although in most cases the documents are based on standard industry models. The timing of the actual payment of moneys committed during the investment round depends upon the nature of the round. In friends and family rounds, you may be able to receive funds as they are committed. In a traditional angel round, there will be a targeted range that you try to reach, as well as a minimum amount needed to close. Once that minimum is reached, a closing is held at which all the funds are released to the company.

In the past, a closing involved sending paper back and forth for signatures and using overnight delivery services to send checks to the company's bank. Today, the trend is toward fully electronic/digital closings, in which the requisite documents are electronically signed by all parties and funds are wired directly into the company's bank accounts.

Escrow

Depositing funds into an escrow account is often required during a large funding round involving several investors, in cases where investors only want to fund if the company is sure to get all the money it needs to execute its plan. Otherwise, if the money came in dribs and drabs, the company might get partway down the road, run out of money, and go broke. So investors say, in effect, "Okay, I'll put the money in escrow with your lawyer (or an online platform), so you know that you'll have my money. But you can't get your hands on it until I know that you will be successful in raising the full amount you say you need."

Another situation in a round like this is that everyone wants to invest simultaneously with everyone else, but logistically the signatures come in at different times; there may be changes in the paperwork until the last minute. So everyone signs the signature pages, and the signatures are held in escrow until everyone gives permission to release, at which time the deal is closed.

The Due Diligence Investigation

On the way to closing your funding round, you will probably be required to provide the investor(s) with significant, detailed information about your business—even more than you gave them during the pitch meetings. "Due diligence" refers to the practice of the investor carefully checking the details of any claims made by the company.

The precise nature of the due diligence process may vary. In an investment round made up of accredited investors, there is no legal requirement for you to provide a prospectus or specific disclosure schedules. These documents are therefore rarely, provided for an angel investment round.

Where the schedules and lists do appear, however, is in the due diligence requests from serious investors, which they will provide to you before the closing of the investment deal. Depending on the size of the round and the size and professionalism of the investors (and the budget of their lawyers), the information you'll be asked to provide will range from nothing more than a business plan and a slide deck (for an informal seed round) up to a voluminous amount of material (for a later stage venture round from a top-tier venture capital fund). A sample comprehensive due diligence request list is included in Appendix B.

The closing documents will generally include a representations and warranties clause, in which you as the entrepreneur are required to swear on a stack of Bibles (backed up by severe economic penalties) that everything you have told the investors is true . . . including such promises as "We own all our code" and "We are operating perfectly legally." This suggests the first and most important rule for surviving the due diligence process: Tell the truth, the whole truth, and nothing but the truth.

Most investors are aware of the vital importance of due diligence to the financial success of their undertakings. They take the process seriously and will expect the same from you as their potential entrepreneurial business partner.

Areas Covered in Due Diligence

The things investors look for during the diligence process generally fall into three main categories:

Market diligence refers to an independent review of the claims that you and your company are making regarding the industry into which you are entering. Your investor will want to verify the market size, the current competitive players in the market, and the overall industry trends that might affect your company's planned products and/or services road map. The investor will conduct online research, talk to other people knowledgeable in the field, review the reports of analysts, and more.

Business diligence looks into the specific claims that you and your company make about your business operations. These include your customers, your revenues and expenses, your background, and the background of the other company founders. To check these claims, your investor will probably call some of your customers to verify that they are, indeed, your customers and that they are happy with your products or services. The investor will also look at your accounting statements, and will at least spot-check some of the details about your career background by speaking to one or more of your previous business associates.

Legal diligence focuses on your company's structure, documentation, and history, verifying that everything is as claimed. The last thing an investor wants is to find out after the closing that the company's entire source code is actually owned by an outside programmer because you, the company founder, never effectively acquired ownership of it! Because legal diligence is factual and can be backed up by documents, this is one area where the lawyers on both sides can do much of the heavy lifting.

23

Get the Most from Your Investors, Now and in the Future

WHEN YOU HAVE ASSEMBLED a group of investors who believe in your company's future and have demonstrated their faith by providing you with capital, you're in a fortunate position—one that most entrepreneurs never experience.

This positive development carries with it new challenges. The main one is simultaneously obvious and underestimated in both directions—namely, the need to keep your investors engaged in a positive way, taking full advantage of the wisdom and insights they have to offer while not being distracted from the day-to-day responsibilities of running your business.

Suppose that you've been fortunate enough to win the support of a number of angel investors—ones who came to you prepackaged through an organized angel group or ones whom you pitched individually. You likely now have anywhere from 5 to 25 partners, each of whom has taken somewhere between $10,000 and $100,000 from his or her carefully guarded wallet and entrusted it to you to steward.

The good side is that you now have 5 to 25 smart, connected people rooting for you, and—quite literally—invested in your success. If

225

you handle this correctly and make the relationship expectations clear up front, they can be a major asset when it comes to introductions, connections, advice, and follow-on funding.

The not-so-good side is that you now have the same number of people with a legitimate interest in the details of your business, people to whom you have a fiduciary responsibility to safeguard their money and keep them informed. While this usually works out well for everyone, I've seen cases where a few small investors can aggravate the CEO by constantly calling with questions, intruding with operating advice and generally being pains in the neck.

The solution, however, is straightforward, provided you treat the care and handling of your investors with the importance it deserves.

Best Practices for Dealing with Your Investors

Your lead investor is key. Make sure you have a good working relationship with your lead angel, who will often be on your board. This may or may not have been the person who brought all the other angels in this round to the table, but try to establish up front that he or she will be one of your primary interfaces with the group. Do NOT, however, relate only to your lead and ignore everyone else. That sends a bad signal and is almost as bad as not communicating at all.

Communicate early, often, and fully with all your investors. If your term sheet calls for quarterly reports to investors, send them! And make sure that financial reports are accompanied by a management letter explaining what's actually happening. Despite the fact that every single company in which I have invested requires quarterly or annual reports, the number of companies that don't send them is shockingly high. You can be sure that those are the companies that are unlikely ever to get another penny from me and that will not be top of mind when I have good things to offer.

Use an investor relations platform to keep all your investor material, reports and contact info up-to-date. In the case of an organized angel group, that is likely what the group is already using to collaborate with one other. If your investors don't bring their own, then you should find something to streamline your communications with them. It can be as simple as a Google Groups mailing list or as comprehensive as Gust, but make it a point to keep the communications lines open.

Some of the specialized services used for this purpose are Venture360, Seraf, or AngelSpan, as well as general-purpose communication tools, like mailing list programs and social networking groups.

Regularly schedule conference calls with your early investors as a great way to keep them in the loop and let them ask questions. Whether they actually get on the call, just the fact that you are inviting them is a major plus and will keep you at the forefront of their minds. One of my portfolio companies has had quarterly calls for its early angels for over six years, and although by the second year almost no one was taking the trouble to dial in any longer, everyone appreciated the fact that they could if they wished. My gut tells me that quarterly calls are probably too frequent. Semiannually may be about right, and annually should be a mandatory minimum.

Make it a point to reach out to your investors when you need something, including introductions, sales leads, team members, and so on. Here is where most founders drop the ball. These are people who have a vested interest in your success! In most cases, investors probably won't be able to help, but even if each request to the investor base results in only one referral or contact, you'll be ahead of the game. I am a partner in one "super angel" venture fund whose competitive advantage is that all the investor partners have a conference call with every CEO every quarter and are asked what introductions they can make. While that may be overkill for your startup, sending a quarterly e-mail (or using an investor relations platform to post your current needs) is fundamental to making the best use of your investors.

For startups that are LLCs, **give your investors their K-1s in good time to file their taxes** . . . you run the risk of being burned in effigy. This doesn't apply to startups that are C corporations and issue stock, so if you've followed my advice, it probably doesn't apply to you. But, if for some reason you are an LLC or partnership, your investors will not be able to file their tax returns on time if you don't get them the information they need . . . which is the official tax record of their profit or loss from your venture in the previous year, known as form K-1.

Make sure to **keep all your books and records accurate and up-to-date**. In addition to your legal documents, contracts, leases, and intellectual property assignments, this includes your option plan records cap table, and 409(a) valuations. Thus you can respond quickly and professionally when your investors request information to establish valuations for their portfolios. In many cases, they are required by law or SEC regulation to do this and you are required to provide them with the information they need (subject to them agreeing to sign a nondisclosure agreement). The process is becoming easier as the accounting and equity platforms on both sides of the investment go online and work together.

From the beginning, **make clear what you expect** from your relationships with your investors, promising regular communication to them in exchange for putting rational limits on communication from them. It's a one-to-many relationship, so that is the only way it can work.

When an Investor Becomes Excessively Demanding

On occasion, one or more of your investors may turn out to be a problem for you as the founder. You may have an investor who is taking up too much of your time and energy with unrealistic demands, never-ending questions, strategic advice that is unhelpful, or criticisms that are off base. When this happens—provided you have checked your perceptions with others who know the situation—you may need to take steps to remedy the situation.

The first approach is to enlist the help of an intermediary. Does your company have a board of directors? Are there any investor representatives on it? Is there, as I have suggested, a lead investor with whom you have a good relationship? You might have one of these act as your front person. Sometimes, putting a new face on a problem is enough to lower the emotional temperature and reduce the issue from a chronic nuisance to an occasional inconvenience.

If this approach is impractical, or if you have tried it and failed, you might send all your investors a message that reads something like this (which I suggested to a founder who had bent himself into a pretzel trying to appease one intrusive investor):

Dear NewCo Investors,

Given the circumstances of our company's founding and seed funding, we have been blessed with an amazing group of value-adding investors. In turn, we have established a virtually unprecedented communications program with our investors, including weekly reports, monthly in-person meetings, and frequent phone calls.

This has been a great boon for NewCo during our formative period, and we look forward to continuing our frequent and regular investor communications as we continue to grow. However, we have now come to a point where I need to be able to focus directly on running the business rather than spending nearly a full day a week on the phone with my wonderful investors.

Therefore, beginning this week, we will need to limit our investor communications to the weekly reports and monthly meetings. Of course, if anything urgent arises requiring your advice, I will be sure to reach out to you immediately. But otherwise, I respectfully ask your support in allowing me to dedicate my full time to enhancing the value of your investment.

Warmly, and with great appreciation for your support,

John Doe

CEO

From that point on, don't take any calls from your problem investor.

Reaching out for a Follow-on Round

Your ability to entice your existing investors to pony up a follow-on investment will be influenced by the following factors (ordered from my personal experience with over 100 startups):

1. How well the company is doing
2. How well you have previously treated your investors
3. How the valuation of the new round compares to the original valuation when they invested
4. What the terms are for the new round, including any carrots or sticks
5. How liquid each investor is feeling (that is, how much cash he or she has available to invest at this time)

Although most novice investors (to be fair, many experienced ones as well) expect that they will write one check up front and then sit back until your IPO or acquisition, in the majority of cases the real world intervenes, and your venture will require additional funding. When this happens, there are not many other sources of cash immediately at hand, so your eyes will inevitably turn to your original angels. Here is where follow-on investments can become important.

A follow-on investment is simply an additional investment in your venture by a current investor. It can be structured in a number of ways, depending on the particular circumstance (inside/outside, up/down/flat, bridge/equity, etc.). In general, however, it takes its cue in form, if not valuation, from the previous round. So if you have previously done a Series A convertible preferred stock financing round with investors putting in $5 million, and it is now going to be followed by an investor putting in an additional $2 million, the follow-on investment might be structured in any of the following ways:

- All of the existing Series A preferred investors and the new investor and the company could agree to open Series A, with the same exact equity sold at the same valuation to the investor. Depending on how much time elapses between the two investments, it could be considered part of the same round. This would be used primarily in a case where the same investor had all of the original Series A, because by purchasing the same equity (the Series A convertible preferred stock), the new investor's liquidation preferences would be *pari passu* (that is, side-by-side in liquidation preference) with the earlier investors. (In financings, the rule is "last in, first out," so this would benefit the original Series A at the expense of the later investor.)
- The company could issue a Series B convertible preferred stock identical to the Series A, except that it has liquidation priority (remember, last in, first out). This might be used in a case where a follow-on investor didn't own all of the Series A and wanted to be sure to get all the new money out before the Series A holder(s) were paid back. This would be considered a new follow-on, flat round.
- If the company is doing well, you could issue a new Series B identical to the Series A, except for its liquidation priority and a *higher* valuation. This would be considered a new follow-on, up round.
- If the company is doing poorly, but the investor still has faith that you can pull the chestnut out of the fire, he or she might be

willing to invest in a Series B at a *lower* valuation. This would be a follow-on, down round and would not be a good thing for the company, because it would trigger the (almost inevitable) antidilution clauses in the Series A round, resulting in the common stockholders (i.e., you and your employees) taking an even bigger hit than the new investment by itself would warrant.

■ Finally, if everyone believes that the company will be able to raise a new round from some third-party investor, hopefully at a higher valuation, but you need some operating cash to keep going until that investment closes, the investor might be willing to put in the $2 million as a convertible note to bridge the company to the outside Series B. In that case, the money would go in as a loan and convert (possibly/probably at a discount) to whatever form of equity is being sold to the new investor. In that case, the $2 million would be considered a follow-on investment in the new round.

When Things Go *Really* Badly

A *pay-to-play* down round may occur when a company has not met expectations and needs to raise additional capital to keep going. But because it isn't doing well, the valuation of the company used for the new investment is lower than the valuation used for the last round of investment. This is a down round, as described above, which means new investors end up buying more shares of the company for each of their dollars than did the earlier investors.

While this seems like a good incentive to get all of the company's existing investors to put in more money, often it is not enough. Many investors are quick to cut their losses in troubled companies, and might regard this as throwing good money after bad or trying to catch a falling knife. So an additional incentive is needed.

As a Hail Mary pass, you as the founder, together with whichever investor(s) is/are prepared to commit cash in this round, issue an ultimatum like the following to the other investors:

"We would like every current investor to invest new money as part of this round, in the same proportion as the amount of equity you currently own (known as your "pro rata").

"To provide you with a little incentive to do the right thing, we're going to up the ante:

"If you are an existing investor, you currently own shares of convertible preferred stock. Those have all sorts of good features, both economic and protective. If you do *not* participate in this round (your prerogative, of course), then we are going to convert your preferred stock into common stock, taking away all of your protective and control provisions. In addition, you will suffer dilution of your ownership, in favor of those who do invest.

"Now, would you like to reconsider your decision?"

This sets up a situation where, if existing investors wants to continue to have a meaningful interest in the future of the company (playing), he or she needs to cough up new cash to invest in this round (paying). Hence, a pay-to-play down round.

But heed this warning: that action should be used only as a last-gasp resort when everything else has failed—because I guarantee you that all investors who do not take part in the round will forever feel that you have completely screwed them, and will become your worst enemies, no matter how graciously they seem to act at the time.

And that is something that you really do not want.

24

Understand Your Company's Valuation

THE VALUATION OF startup companies before they have generated any profits—and sometimes afterward, too—is a cross between black magic, hard math, market dynamics, investor return calculations, and entrepreneurial hubris. As a result, it is the most confusing, debated, and variable number in the world of investing.

As the entrepreneur, you want the investor to value your company based on its (potentially sky-high) future value. The investor wants to value it based on its (much more modest) current value. Neither approach is objectively right or wrong. In most cases, the valuation of a company still in the early days of its history, but one that the founders and the investors think should be able to grow very big, lies somewhere in between.

The number that is ultimately agreed upon will reflect not only the number of customers, the total revenues, the user and revenue growth curve (if any), the business model, the market niche, the intellectual property value, and much more, but also the relative bargaining power of those doing the negotiating. Which generally means—given the huge imbalance between the vast number of companies seeking investment funding and the relatively small number of investors with real money to invest—that, in the end, the valuation assigned to a company reflects the price that investors are willing to pay for it.

Ultimately, an investment in a startup is a market transaction in which both sides need to believe that it is getting appropriate value for what it is giving up. Because the form of the investment is the investor putting in X amount of cash and getting Y percent of the company, the effect is a math equation that lets you figure out, for any given investment, what the value of your company would be today, before the investment. If you and your investor agree on that, then you can negotiate a deal. If you don't, then you can't.

Let's say that a potential investor offers to invest $1 million in exchange for 25 percent ownership in your company. This means the investor is saying that, as of this moment, you have created something that is worth $3 million dollars.

"Huh?" I hear you ask. "If the investor's million dollars gets a quarter of the company, doesn't that mean the company is worth $4 million? That's the way they do it on *Shark Tank*!"

Well, that may be the way they do it on TV, but that doesn't make it right. Here's the math: If $1 million = 25 percent of the company, then the whole company is worth $4 million. But since that would be after the investment—what is known as the postmoney valuation—we have to back out the $1 million cash that just came in, because the company after the investment is worth whatever it was worth the day before the investment, plus the investor's million dollars that is now sitting in the company's bank account! So $4 million – $1 million = $3 million . . . which is the "premoney" valuation, or what the company is worth today, before the investor arrives on the scene.

The investor will decide how much a company is worth on the basis of many factors, including how far the business has come (Is it just a business plan? Is it already profitable? Is it somewhere in between?) and how far it can go (Given perfect execution, does this have the potential to be a billion-dollar business? Or is it more likely to top out at $20 million?)

Further complicating the calculation is the question of incentive for you, the founder. If the real value of what you have created so far is, say, $500,000, and the business needs $4.5 million to get to the point where the additional value would allow it to raise more money at a higher valuation, then the math would say the investor should get 90 percent of the company. Since that would leave you with only 10 percent—likely less, after taking in future investment rounds—the odds are that you would not be willing to take it and instead would close the company and go on to do something else.

All of these factors make the valuation decision inherently complicated, and in part subjective—despite the various objective quantitative elements that unquestionably play a role.

Business Valuation Methods for Investment

There have been many attempts to develop normalized models to provide a starting point for the negotiation. The best summary of the different approaches has been written by my friend Bill Payne, the world's leading trainer of angel investors (and who taught me much of what I'm now teaching you). What follows, adapted with permission from his books, articles, and website, is an overview of various valuation methods.

Scorecard Valuation Methodology

This method compares the target company to typical angel-funded startup ventures and adjusts the average valuation of recently funded companies in the region to establish a premoney valuation of the target. Such comparisons can only be made for companies at the same stage of development—in this case, for prerevenue startup ventures.

The first step in using the scorecard method is to determine the average premoney valuation of prerevenue companies in the region and business sector of the target company. Premoney valuation varies with the economy and with the competitive environment for startup ventures within a region. In most regions, the premoney valuation does not vary significantly from one business sector to another.

As of 2015, the range of data aggregated from various surveys by the Angel Resource Institute, CB Insights, Gust, and Bill Payne himself goes from a low premoney valuation of $500,000 to a high of $3 million for seed stage, prerevenue companies. For our purposes, we will assume that the premoney valuation of prerevenue companies ranges from $1 million to $2 million and that a typical premoney valuation for such firms is

$1.5 million. (For context, CB Insights seed stage valuation numbers for 2013 were an average of $1.9 million and a median of $600,000.)

The next step is to compare your company to your perception of similar deals done in your region. This task requires you to measure the strength of your business objectively against those of other businesses in the same or related industries—not an easy job for most entrepreneurs, who (understandably) tend to fall in love with their own businesses. Cross-check your perceptions with those of other observers to bring them in closer alignment with reality.

To provide an example, let's assume there is a company with an average product and technology (100 percent of norm), a stronger-than-average team (125 percent of norm), and a significantly larger-than-average market opportunity (150 percent of norm). The company can get to positive cash flow with a single angel round of investment (100 percent of norm). Looking at the strength of the competition in the market, you are currently weaker (75 percent of norm), but early customer feedback on the product is excellent ("other" = 100 percent of norm). The company needs additional work on building sales channels and partnerships (80 percent of norm). Using this data, and scaling it with the weight that an investor might assign to each of the factors, we can complete the calculation shown in the following worksheet (Figure 24.1):

Sample Screening and Valuation Worksheet			
COMPARISON FACTOR	SCALE	TARGET COMPANY	FACTOR
Strength of Entrepreneur and Team	30% max	125%	0.3750
Size of the Opportunity	25% max	150%	0.3750
Product/Technology	15% max	100%	0.1500
Competitive Environment	10% max	75%	0.0750
Marketing/Sales/Partnerships	10% max	80%	0.0800
Need of Additional Investment	5% max	100%	0.0500
Other (Great Customer Feedback)	5% max	100%	0.0500
Sum			1.1550

Figure 24.1   Sample Screening and Valuation Worksheet

Multiplying the sum of factors (1.155) times the average premoney valuation of $1.5 million, we arrive at a premoney valuation for the company of about $1.7 million (rounding from the calculated $1.73 million).

Venture Capital (VC) Method

The VC method was first described by Professor Bill Sahlman at Harvard Business School in 1987 in a case study. The concept is simple:

Since return on investment (ROI) = terminal value ÷ postmoney valuation;

Then, postmoney valuation = terminal value ÷ anticipated ROI.

Let me address each of these terms and explain how it is calculated and used.

Terminal value is the anticipated selling price for the company at some point down the road—assume five to eight years after investment. The selling price can be estimated by establishing a reasonable expectation for revenues in the year of the sale and, based on those revenues, estimating earnings in the year of the sale from industry-specific statistics. For example, a software company with revenues of $20 million in the harvest year might be expected to have after-tax earnings of 15 percent, or $3 million. Using available industry-specific price/earnings ratios, we can then determine the terminal value. For example, a 15× price/earnings ratio for the software company would give an estimated terminal value of $45 million.

Another way to look at it is that, since software companies often sell for two times revenues, in this case the terminal value would be $40 million. Splitting the difference, we arrive at a terminal value of $42.5 million.

Anticipated ROI: Since most early stage investors look for the possibility of a 10× to 30× return on each of their investments, assume 20× for the purpose of this example.

We can use this information to calculate the premoney valuation of the company—that is, what the company is worth before the investor arrives.

Assuming you need $500,000 to achieve positive cash flow and will grow organically thereafter, here's how the investor would calculate the premoney valuation of this transaction:

Postmoney valuation = terminal value ÷ anticipated ROI = $42.5 million ÷ 20×;

Postmoney valuation = $2.125 million;

Premoney valuation = postmoney valuation – investment = $2.125 – $0.5 million; therefore,

Premoney valuation = $1.625 million.

Okay . . . but what if the investors anticipate the need for subsequent investment? One easy way is to adjust the premoney valuation of the current round, reducing the premoney valuation by the estimated level of dilution from later investors. If investors in this round anticipate eventually being diluted by half, the premoney valuation for the current round would be about $800,000.

Dave Berkus Method

My friend Dave Berkus is a lecturer and educator, and a founding member of the Tech Coast Angels in Southern California, who has invested in more than 70 startup ventures. Dave's valuation model first appeared in a book published by Harvard's Howard Stevenson in the mid-90s, and has been used by angels since. Here is the latest version, updated by Dave in 2009.

Start with a premoney valuation of zero, and then assess the quality of the target company in light of the characteristics shown in the following table (Figure 24.2):

Characteristic	Add to Premoney Valuation
Quality Management Team	Zero to $0.5 million
Sound Idea	Zero to $0.5 million
Working Prototype	Zero to $0.5 million
Quality Board of Directors	Zero to $0.5 million
Product Rollout or Sales	Zero to $0.5 million

Figure 24.2   Berkus Valuation Factors

Note that the numbers are the maximum for each class (not absolutes), so a valuation can be $800K (or less) as easily as $2.5 million. Furthermore, Dave reminds us that his method "was created specifically for the earliest stage investments as a way to find a starting point without relying upon the founder's financial forecasts."

The Risk Factor Summation Method

This approach considers a broader set of factors in determining the premoney valuation of prerevenue companies. The Ohio Tech Angels, who developed it, describe the method as follows:

> "Reflecting the premise that the higher the number of risk factors, then the higher the overall risk, this method forces investors to think about the various types of risks that a particular venture must manage in order to achieve a lucrative exit. Of course, the largest is always "management risk," which demands the most consideration, and investors feel is the most overarching risk in any venture. While this method certainly considers the level of management risk, it also prompts the user to assess other risk types."

The list of risk types to be considered when using this method includes:

- Management risk
- Stage of the business risk
- Legislation/political risk
- Manufacturing risk
- Sales and marketing risk
- Funding/capital raising risk
- Competition risk
- Technology risk
- Litigation risk
- International risk
- Reputation risk
- Potential lucrative exit

Assign a score to each risk as follows:

+2 very positive for growing the company and executing a wonderful exit

+1 positive

0 neutral

−1 negative for growing the company and executing a wonderful exit

−2 very negative

The average premoney valuation of prerevenue companies in your region is then adjusted positively by $250,000 for every +1 (+$500K for a +2) and negatively by $250,000 for every −1 (−$500K for a −2).

Emerging Valuation Techniques

The preceding methods are ones that angels and other early stage investors have been using over the past few decades to evaluate startup investments. But advancing technology, the rapid rise in the use of online platforms, and the advent of big data analytics is about to change the nature of the analysis. With transactional platforms able to track the actual valuations at which investments are being made, while at the same time having access to the specific metrics of the companies being valued, it is possible—in a completely anonymous but highly accurate manner—to come up with mathematic calculators that can look at the real metrics of a business, combined with objective, third-party analysis of intangible factors, and deliver remarkably accurate valuations . . . at least within a defined range of early stage, high-growth, scalable businesses. These new valuation methods are still in the formative stages, but within a few years they are likely to revolutionize the field, making it less of an art and more of a science.

The Perils of Misvaluation

Valuing your business accurately is crucially important. Failure to do so will impact the future of the company significantly. If a startup has an unreasonably high valuation in its friends and family round, angels and VCs considering a later investment are likely to be concerned. In fact, in my experience, that may be the number one killer of deals that should otherwise happen.

Consider the math: If the friends and family round is $60K for one percent of the company, that means the postinvestment valuation of the company is $6 million. The company might now approach a professional investor, such as a VC, angel group, or serious angel. Let's say that this new investor is prepared to put in $400,000, but, based on his experience and knowledge of the market, he is only willing to do so at a premoney valuation of $1.2 million (that is, he expects to get 25 percent of the company for his investment).

This sets up an uncomfortable situation for you as an entrepreneur, with only three possible outcomes—none of which is good:

- Take the money from the new investors, and don't do anything to the friends and family investors. Result: Your uncle has just lost 80 percent of the value of his investment because he had the faith to make a bet on you when you were starting out . . . and now he feels you cheated him by overstating the value of your venture. How comfortable do you think the next family dinner is going to be?

- Take the money from the new investors, but retroactively adjust the valuation of the company used for the friends and family investors so that the value of their holdings remains intact (this is technically called "full ratchet antidilution protection"). Result: If the two ends are being held constant, the only place from which to take the makeup value is from the pocket of the founder, which means that you personally take four percent of the equity from your share and give it to your uncle (which, added to the one percent he already had, brings him to five percent, which is what his $60K investment should have gotten him in the first place).

- If the first is too painful, and the second too expensive, then you do neither . . . which means that the new investor walks away, and the company has locked itself into a position from which it will be unable to raise additional financing.

For precisely these reasons, it is advisable to do friends and family rounds as convertible notes with a 10 to 20 percent discount. This leaves the valuation exercise to the professional investors, gives the friends and family an immediate uptick in the value of their investment, and is efficient and cost-effective from a legal documentation standpoint.

There are a few companies, mostly on the West Coast, that have done convertible rounds with differing caps for different investors—but it is unusual, tricky, and not something that will endear you to the less fortunate investors.

If you find yourself in a situation where (1) you absolutely need/want the $4 million investor and (2) those are the only terms on which she or he will come in, then you would be well advised to unilaterally lower the cap for all other investors in the round as well.

The alternative that is sometimes used in cases like this (particularly where it is apparent to everyone that the investor will really be adding ongoing value) is to do the round at the same $6 million cap as everyone else, but put the investor on the company's advisory board, for which service some additional equity is granted.

25

Keep Your Eye on the Exit and Reap the Benefits of Success

THE WHOLE PURPOSE of founding and building a scalable, high-growth startup is to benefit from the growth in its value that you have created. While it is possible to build a big company and continue to own and operate it for the rest of your life while making a handsome living off the profits it generates, that option becomes less available as more and more people begin to have an economic interest in the venture's outcome.

The kind of high-growth enterprise that I have been discussing throughout this book is one that has received economic investments from angels and venture capitalists. It has recruited top-notch talent who are incentivized, at least in part, by stock options. Perhaps it has acquired other companies along the way in exchange for shares of its stock. These other players now have an interest in the outcome of the business, and virtually all of them, for legal, personal, or other reasons, have entered into relationships with you with the expectation that you will guide the business to an exit.

In practice, most employees in high-growth businesses receive stock options that vest over four years. At the end of that period, the company will need to grant them additional options as an incentive to stay, or else they will move on to another company. Angel investors assume that the companies they back will return their funds, plus profits, within six to nine years. Similarly, venture capital funds raise money from their investors (known as limited partners) with the promise that the money will be returned, along with significant profits, within 10 years. That means a typical fund spends five years actively investing and the next five years encouraging their portfolio companies toward an exit.

With those other players ultimately holding what is likely a majority of the company's equity (at the time of an exit, the typical founder might have retained 15 to 25 percent ownership of the enterprise), the expectation on everyone's part is that the goal of the high-growth startup is to have a "liquidity event" within 5 to 10 years of founding. While every large and successful startup will live beyond that time frame, in the twenty-first century, it is a reasonable assumption that the business will do so as either a publicly held company (Twitter, LinkedIn, Facebook, Apple, Microsoft, Yahoo!) or as a division of a larger company (YouTube, WhatsApp, Skype, Periscope, LearnVest, Business Insider, Nest, Beats).

This means that, as a founder, you are inevitably going to find yourself with one of three outcomes for your startup within a period of less than 10 years:

Outcome	Likelihood
IPO	0.1%
Acquisition	40%
Out of business	50%
Anything else	9.9%

Going Public

Launching the business into the open market through an initial public offering (IPO) is the exit option that most entrepreneurs dream about. In this scenario, your business becomes a publicly traded company, which means that all of its stock can be bought and sold through the public stock market. If this happens—and if you as the company founder continue to control a sizeable portion of the business's equity after several investment rounds—your ownership in the company will now be liquid and can be converted into cash at any time just by calling your stockbroker. An IPO can also raise a large sum of capital for the business, thereby facilitating enormous future growth.

The challenge is that an IPO is an extremely complex process, costing an average of $3 million and requiring a large team of lawyers, accountants, and investment bankers, as well as compliance with a host of onerous legal requirements. More difficult, however, is the lengthy, challenging task of attracting interest from Wall Street investment firms through a "road show" in which you present your company's story scores or hundreds of times. Think of it like as a crowdfunding campaign multiplied 100-fold. Only a tiny fraction of the companies launched in any given year are likely to end up going public—but the handful that do often garner headlines and, in some cases, create great fortunes. In 2016, it would be unrealistic to expect to file for an IPO with revenues of less than $100 million.

Acquisition

Given the odds against an average company being able to achieve an IPO, the most common way a positive outcome occurs for a high-growth startup is through an acquisition of the company.

For a startup whose product is a natural extension of the acquirer's own products, or provides traction in a market that the acquirer needs to enter, the startup is usually folded into the larger company.

If it's a big acquisition (such as Instagram, the photo-sharing service purchased by Facebook in 2012 for a billion dollars, or YouTube, the video service purchased by Google in 2006 for $1.65 billion), the startup is generally kept in one piece and the CEO can take on an important role in the acquiring business. If it's a smaller acquisition, the startup's product is often just abandoned, and the startup team members are added to the company's existing teams working in a similar area. If the key reason for the purchase was one or more specific people in the startup, that's colloquially known as an *acquihire*, and often the original startup is shut down and some or all of the employees are put to work on other projects for the bigger company.

There are a few cases where the primary motivation for the acquisition is purely the intellectual property, and in those cases the startup team may not even go to the new company . . . but those situations are relatively rare. Meanwhile—and more important to you as the founder—is what happens to the money that changes hands when the acquisition takes place.

Since all companies are ultimately owned by individual people and/or other entities (through the ownership of stock), the acquirer is buying the target company from its owners, not from the company itself. As such, the founders of—and early investors in—Instagram made a lot of money on its sale to Facebook, because Facebook purchased the company from them for cash and stock.

Pure cash exits (particularly for founders, as opposed to investors) are typically restricted to those cases where the acquirer is looking for value that the startup has already created, as opposed to people who will create more value in the future. That could mean high-value users (for example, subscribers paying big dollars on an automatically recurring basis, as with mobile phones or cable television), monopolistic market rights (such as a transferable exclusive license to a patent, brand, or sales channel), or technology that would be expensive or time-consuming to replicate (such as a high-frequency trading system or a complex predictive algorithm). From these descriptions, it's obvious that in most cases the startup wouldn't have been around long enough to create that kind of value. So why the acquisition?

In the case of the vast majority of tech startups acquired by large industry players for something in the range of $10 million to $40 million, the justification is more of an acquihire, where the larger company is looking to bring on the team, the ideas, and the fresh blood of the upstart to augment its own activities, or to serve as the core of a new product offering or line of business. In that case, very little value is assigned to the company itself, and most of the value is attributable to the team. In those cases, the last thing the acquirer wants is to give the founders of the company "walking-away money," because the goal is to lock them into contracts with the company for at least the next two to four years.

Indeed, even in most of the cases where an acquisition is for all cash, a majority of the cash that the founders would get is locked up and payable only after they've spent some years with the acquirer. The investors, however, would get their cash up front (except for a small holdback percentage to cover any postclosing surprises).

In the case of a company acquiring a startup for stock, one of two situations likely applies: either the company doing the acquiring is a very large one (Google, Facebook, etc.), where the stock has real, determinable value and is therefore effectively the same as cash, the company is a much smaller one (perhaps only a bit larger than the target), where cash is tight and the stock it's paying with is the only way it can do the deal. In that situation, everyone effectively becomes partners and is incentivized to help the combined company grow rapidly.

Occasionally a startup is acquired for less money than it raised from its investors. As I've discussed, every investment round in a company is made on the basis of extensive paperwork (often upward of 100 pages), with the most important part of the legalese specifying precisely what happens when it comes time to pay out the proceeds (if any) from the sale or dissolution of the company. Since all prior investors sign such agreements (or are otherwise legally bound by them) with every new financing round, there is never any confusion about exactly what will happen under any particular outcome.

Who Gets What: The Liquidation Waterfall

In many (if not most) seed and early stage funding scenarios, the investments are structured in LIFO order: last in, first out. The technical term for the structure is the *liquidation waterfall*, because in a liquidation event (whether good, as in a large buyout, or bad, as in a distress sale), investors (and others) are paid out in a specified order. After one pool of investors (say, all those in the Series A round) is filled up, any remaining cash falls down to the next pool, until that pool is filled up . . . and so on, all the way down the line. (In other cases, all preferred investors are treated *pari passu*, so steps 6 and 8, and 7 and 9 below would be combined into one.)

Also, in some cases, the investors may choose to provide an incentive to the management team in order to ensure that the sale goes through quickly. That is usually done by setting aside a fixed amount, or a percentage of the purchase price, which is divided among the management team and paid out before the investors start getting paid back.

Here is the typical payout order, from first to last:

1. Salaries owed to employees
2. Secured creditors
3. Unsecured trade creditors
4. Note holders (convertible and other)
5. Management carve out (if any)
6. Senior preferred stock and warrants
7. Any preference multiple on (6)
8. Junior preferred stock and warrants
9. Any preference multiple on (8)
10. Common stock (including any preferred that converted to common, any exercised options, and all founders' stock) and common stock warrants

If a company hasn't taken in any outside financing, things are very simple because the liquidation waterfall jumps directly from (1) down to (10). But for a high-growth company with multiple rounds of equity and/or debt funding, things can rapidly get so complicated that the only way to figure out who gets what, and when, is to use a specialized computer- or web-based program. These waterfall calculators are included in the cap table and equity management programs discussed in Chapter 18.

As the founder of an acquired company, the good news is that you will forever have on your resume that you pulled it off: you envisioned, founded, built, and shepherded to an exit a successful high-growth company.

Even better news is that, as an entrepreneur, you will have the extraordinary feeling of satisfaction that comes from having your vision realized and the value you created recognized and continued into the future.

Best of all are the tangible rewards that come with an acquisition. If the transaction was essentially an acquihire, you will have a highly compensated job with a larger, stable company for several years. But if, after all your hard work, your startup has blossomed into the proverbial home run, along with your new role may come a great deal of financial benefit in the form of cash or, more likely, stock. You'll dive into the task of integrating your team into the acquirer, you'll take on the challenge of bringing new energy and vision to your parent company, and you'll have a productive and interesting two years while you earn out your share of the acquisition proceeds.

And then?

Well, if you're like 95 percent of the successfully acquired entre-preneurs I know . . . it's back to Chapter 1: Translate Your *Next* Idea into *Another* Compelling Business!

The Startup Checklist Online
gust.com/checklist

IF YOU HAVE read all the way through this book, you will no doubt have come to the conclusion that starting up a high-growth company the right way (1) is non trivial, (2) is not cheap, and (3) requires that you find a lot of different players and get them all working together. And even then, keeping an ongoing tight handle on all of the various pieces, from your Business Model Canvas and lean plan, to your cap table and option plan, to your employees and legal agreements, to your finance and accounting issues, is enough to make anyone want to hide under the covers.

Coinciding with the publication of this book is the launch by Gust of a companion web site: a powerful new platform that pulls together everything that you have been reading about and provides a single online tool to manage your startup from the Big Idea to the Big Exit.

At gust.com/checklist you will find a free, cloud-based version of the checklist to help you keep track of your progress, along with updates to the book, downloadable copies of supplementary materials, and links to a wide variety of tools to help you at every step of the startup progress.

Good luck with your scalable, high-growth business!

The Startup Checklist

- ☐ Develop and iterate your Business Model Canvas
- ☐ Craft and maintain your lean business plan
- ☐ Find and monitor your competitors
- ☐ Find and collaborate with your founding team
- ☐ Establish and maintain your founder accord
- ☐ Track and monitor your lean startup experiments
- ☐ Establish your online profiles
- ☐ Network within the entrepreneurial ecosystem
- ☐ Incorporate your venture as a Delaware corporation
- ☐ Work with your startup lawyer for incorporation and financings
- ☐ Recruit and communicate with your board and advisors
- ☐ Manage your financial accounts and accountant
- ☐ Establish and manage your credit profile
- ☐ Establish your bank, credit card, and merchant accounts
- ☐ Integrate your key online platforms and vendors
- ☐ Measure your business with data analytics
- ☐ Hire your team for best fit and work with freelancers
- ☐ Establish and maintain your stock option plan
- ☐ Assess your funding readiness and develop your fund-raising pitch
- ☐ Reach out to investors and manage your investor pipeline
- ☐ Raise funds online from the crowd, angel investors, and VCs
- ☐ Execute your investment term sheet and manage all due diligence
- ☐ Manage your investor relations
- ☐ Keep your 409(a) valuations current
- ☐ Plan for a strategic merger or acquisitions or an IPO

Appendix

The Startup Reading List

THE E-MYTH REVISITED: Why Most Small Businesses Don't Work and What to Do About It, by Michael E. Gerber (HarperCollins, 1995)

For anyone considering starting his or her own business, this classic is an absolute must; read it before you do anything. It lays out in explicitly stark terms the difference between small business ownership and entrepreneurship. After you finish this, you should have a pretty good feel for whether you have what it takes to create a high-growth business.

The Lean Startup: How Today's Entrepreneurs Use Continuous Innovation to Create Radically Successful Businesses, by Eric Ries (Crown Business, 2011)

This book, based on the experiences of Eric Ries (my successor as entrepreneurship chair at Singularity University), and Steve Blank (originator of the Customer Development approach) has sparked the most significant revolution in the startup world since the rise of venture capital funding in the 1950s. Its premise is simple and stark: Build, measure, learn . . . and then keep repeating. As Eric describes, the first steps in the lean approach are figuring out the problem that needs to be solved and then developing a minimum viable product (MVP) to begin the process of learning as quickly as possible. Once the MVP is established, a startup can work on tuning the engine by continually measuring, learning from the measurements, and then changing the product in response to what you have learned. I discuss the lean methodology at greater length in Chapter 6.

The Startup Owner's Manual: The Step-By-Step Guide for Building a Great Company, by Steve Blank and Bob Dorf (K & S Ranch, 2012)

This guide takes the lean theories and shows you how to put them into practice, based on the seminal Lean LaunchPad course that Steve developed for the National Science Foundation and that is taken by thousands of startup entrepreneurs (and corporate "intrapreneurs") every year.

Business Model Generation: A Handbook for Visionaries, Game Changers, and Challengers, by Alexander Osterwalder and Yves Pigneur (John Wiley & Sons, 2010).

One of the tools Steve discusses that has become a hallmark of the lean methodology is the Business Model Canvas. This book is where it all started and uses a deceptively simple graphic visualization of all parts of a business to help you figure out the whys and hows of your business proposition. I explore the Canvas in some detail in Chapter 1.

Lean Customer Development, by Cindy Alvarez (O'Reilly, 2014), and **Traction: How Any Startup Can Achieve Explosive Customer Growth**, by Gabriel Weinberg and Justin Mares (Portfolio, 2015)

These are great books to help you rapidly get sales and traction during your lean development process.

The Customer-Funded Business: Start, Finance, or Grow Your Company with Your Customers' Cash, by John Mullins (John Wiley & Sons, 2014)

This should be mandatory reading for every startup convinced that the only path to success runs through angel or venture capital. In fact, only a tiny subset of companies will successfully raise money from angel investors, and an infinitesimally small number from venture capitalists. John lays out practical, effective strategies for bootstrapping your startup without investors—which paradoxically is also often the best way to get investors.

From Impossible to Inevitable: How Hyper-Growth Companies Create Predictable Revenue, by Aaron Ross and Jason Lemkin (John Wiley & Sons, 2016)

The ultimate guide to massively scaling up your sales enroute to becoming a unicorn, this book by the team that created the famous SaaStr blog on Quora is mandatory reading for every Software as a Service business, and highly recommended for everyone else as well.

The Definitive Guide to Raising Money from Angels, by Bill Payne (billpayne.com, 2007), is the basic primer on startup fund-raising.

My own book *Angel Investing: The Gust Guide to Making Money & Having Fun Investing in Startups* (John Wiley & Sons, 2014) has become the official textbook for how to be an angel investor—and therefore will be of even greater value to you as an entrepreneur, because it gives you the ability to effectively read the mind of a prospective angel investor.

Finally, if you're in the tiny group that can indeed attract a venture capitalist, before you have your first meeting you should read *Venture Deals: Be Smarter Than Your Lawyer and Venture Capitalist*, by Brad Feld and Jason Mendelson (John Wiley & Sons, 2012) which will let you know what to look for . . . and why.

With all that guidance under your belt, I suggest rounding out your pre-education by sitting down with smart people who have been through this route before and have learned the hard way. While few of us will have the opportunity to do this in person, the next best thing is sitting down with them vicariously.

The Startup Playbook: Secrets of the Fastest-Growing Startups from Their Founding Entrepreneurs, by David Kidder (Chronicle Books, 2013), is a series of interviews with the founders of companies like PayPal, LinkedIn, AOL, TED, and Flickr. Like you, they all began as first-time entrepreneurs, and here they share many of the painful lessons they have learned along the way. Read this along with the shortest book on this list: *Lucky or Smart?: 50 pages for the First-Time Entrepreneur,* by Bo Peabody (BookSurge, 2008). A tale from one of the first successful Internet entrepreneurs who found himself rocketed from his dorm room to an IPO in the earliest days of the web, Bo's lessons are simple, wise, and an easy read.

Two other collections of very useful tips from successful entrepreneurs and early stage investors are **INSIGHTS: *Reflections from 101 of Yale's Most Successful Entrepreneurs,*** edited by my former associate Chris LoPresti (Merry Dissonance Press, 2015), and **Basic Berkonomics**, edited by my good friend, super angel Dave Berkus (The Berkus Press, 2012).

The above handpicked collection of wisdom, guidance, and cautions will at least get you up to speed on what some really smart people think is important. Together, these books will form the backbone of your entrepreneurial library, give you an understanding of the basic terminology of the field, and hopefully prevent you from making a ton of rookie mistakes.

(By the way, if you are an insatiable reader looking for more suggestions for the high-growth entrepreneur, you might want to check out the reading list that I prepared for my finance, entrepreneurship, and economics students at Singularity University. It includes books on entrepreneurship, presentation skills, global economics, the coming technological singularity, and much more. It is available online at http://amzn.to/1mzQ6US.

Appendix

B

Sample Due Diligence Request

BELOW IS A preliminary list of documents and other information that Investor and its outside counsel will need to review in connection with the proposed investment. This is a preliminary document request and upon review of any materials provided to us hereunder, additional requests for documents or information may be forthcoming.

Please furnish for our review copies of the following documents or indicate in writing on a copy of this list that none exist. In addition, please provide a written summary of each oral agreement or arrangement which is responsive to the requests set forth below. We would like to receive all materials responsive to this request at our offices. Any documents identified as originals will be returned to you promptly.

Unless otherwise indicated, (i) all requests are for any matters which are currently existing and in effect or which occurred at any time since the Company's incorporation but which are not now existing or in effect, and (ii) each request applies to all past and present direct or indirect subsidiaries (if any), and all predecessors, whether corporations, partnerships, or joint ventures. For purposes of this request, all such entities are included in the term "Company." Where there is no information responsive to the request, please so indicate by writing "N/A" or the equivalent in the margin.

I. **Corporate Records.**
   A. Chart showing, or a narrative description of, the corporate, partnership, limited liability company structures (parents, all subsidiaries, and other financially or legally related entities) and ownership (including the number of shares and/or percentage of ownership) of the Company.
   B. Copies of the certificates of incorporation, bylaws, partnership agreements, operating agreements, and other similar organizational documents of the Company.
   C. Stock record books and copies of all stock certificates, including reverse sides, of the Company and affiliates.
   D. List of all subsidiaries and affiliates of the Company, if any.
   E. List of jurisdictions in which the Company is qualified or has applied for qualification to do business and evidence of such qualification or application.
   F. List of jurisdictions where the Company has substantial contacts (e.g., real or personal property owned or leased, employees, sales representatives, etc.).
   G. List of the Company's current shareholders, the numbers of shares owned, and the consideration paid for such shares.
   H. Warrants, stock options, agreements relating to any warrants or options to purchase securities, any convertible security, and other rights to subscribe for or purchase securities.
   I. Schedule of all outstanding stock options and warrants, including name of individual, grant date, expiration date, and exercise price, of the Company.
   J. Voting agreements, voting trusts, shareholder agreements, or other similar arrangements with or among shareholders or equity owners of the Company.
   K. Stock purchase and repurchase agreements.
   L. Stock restriction agreements.
   M. Registration rights agreements.
   N. Minutes or other records of meetings of the Board of Directors, committees of the Board of Directors, or shareholders of the Company.

O. All materials distributed to members of the Board of Directors, committees of the Board of Directors, or shareholders of the Company since incorporation or organization (or written consents in lieu of meetings).

II. Employee Benefit Plans and Other Employment Matters.

A. Employment, consulting, compensation, or other agreements or arrangements to which any director, officer, or employee of the Company is a party.

B. Copies of any provisions of any contract or arrangement, pursuant to which any director or officer (or other applicable principals, partners, or members) of the Company is insured or indemnified in any manner against liability.

C. All documents relating to pension, deferred compensation, stock option (including SARs), profit sharing, and any other similar plans of the Company; all IRS determination letters relating to the foregoing; and the most recent actuarial report for any defined benefit pension plan for the Company.

D. All other employee compensation, bonus, incentive, benefit (e.g., life or health insurance), or similar plans of the Company, including plan evaluation and actuarial evaluation reports.

E. Any standard form employment agreements used by the Company as well as any agreements that deviate in any material respect from such standard forms, and all severance or special termination agreements with senior management of the Company.

F. Information with respect to any pension benefit plan subject to Title IV of ERISA maintained by an entity other than the Company which is, or was within the past five years, in a single controlled group with the Company.

G. All collective bargaining agreements to which the Company is a party or by which it is bound, including any side letters.

H. Any policy manuals or materials with respect to trade or employment practices of the Company.

I. Confidentiality, proprietary rights, and noncompetition agreements (i) between the Company and any officer, director, employee, consultant, representative, supplier, or customer or (ii) which the Company's employees or consultants have entered into with a prior employer.

J.   Information as to employment arrangements and/or compensation plans where any benefits or rights are triggered by a change in control of the Company, including any so-called golden parachute or similar arrangements.

K.   Information as to employment arrangements and/or severance plans where any benefits or rights are granted upon severance or termination of an employee, whether or not in connection with a change in control of the Company.

L.   Any contracts for consulting or management services.

III. Regulatory Matters.

All applications, filings, findings, reports, registration statements, correspondence, complaints, consent decrees, determinations, orders, etc. relating to federal regulatory agencies and all foreign, state, and local agencies performing similar functions. Include all exhibits for all filings, unless duplicative of material requested elsewhere.

IV. Properties, Assets, and Leases.

A.   List of all real property owned, leased (as lessee or lessor), or used by the Company, including all documentation of ownership, leasehold interest, any encumbrances or restrictions against transfer on such property, and any title insurance policies or title searches.

B.   List of all intangible or intellectual property—e.g., patents, trademarks, copyrights, trade names, trade secrets, and customer lists—owned, leased, licensed, or used by the Company and any patent or trademark registrations or similar documents in any domestic or foreign jurisdiction. Please include any required permits, licenses, approvals, related regulatory reports, or agreements and any actual or threatened claims of infringement or misappropriation.

C.   List of all fixed assets, personal property, and equipment owned, leased, or used by the Company, including all documentation of ownership, leasehold interest, or any encumbrances or restrictions against transfer of such property.

With respect to all of the properties and leases described in this Item IV, please identify any officers, directors, shareholders, or employees of the Company holding an interest in such properties or leases.

V. **Material Agreements and Financing Documents.**
A. Loan agreements, lines of credit, indentures, revolving credit agreements, note purchase agreements, notes, other evidence of indebtedness, and all related documents concerning any debt financing.
B. Venture capital financing documents.
C. Any agreements in principle or otherwise with respect to mergers, acquisitions, divestitures, or sales of material assets of the Company, whether or not consummated.
D. Mortgages, security agreements, pledges, and other evidence of liens or letters of credit securing any obligations of the Company.
E. Corporate and personal guarantees of any obligations and powers of attorney executed in the Company's name.
F. Schedule and copies of all contracts, agreements, arrangements, or understandings under which the Company (i) has any surviving representations or warranties or any ongoing obligation to indemnify, defend, or hold harmless any party; (ii) is subject to any other material commitment, contingency, or liability; or (iii) which restrict in any manner the right of the Company to conduct its business or to compete with any party.
G. List of bank accounts belonging to the Company and its affiliates.
H. Correspondence and internal memoranda relating to any documents requested in this Item V.

VI. **Marketing, Sales, and Operations.**
A. Licensing agreements (including inter company).
B. Patents, patent applications, trademarks, trademark applications and copyrights (domestic and foreign), service marks (domestic and foreign), and documents relating to know-how, trade secrets, and other proprietary information used by the Company.
C. Promotional material, sales literature, and other advertising documents distributed to potential customers.
D. Agreements with any educational institutions or relating to the Company's provision of private student loans.
E. Joint venture, partnership, and limited partnership agreements.

    F. Agency, commission, distribution, franchise, or sales representative agreements.

    G. Governmental contracts, agreements, or purchase orders.

    H. Agreements under which the company is obligated to provide or purchase a material amount of goods or services.

    I. All other contracts (including executory contracts) material to the Company.

VII. **Accounting, Financial, and Insurance Matters.**

    A. Previous year annual and current year to date monthly financial statements (including balance sheet and income statement).

    B. All documentation relating to any transaction between the Company and any director and officer, including any loans or similar arrangement.

    C. Budgets, fiscal projections, and strategic plans, together with a review of or comparison with actual results, if available.

    D. Summary of federal, state, local, and foreign income tax status, including consents and agreements with any tax authority or any pending or threatened disputes concerning tax matters and all audit papers and communications between the Company and the Internal Revenue Service.

    E. Any documents relating to liabilities and obligations, including material contingent liabilities, write-downs, or write-offs of notes or accounts receivable, incurred otherwise than in the ordinary course of business since formation.

    F. Copies of all insurance policies and a history of insurance claims, with details of any pending claims or incidents which may arise in claims.

VIII. **Legal Proceedings.**

    A. List and description of all material litigation, administrative proceedings, arbitration proceedings, investigations, claims, or disputes (including pending or threatened litigation or claims) involving the Company or any principal shareholder, officer, director, principal, partner, or member of the Company as a plaintiff or defendant.

B. All consent decrees, judgments, other decrees or orders, settlement agreements, injunctions, or similar matters (continuing or contingent) to which the Company is a party or involving any person in his capacity as a shareholder, officer, director, principal, partner, member, or employee of the Company.

C. Documentation with respect to any pending or threatened disputes with any governmental agency to which the Company is or may become a party.

D. All correspondence dealing with actual or alleged infringement of patents, trademarks, and copyrights.

E. Any waivers or agreements canceling claims or rights of substantial value other than in the ordinary course of business.

IX. All other materials and documents involving the Company, not otherwise covered by the foregoing items, which, in your judgment, may be material to the business of the Company or which should be reviewed in making disclosures regarding the business and financial condition of the Company.

Appendix

C

Starting a U.S. Corporation from a Foreign Country

MANY OF THE discussions in this book pertaining to incorporation, stock option plans, term sheets, and exits relate specifically to U.S. companies. The United States has a long history of supporting entrepreneurship, stable corporate law, and a robust ecosystem of investors who fund scalable, high-growth companies. Indeed, each year more than $50 billion is invested by American business angels and venture capitalists into early stage businesses.

Because the United States has such a standardized structure for early stage investments (relatively speaking), because U.S. investors are familiar with it, and because there are so many local opportunities for early stage investments (over 700,000 incorporated employer businesses are founded each year in the United States), most American business angels and venture funds invest primarily domestically. For them, the challenges of making international seed investments are typically not worth the trouble and unfamiliarity of dealing in another country.

For that reason, many international founders who are interested in approaching the U.S. investor market have begun to consider incorporating their venture in the United States and then operating the business in their home country as a subsidiary of the U.S. parent. This makes it just as easy for American investors as it would be if the firm had been a domestic company formed by an American citizen.

What's interesting is that it turns out this is not as difficult as it might sound! The process of forming a Delaware C corporation, as I discussed in Chapter 9, is exactly the same for a nonresident alien as it is for an American citizen. All you need to do is ensure that you provide your real name and real foreign address as the responsible party who will be running the company. You would then form a subsidiary company in your home country, owned entirely by the Delaware corporation. That process is regulated by your own government, with the only wrinkle being that you will need to get your Delaware documents "apostilled" (a somewhat cumbersome process through which the state of Delaware certifies that your corporate documents are legitimate).

Where things begin to get a little tricky, however, is when it comes to financial transactions. If you find American investors who are willing to wire their funds to your overseas bank account, that should be fine. But if instead they insist upon only funding in the United States, you will need to open an American bank account.

It is here, because of the strong anti–money laundering and tax regulations in the United States, that you will have to jump through several bureaucratic and security hoops. Specifically, all U.S. banks are required to know their customer, which means that they are required to do *very* detailed background checks on all of their account holders. You will need to prove your identity, sources of income, address, and more . . . and in many cases do so with original documents or certified copies. This can be a challenge.

Then, once you have convinced the bank that you are who you say you are, you will need to given them the U.S. Employer Identification Number (EIN) for your company in order to open your account. EINs are provided by the U.S. Internal Revenue Service (IRS), the federal government's tax agency, and are typically procured right after your company is incorporated and often by the same registered agent service that handled your incorporation.

The problem is that getting an EIN requires you provide the IRS with a U.S. Social Security Number (SSN), or an Individual Taxpayer

Identification Number (ITIN). While all U.S. citizens will have one (so it's not a problem for them), *you* won't. That means you will need to apply to the IRS to give you one. And while this is certainly not impossible, or even improbable, it can be time-consuming, bureaucratic, and a major pain. But it *can* be done, so follow the instructions at https://www.irs.gov/Individuals/International-Taxpayers/Obtaining-an-ITIN-from-Abroad, and keep your sense of humor while exercising patience.

Appendix

Sample Convertible Preferred Stock Term Sheet

This term sheet for financing early stage companies with investments from sophisticated angel investors was developed by Gust, the platform powering over 90 percent of the organized angel investment groups in the United States. The goal was to standardize on a single investment structure, eliminate confusion, and significantly reduce the costs of negotiating, documenting, and closing an early stage seed investment.

For those familiar with early stage angel transactions, this middle-of-the-road approach is founder friendly and investor rational, intended to strike a balance between the Series A model documents developed by the National Venture Capital Association (NVCA) that have traditionally been used by most American angel groups (which include a 17-page term sheet and 120 pages of supporting documentation covering many low-probability edge cases), and the one-page Series Seed Term Sheet, version 2.0, developed in 2010 by Ted Wang of Fenwick & West as a contribution to the early stage community (which deferred most investor protections and deal specifics until future financing rounds).

Terms for Private Placement of Seed Series Preferred Stock of
[*Insert Company Name*], Inc.

[Date]

The following is a summary of the principal terms with respect to the proposed seed series preferred stock financing of _____, Inc., a [Delaware] corporation (the "*Company*"). Except for the sections titled "Expenses," "No Shop/Confidentiality," [and "Special Terms"], such summary of terms does not constitute a legally binding obligation. Any other legally binding obligation will only be made pursuant to definitive agreements to be negotiated and executed by the parties.

Shares of stock are only applicable to an incorporated company, which means that this term sheet is only applicable to a C Corporation. (Angel investments in a limited liability company are more complex and require a different structure.) Delaware is the favored state of incorporation for U.S. businesses (including more than half of the Fortune 500) because it is considered corporate friendly, with well-established case law. While not required either by law or by this term sheet, incorporation of the company in Delaware is strongly advised. Recently, Nevada has developed a similar reputation and is sometimes used as the incorporation venue for companies based on the West Coast.

This term sheet is, for the most part, "nonbinding," which means that it is used only to document the general meeting of the minds between the two parties and not to serve as the legal basis for the investment. However, its first paragraph makes clear that the three specific sections referenced, "Expenses," "No

Shop/Confidentiality," and "Special Terms" (if such a section is included), ARE legally binding, and once this term sheet is signed by both parties, those sections only are immediately in force. Therefore, regardless of whether the investment is ultimately made, any breach of things such as the confidentiality provisions, or the requirement to pay legal fees, can subject the breaching party to legal action by the other.

Note that the company name should be inserted in both the title and in the first paragraph, the state of incorporation should be inserted where indicated, and the brackets should be removed. If there is a Special Terms section added to the document, the brackets around that phrase should be removed; otherwise delete the whole bracketed phrase.

Offering Terms

Securities to Issue: Shares of seed series preferred stock of the Company (the *"Series Seed"*).

> In exchange for their financial investment, the investors under this term sheet are acquiring shares of stock in the company. Unlike common stock (which is what is usually purchased on the public stock markets), this term sheet specifies preferred stock. The difference is that in the case of a sale, liquidation, or winding up of the company, the preferred stock gets paid back first, before any common stock (which is typically what founders and employees of the company hold). However, because preferred stock gets back ONLY the amount invested, all of the upside goes to the common stock holders. For that reason, a subsequent section of this term sheet provides for the option of the investors to convert the preferred to common, if such conversion would be in the investors' interest.
>
> Note that the class of stock being purchased in this investment round is named "Series Seed." This is a purely arbitrary name, for reference purposes. Traditionally, a first, relatively small investment round from angel investors or a seed fund would be called a Series Seed. The first institutional investment round from a venture capital fund would be called a "Series A," with each subsequent round incrementing one letter (Series B, Series C, etc.).

Aggregate Proceeds: Minimum of $_____ [and maximum of $_____ in aggregate].

> This sets forth how much money the company is planning to raise in this round. Investors typically would not want to fund their commitments until they are sure that the company will receive enough money to be able to achieve its objectives for this round. As such, even if the investors and the company sign the term sheet today, no money will change hands until at least the minimum amount is committed by adding additional commitments from other investors. If the company and investors have agreed upon a maximum amount to be raised, insert it here and remove the brackets. If there is no maximum, delete the bracketed phrase.

Lead Investors: _____, who will invest a minimum of $_____

> This sets for the identity of the investor(s) who are signing this term sheet and committing to invest in the company. While other investors may participate in the funding, the primary investor (whether individual, fund, or group) may (but need not) be granted additional rights in the term sheet. The amount here is the minimum amount that the lead investor(s) are committing to this round, and is distinct from the minimum amount required to consummate the investment.

Price per Share: $_____ (the *"Original Issue Price"*), based on a premoney valuation of $____, calculated based upon the capitalization of the Company as set forth in Exhibit A inclusive of an available postclosing option pool of 15 percent after receipt of maximum aggregate proceeds.

> The price that investors will pay for each share of preferred stock is calculated on the basis of the other factors noted in the term sheet, as well as the number of shares that the company has authorized (or will do so as part of this round). This price is usually filled in last, with the important number in this paragraph being the premoney valuation. This is the amount that the founders and investors agree that the company is worth as of the date the term sheet is signed, before the investors' money is received by the company.

To make this section absolutely clear for everyone, it refers to Exhibit A to the term sheet, which is a capitalization table for the company, showing in names and numbers exactly who owns what shares, both before and after the investment.

In the second part of the sentence the parties agree that before the investment happens, the company will set aside extra shares of common stock that will be used to attract and compensate future employees. This is known as the "unallocated, postclosing option pool." The important thing to understand here is that the 15 percent for the option pool is what will exist AFTER the investment, but the calculation is done BEFORE the investment is made. That means all of the shares for the option pool come out of the founder's shares, not the investors'.

Here is an example: A founder owns 100 percent of a company. Investors put in $350,000 in exchange for 35 percent ownership. That means the postmoney valuation of the company is $1 million, and the premoney valuation (after subtracting out the $350,000) is $650,000. However, as the term sheet indicates, there needs to be a pool of 15 percent of the stock available for employee options. This means the postclosing cap table shown in Exhibit A will show 35 percent for the investors, 15 percent for the option pool, and 50 percent for the founder.

Dividends: Annual 5 percent accruing cumulative dividend payable when as and if declared, and upon (1) a redemption or (2) a liquidation (including a Deemed Liquidation Event) of the Company in which the holders of Series Seed receive less than 5 times the Original Issue Price per share (the "Cap"). For any other dividends or distributions, participation with common stock on an as-converted basis.

A dividend on preferred stock is roughly equivalent to interest on a loan. This paragraph says that investors are entitled to a 5 percent dividend each year on their investment but that the company's Board decides when, as, and if dividend payments are actually made. Since growing companies always need cash, it would be extremely unusual for a Board to declare a dividend payment during the early years. However, "accruing cumulative dividends" means that if the dividends are not paid each year, they continue to accrue until such time as they are.

> This paragraph sets out a couple of additional cases where the accrued dividends must be paid: (1) is the highly unusual case in which after seven years (as laid out in a subsequent section) the company is successful but the investors have not been able to get their money out, and therefore require the company to repurchase their stock, and (2) a sale or other winding-up of the company . . . but only in a case where the investors would otherwise receive less than a 5× return.
>
> Finally, the last sentence says that if the common stock (usually held by the founders) gets a dividend, so does the preferred stock held by the investors.

Liquidation Preference: One times the Original Issue Price plus any accrued and unpaid dividends thereon (subject to the Cap) plus any other declared but unpaid dividends on each share of Series Seed, balance of proceeds paid to common. A merger, consolidation, reorganization, sale, or exclusive license of all or substantially all of the assets or similar transaction in one or a series of related transactions will be treated as a liquidation (a "Deemed Liquidation Event").

> This paragraph says that if the company is converted to cash ("liquidated") whether for happy reasons, such as getting acquired for a billion dollars, or sad ones, such as going out of business and selling the furniture, after paying all of its debts (which always get paid before equity) any remaining money first goes to pay back the amount put in by the investors and then goes to pay the accrued dividends. After that, everything and anything that's left goes to the common stock holders (typically the founders and employees).
>
> While this sounds good for investors in the sad case, it means that in the happy case, even if the company is sold for a billion dollars, the only money the investors will get back is their original investment plus the 5 percent dividend. That's the reason for the next section: Conversion.

Conversion: Convertible into one share of common (subject to proportional adjustments for stock splits, stock dividends and the like, and broad-based weighted average antidilution protection) at any time at the option of the holder.

> Here's where investors get their return: While preferred stock gets paid off first, it doesn't participate in any upside benefits. On the other hand, common stock gets a proportional share of any incoming money (such as a from the proceeds of an acquisition) but has to stand in line behind the preferred. So this paragraph says that investors who hold preferred stock can choose at any time to convert it into common stock. The result is that in a bad scenario (the company is going out of business) the investors stay with preferred and get the first money out. But in a good scenario (an acquisition at a high price), they will choose instead to convert to common and share in the good things.
>
> The "broad-based weighted average antidilution protection" means that if the company at some point in the future raises money at a lower valuation than that being used for the current round, the current investors will be partially protected. This provision is a middle-of-the-road industry standard, halfway between the founder-biased "no antidilution" approach and the investor-biased "full ratchet antidilution" version.

Voting Rights: Votes together with the common stock on all matters on an as-converted basis. Approval of a majority of the Series Seed required to (i) adversely change rights of the Series Seed; (ii) change the authorized number of shares; (iii) authorize a new series of preferred stock having rights senior to or on parity with the Series Seed; (iv) create or authorize the creation of any debt security if the Company's aggregate indebtedness would exceed 50 percent of the aggregate proceeds of the Series Seed; (v) redeem or repurchase any shares (other than pursuant to the Company's right of repurchase at original cost); (vi) declare or pay any dividend; (vii) increase in the option pool reserve within two years following the closing; (viii) change the number of directors; or (ix) liquidate or dissolve, including any change of control or Deemed Liquidation Event.

> This is where most of the protective provisions for investors are found. It says that even though investors hold preferred stock, when it comes to voting we will treat them as if they had converted to common stock so that everyone who owns stock (founders, investors, et al.) gets to vote together on things requiring shareholder approval. However, in addition to their voting alongside every other shareholder, this paragraph provides for a Series vote on certain issues. That is, even if the Board of Directors and 100 percent of all the other shareholders voted to do something in one of these areas, it wouldn't happen unless a majority of the investors in this round agreed. The subjects requiring a Series vote are generally ones that protect the investors from having their rights stripped, having their voting power diluted out of existence, or having the money they just put in go to someone else.

Documentation: Documents will be based on Seed Series preferred stock documents published at http://gust.com /SeriesSeed, which will be generated/drafted by Company counsel.

> A term sheet lays out the general outline of an investment, but the devil is in the details. Once the term sheet is signed and the company and investors proceed to a closing, the lawyers then draft dozens of pages of documentation, including an amended certificate of incorporation, a shareholders agreement, an investors' rights agreement, and so on. The Gust website has a set of standard model documents that match the provisions of this term sheet and make it very easy for an attorney to use them as the basis for his or her work.
>
> While nothing will be signed and finalized until both the parties and their respective attorneys are satisfied, someone has to take the first step in drafting the documents. This paragraph says that the Company's counsel will do so, based on the Gust standard docs.

Financial Information:	All investors will receive annual financial statements and narrative update reports from management. Investors who have invested at least $25,000 ("**Major Investors**") will receive quarterly financial and narrative update reports from management and inspection rights. Management rights letter will be provided to any investor that requires such a letter. All communications with investors shall be conducted through Company's secure investor relations deal room on the Gust platform, which Company shall be responsible for maintaining with current, complete, and accurate information.

> Because private companies are not required to file any statements with the Securities and Exchange Commission, this section lays out what information the company will be required to provide to its investors so that they are aware of what is happening with their investments. It provides for annual financial and written update reports from the company's management be sent to all investors. In addition, investors who have put in more than $25,000 are entitled to quarterly reports, and have the right to visit the company on request and see the corporate books and records (subject, of course, to confidentiality).
>
> A management rights letter is a particular document required by certain venture funds.
>
> To ensure timely communications with investors, the company is required to keep its information updated and current in its Gust deal room, which will greatly enhance both the company's investor relations and the investors' portfolio management activities.

Participation Right:	Major Investors will have the right to participate on a pro rata basis in subsequent issuances of equity securities.

> If the company sells additional stock at any time in the future, this says that each investor has the right (but not the obligation) to participate in such future rounds on the same terms as the new investors, at least up to an amount that will enable them to maintain the same percentage ownership after the new investment that they had before.

Redemption
Right:

The Series Seed shall be redeemable from funds legally available for distribution at the option of the holders of a majority of the outstanding Series Seed commencing any time after the seventh anniversary of the closing at a price equal to the original purchase price plus all accrued but unpaid dividends and any other declared and unpaid dividends thereon. Redemption shall occur in three equal annual portions.

> If, after many years, the company ends up as a lifestyle business, where it is profitable but not likely ever to have an exit, this paragraph gives the investors the right to require the company to buy back their stock for what they paid for it (plus dividends). The repurchase (known as "redemption") would take place over three years, starting at the investor's option any time after the seventh year.

Board of
Directors:

Two directors elected by holders of a majority of common stock, one elected by holders of a majority of Series Seed. Series Seed director approval required for (i) incurring indebtedness **[exceeding $25,000]** for borrowed money prior to the Company being cash flow positive; (ii) selling, transferring, licensing, pledging, or encumbering technology or intellectual property, other than licenses granted in the ordinary course of business; (iii) entering into any material transaction with any founder, officer, director, or key employee of the Company or any affiliate or family member of any of the foregoing; (iv) hiring, firing, or materially changing the compensation of founders or executive officers; (v) changing the principal business of the Company; or (vi) entering into any Deemed Liquidation Event that would result in the holders of Series Seed receiving less than five times their original purchase price.

> The Board of Directors of a company is in charge of making all major decisions, including hiring/firing the CEO. This paragraph establishes a three-person board, with two of the members appointed by the common stock holders and one by the investors in this round.
>
> While this 2:1 ratio means that the directors appointed by the commons (usually the founder[s] themselves) could always outvote the investor, the term sheet equalizes things by setting forth a number of areas in which not only does a majority of the board have to approve, but the director appointed by the investors must also specifically approve. The $25,000 limit on borrowing is rational for smaller deals but can be increased for larger ones.

Expenses: Company to reimburse investors a flat fee of $_____ for background check expenses, due diligence and review of transaction documentation by Investors' counsel. Company shall be responsible for expenses related to Company's Gust investor relations deal room.

> Out-of-pocket expenses related to closing an investment are typically picked up by the company out of the investment proceeds. Given no deviation from this standard term sheet, a moderate flat fee for all of the investors' legal work is eminently reasonable, likely much less than the $20,000 or more when a full-scale NVCA term sheet is used. Including the cost of maintaining the company's investor relations site means that investors are assured of always getting up-to-date information in a form that is immediately usable to them.

Future
Rights: The Series Seed will be given the same contractual rights (such as registration rights, information rights, rights of first refusal, and tagalong rights) as the first series of preferred stock sold to investors on terms similar to, or consistent with, NVCA or other standard documents customary for venture capital investments by institutional investors.

> This is the magic paragraph that ensures investors are protected with all the provisions included in the NVCA model documents, assuming that the company does a follow-on investment round with an institutional investor, such as a traditional venture fund. It is what allows us to cut 14 pages' worth of detail out of this term sheet, compared with the NVCA one.

Founder Matters:

Each founder shall have four years vesting beginning as of the closing, with 25 percent vesting on the first anniversary of the closing and the remainder vesting monthly over the following 36 months. Full acceleration upon "Double Trigger." Each Founder shall have assigned all relevant IP to the Company prior to closing and shall have entered into a nondisclosure, noncompetition, and nonsolicitation agreement (to the fullest extent permitted by applicable law), with such noncompetition and nonsolicitation covenants to be applicable during the term of his or her employment by the Company and for one year after the termination thereof. Founders shall be subject to an agreement with the Company pursuant to which the Company shall have a right of first refusal with respect to any proposed transfer of capital stock of the Company at the price offered.

> This section provides for what is called "reverse vesting" for the company's founders. Even though they may start out owning 100 percent of the company's stock, this gives the company the right to repurchase the stock owned by the founder(s) if they leave the company. The terms are the standard four-year vesting/one-year cliff, which means that if the founder leaves within the first year after the investment, the company can reacquire all of his or her stock, and after the one-year anniversary, the remaining stock vests monthly over the next three years. While some founders initially find this onerous, it is actually *very* much in each founder's best interest, because otherwise one cofounder (say, out of two) could theoretically walk away from the company the day after the closing and retain nearly half of the equity . . . something that would be manifestly unfair to the other founder.

> The "full acceleration upon Double Trigger" means that if the company is acquired before the four years are up, and the new owners terminate the founder, all of the remaining stock owned by the founder immediately vests.
>
> Other provisions of this section ensure that the founder(s) have fully assigned all of their intellectual property so that it is owned by the company, that they have entered into an employment agreement providing for nondisclosure of confidential information, and that if they leave the company, they are restricted for a year from either directly competing with the company or poaching its employees.
>
> Finally, this section says that if founders want to sell any of their stock, they are required to first offer it to the company.

No Shop/ Confidentiality: The Company and the founders agree that they will not, for a period of 60 days from the date these terms are accepted, take any action to solicit, initiate, encourage, or assist the submission of any proposal, negotiation, or offer from any person or entity other than the investors relating to the sale or issuance of any of the capital stock of the Company and shall notify the investors promptly of any inquiries by any third parties in regards to the foregoing. The Company and the founders will not disclose the terms of this term sheet to any person other than officers, members of the Board of Directors, the Company's accountants and attorneys, and other potential investors acceptable to the investors, without the written consent of the Investors.

> The idea behind a No Shop provision is that investors do not want to be used as a straw man for helping the company get a better deal from someone else. So there can be as much discussion as necessary, and as many unsigned drafts of the term sheet exchanged as necessary, but the minute the company signs this term sheet, they are agreeing that for 60 days they won't talk to anyone else about investing, without the investors' approval.

Special Terms: [Deal-specific comments/conditions inserted here. Otherwise delete this section.]

> In order to keep the rest of the term sheet absolutely standard and reduce legal and drafting costs, there should be absolutely NO modifications within the text of the other sections of the term sheet. This "Special Terms" section is the one place that anything unusual or specific to this particular investment should go, although the more special terms or modifications there are, the longer it will take to negotiate and the more the legal fees will cost. Remember that every page in the term sheet ultimately translates into 10 or more pages of the actual deal documentation, and every new or special provision added requires that the lawyers on both sides write, read, and negotiate something nonstandard. As a rule of thumb, every time the documents need to go back and forth between the lawyers, it adds approximately $5,000 to the overall legal costs for the transaction.

Company: [_____, Inc.]

_____

Name: _____
Title: _____
Date: _____

FOR THE INVESTORS:

_____

Name: _____
Title: _____
Date: _____

Since parts of the term sheet are legally binding, it should be signed by someone legally able to bind both parties. This would normally be the CEO of the company and a lead investor who is firmly committed to investing in the company on these terms.

This sample term sheet was developed by Gust with the legal support of Lori Smith, Esq. of White and Williams, and extensive comments from the members of the New York Angels Term Sheet Committee, including Larry Richenstein, Jeffrey Seltzer, and Mark Schneider. Annotations and commentary copyright © 2013 by David S. Rose.

Appendix

Sample Convertible Note Term Sheet

Terms for Convertible Note Bridge Financing of NewCo, Inc.

_____, 20__

The following is a summary of the principal terms with respect to the proposed convertible note financing of NewCo, Inc, a Delaware corporation (the "**Company**"). Except for the sections entitled "Expenses" and "No Shop/Confidentiality," such summary of terms does not constitute a legally binding obligation. Any other legally binding obligation will only be made pursuant to definitive agreements to be negotiated and executed by the parties.

Securities to Issue:	Convertible promissory notes of the Company (the "Notes").
Aggregate Proceeds:	Minimum of $_____ and maximum of $_____ in aggregate, including the conversion of any prior convertible notes outstanding as of the Closing.
Lenders:	Nice Guy Angels, LLC (the "**Lead Lender**"), who will lend a minimum of $_____, and other lenders acceptable to the Company and the Lead Lender.

Purchase Price:	Face value.
Interest Rate:	Annual 5 percent accruing cumulative interest, payable at maturity.
Term:	All principal, together with accrued and unpaid interest under the Notes, is due and payable on the date that is 12 months from the Closing (the "**Maturity Date**"). The Maturity Date may be extended by the consent of holders of the Notes that hold a majority of the aggregate outstanding principal amount of the Notes (a "**Majority Interest**").
Note Priority:	Notes shall be senior to all other indebtedness. All unsecured indebtedness of the Company for borrowed money will be fully subordinated to the prior payment of all principal and interest on the Notes.
Prepayment:	The Notes may not be prepaid without the consent of a Majority Interest.
Conversion:	The "**Conversion Sales Price**" shall be a price per share equal to the lesser of (i) 80 percent of the lowest price per share paid by any other party purchasing common or Preferred Stock upon a Conversion Event as defined below or (ii) the price obtained by dividing (x), $_____ (the "**Valuation Cap**"), by (y), the number of Fully Diluted Shares outstanding immediately prior to the Conversion Event. "**Fully Diluted Shares**" shall mean the number of shares of Common Stock of the Company outstanding at the applicable time assuming full conversion or exercise of all the outstanding options, options reserved for issuance, warrants, and convertible securities (other than the Notes).

A "**Conversion Event**" shall mean any one of the following events:

(i) *Qualified Financing.* The Company consummates, on or prior to the Maturity Date, an equity financing pursuant to which it sells shares of a series of its preferred stock ("**Preferred Stock**") with an aggregate sales price of not less than $_____ (excluding all indebtedness other than the Notes that are converted into Preferred Stock in such financing) with the principal purpose of raising capital (a "**Qualified Financing**").

(ii) *Nonqualified Financing.* The Company consummates, on or prior to the Maturity Date, an equity financing pursuant to which it sells shares of a series of Preferred Stock, which is not a Qualified Financing (a "**Nonqualified Financing**").

(iii) *Change of Control.* On or prior to the Maturity Date and prior to the consummation of a Qualified Financing, the Company consummates a change of control or sale transaction of its Common Stock (a "**Change of Control**").

(iv) *Maturity.* The Company has not consummated a Qualified Financing or a change of control or sale transaction on or prior to the Maturity Date, and the Maturity Date has not been extended by a Majority Interest.

Conversion under   (i) shall be automatic. Conversion under (ii)–(iv) shall be at the option of a Majority Interest.

In the event of a financing conversion described in (i) or (ii) above, the Notes shall convert into a series of Preferred Stock that is identical to the securities issued in the Qualified or Nonqualified Financing and on the same terms as the other parties purchasing such stock upon the Conversion Event, except that for the purposes of the Notes, the Original Issue Price in such financing shall be the discounted price actually paid per share by the note holder.

In the event of a Change of Control conversion described in (iii) above, the Notes shall convert into Common Stock.

In the event of a Maturity conversion described in (iv) above, the Notes shall convert into nonparticipating convertible Preferred Stock with a 1× liquidation preference, customary dividend preference, customary broad-based weighted average antidilution protection, and customary protective provisions which will entitle the holder to customary contractual pre-emptive rights and other customary contractual rights (each as provided in the Seed Series Convertible Preferred model documents maintained at gust.com/seedseries) ("**New Preferred Stock**").

Special Approvals: So long as a Majority Interest is entitled to elect a Lender Director, the Company will not, without Board approval, which approval must include the affirmative vote of the Lender Director: (i) incur any aggregate indebtedness in excess of $50,000; (ii) make any loan or advance to any person, including employees, subject to customary exceptions; (iii) make any expenditure not in compliance with the annual budget approved by the Board, including the Lender Director (other than expenditures within 25 percent of budget, individually, and in the aggregate); or (iv) approve or enter into any related party transactions (including any amendment of agreements with the founders).

The Company will not, without the consent of a Majority Interest: (i) approve the voluntary liquidation or dissolution of the Company (or any subsidiary), a sale of all or substantially all of the Company's assets, a merger or consolidation of the Company with any other company, or a lease or exclusive license of the Company's assets (each a "**Liquidation Event**") (other than a Liquidation Event in which net proceeds exceed $_____); (ii) authorize, create (by reclassification or otherwise), or issue any new class or series of shares (including in connection with a Qualified Financing) or debt security; or (iii) declare or pay any dividend or distribution or approve any repurchase of capital stock.

Use of Funds: Proceeds shall be used for general corporate operations, and not for repayment of any existing debt obligations of the Company.

Documentation: Transaction documents will be drafted by counsel to lenders.

Financial Information:	All lenders will receive quarterly financial statements and narrative update reports from management. Lead Lender will receive such information monthly.
Board of Directors:	Following the initial Closing, the Company's board of directors (the "**Board**") shall include one representative designated by the Lead Lender (the "**Lender Director**"), so long as any principal or interest remains outstanding under the Notes.
Expenses:	The Company shall pay the reasonable fees and expenses of a single counsel to the lenders up to $5,000 if the financing closes. If the financing is not consummated, each party will bear its own legal fees and expenses, unless the financing is not consummated by reason of the Company's refusal to proceed, in which case, the Company shall pay the lenders' out-of-pocket expenses, including legal fees.
Founder/ Employees:	Founder(s) and all employees and contractors as of the Closing shall have assigned all relevant IP to the Company and shall have entered into nondisclosure, non-competition, and nonsolicitation agreements in a form reasonably acceptable to lenders, with such covenants to be applicable during the term of their employment by the Company and for one year after the termination thereof.
No-Shop/ Confidentiality:	The Company agrees to work in good faith expeditiously toward a closing of this note financing (the date the earliest Note is issued shall be the "**Closing**"). The Company and its officers and founders agree that they will not, for a period of 30 days from the date these terms are accepted, take any action to solicit, initiate, encourage, or assist the submission of any proposal, negotiation, or offer from any person or entity other than the lenders relating to the sale or issuance of any of the capital stock of the Company or the acquisition, sale, lease, license, or other disposition of the Company or any material part of the stock or assets of the Company, or the execution of any debt instruments of any kind, and shall notify the lenders promptly of any inquiries by

any third parties in regards to the foregoing. The Company will not disclose the terms or existence of this term sheet or the fact that negotiations are ongoing to any person other than officers, members of its board of directors, the Company's accountants and attorneys, and other potential lenders acceptable to the Lead Lender, without the written consent of the Lead Lender.

Expiration: This term sheet expires on _____, 20__, if not accepted by the Company by that date.

This Term Sheet may be executed in counterparts, which together will constitute one document. Facsimile or digital signatures shall have the same legal effect as original signatures.

NEWCO, INC.

_____

Name: _____
Title: Founder and CEO _____
Date: _____

NICE GUY ANGELS, LLC

_____

Name: _____
Title: _____
Date: _____

Appendix

F

Sample Founder Accord

THIS FOUNDER ACCORD among the Founders of XXX, Inc. memorializes the respective rights and obligations of the Founders prior to the creation and execution of customary corporate actions and long-form agreements pertaining to these matters ("Formal Setup"). The terms and conditions specified in this Founder Accord shall control any future disagreements among the Founders with respect to the matters covered herein until such time as the Company completes the Formal Setup consistent with the terms of this Founder Accord to supersede it. The Founders anticipate completing the Formal Setup in connection either with the Company's initial financing or at such time that the Company's revenues are sufficient to permit such expenditures, but desire to enter into this agreement to confirm their collective understanding, and for this agreement to be legally binding, as to the matters sufficiently described herein.

Issue	Agreement	Notes
Company/ Status	To be incorporated as a Delaware corp.	Full organization, capitalization to be completed as determined by the Founders
Business Idea	Half-hour comedy "television" program utilizing overt and exaggerated slapstick humor.	"Television" is an emerging technology that transmits cinematic images directly into a magic box installed in individual homes. These images can then be viewed in your living room.
Founders	Larry, Moe, & Curly	
Equity	Larry: XX% Moe: XX% Curly: XX%	Equity to be allocated upon corporate organization.
Titles	Larry: CTO Moe: CEO & President Curly: Chairman	
Board	Larry, Moe, & Curly	Majority for all Board decisions. Any exceptions TBD.
Vesting	—4-year reverse vesting —1-year cliff; quarterly thereafter	All founders to have reverse vesting.
Vesting Commencement Dates	Larry: as of [date] Moe: as of [date] Curly: as of [date]	—Vesting agreements to reflect vested portion at time that the agreements are created.

		—Continuous involvement required, but full time/exclusive status not required for continuous vesting prior to Formal Setup
Commitment/ Outside activities	Larry: Part-time status (for supplemental compensation) until sufficient initial funding obtained. Moe: Part-time status until sufficient initial funding obtained (for supplemental compensation). Curly: Full-time status	
Salary or Other Cash Compensation	Larry: TBD at Formal Setup Moe: TBD at Formal Setup Curly: TBD at Formal Setup	
Company IP, Confidentiality, etc.	Each Founder will enter into a customary long-form PIIA Agreement in connection with Formal Setup, but each Founder agrees as of the date of this Founder Accord that he: —will not utilize any Company IP for any purpose unrelated to the Company —will assign any IP he created or developed in connection with his relationship with the Company to the Company —will not disclose any confidential information regarding the Company to any third party other than in furtherance of the Company's business.	

| Modifications | Changes to this Founder Accord shall require the consent in writing of all Founders. | |
| Disputes | Should any dispute arise, the Founders shall attempt to resolve it in good faith. If such efforts fail, New York law shall apply and the courts of New York, NY, shall be the forum for any dispute resolution proceeding. | |

January __, 2016   January __, 2016   January __, 2016

Acknowledgments

As WITH MY PREVIOUS BOOK on angel investing, this book is my attempt to codify and explain current best practices in the entrepreneurial finance industry—in this case, the intricacies of starting up a company the right way. As such, virtually none of it is original to me, and I have simply served as the interlocutor who brings together the hard lessons learned over long careers in the startup world by much better entrepreneurs, investors, lawyers, mentors, and advisors than I will ever be. In particular, many chapters owe enormous debts to the leading experts in their respective fields. These include:

Bill Gross, the internationally renowned entrepreneur and CEO of Idealab, who has long been a role model not only for me, but also for millions of entrepreneurs around the world, for graciously contributing the Foreword.

Alexander Osterwalder and Yves Pigneur for their seminal work on the Business Model Canvas described in Chapter 1;

Legendary business planning expert Tim Berry for entire sections of Chapter 2 on creating a lean business plan;

Charles McCormick of McCormick & O'Brien, who created the Founder Accord described in Chapter 4;

Frank Demmler of Innovation Works, one of the most respected startup mentors in Pittsburgh, for his practical Founders' Pie Calculator discussed in Chapter 5;

Eric Ries of lean startup fame (and my successor as entrepreneurship track chair at Singularity University) for the essentials of the lean startup methodology in Chapter 6;

Rick Bell of Harvard Business Services, the ultimate incorporator, for teaching me nearly everything I know about Delaware corporations, which I have now relayed to you in Chapter 9;

The terrific startup attorneys, Lori S. Smith and Dan De Wolf, who made sure that Chapter 10 was indeed "Lawyered Up" correctly, and the inimitable Gil Silberman, who provided pages and pages of detailed, brilliant notes and corrections;

Lex Sisney, the wizard of *Organizational Physics*, who created the Hiring Board methodology covered in Chapter 17; and

Bill Payne, my longtime friend and angel mentor, who is justly regarded as the global dean of angel education, for the various valuation methodologies covered in Chapter 24.

Many, many others have contributed to my education in the startup world. In no particular order just a few of the most notable investors and entrepreneurs include John Huston, Basil Peters, Alan Patricof, Fred Wilson, Josh Kopelman, Chris Fralic, Rob Hayes, Brad Higgins, Brian Cohen, Charlie O'Donnell, Jason M. Lemkin, Jim Silver, Yuval Almog, Candace Johnson, Yossi Vardi, Dušan Stojanović, Philippe Gluntz, Reid Hoffman, Scott Kurnit, and Gideon Gartner.

As with *Angel Investing*, many of the thoughts here found their first appearance on the unique question-and-answer website Quora.com, to which I am *not* addicted (no, really, I'm not!), but where I have answered nearly 5,000 questions from aspiring entrepreneurs and business angels over the past several years. Quora's Marc Bodnick (who also happens to be a venture capitalist himself) was a great help in getting them off-line and into this book, and several entrepreneurs who contribute to the Quora community graciously volunteered to read the manuscript in draft and provide early comments. They include Peter Baskerville, Dominic Brown, Nandan Choksi, CJ Cornell, Archie D'Cruz, Ghassane Hajji, Leonid Knyshov, Arit Raj, Sarang Ananda Rao, and Mayeesha Tashin.

Because of the multiple complex subjects covered in *The Startup Checklist*, this book proved quite challenging to bring together. Fortunately, I was backed up by my top-notch editorial and production team, including acquisitions editor Richard Narramore of John Wiley

& Sons, who greenlighted the project and kept me on track with the help of his brook-no-nonsense assistant, Tiffany Colon; Wiley senior production editor Lauren Freestone who deserves a special prize for her saintly patience with exasperating writers; Dejan Jovanovic of 99designs.com, who designed the cover, with a jacket photo of me by David Noles; my agent, Susan Ginsburg of Writers House; Mark Fortier and his team, who led the launch publicity, together with Group Gordon, Gust's public relations team, led by Zigis Switzer; David Kumin of Blane & DeRosa Productions, who produced the audiobook version for Gildan Media; and the person who lets me get away with nothing, my assistant, Sadie Schley.

A very special thanks must go to my developmental editor, Karl Weber of Book Editors Alliance, who has been my partner from the very beginning of this process. He undertook the daunting task of boiling down my Quora contributions into something usable for a book, did much of the basic research on all of the topics I have covered, and provided the armature to support what he and Richard charitably describe as my "unique voice."

Two groups of very special people have contributed to this book in ways large and small. My colleagues at Gust comprise the most extraordinary team I have ever worked with, and they get up every morning focused on supporting startup founders and investors by delivering on the most comprehensive vision in the industry. I am honored to have an extraordinary board of directors in the legendary Howard L. Morgan, cofounder of First Round Capital; Bob Rice, managing partner of Tangent Capital (and author of *The Alternative Answer*); and Richard Zenker, president of Overbrook Management. Together with David Marrus, Peter Jungen, Richard Katzman, John Katzman, Mark Allison, and Liam Lynch, they keep me on a straight and narrow path and provide deep insights into the private equity industry.

The amazing staff at Gust have spent years working to deliver the unique and comprehensive platform that is debuting along with this book, under the guidance of a leadership team including Ryan Nash, Jess Compagnola, Alan McGee, Keyvan Firouzi, Peter Swan, Todd Mohney, Miklos Grof, Will Brown, Jun Simmons, Mike Frederick, Justin Cina, and former members Rich LaFauci, Lisa Balter Saacks, and Ilana Grossman.

Finally, I owe a greater debt to my family—nuclear and extended—than can ever be repaid. I can say without exaggeration that I am the underachiever among a group of extraordinary people. My father, Daniel Rose (author of *Making a Living, Making a Life*, a Kirkus Best Book of 2015), has always been my role model as a thinker, a doer, an entrepreneur and a mensch. My mother, Joanna Semel Rose, widely regarded as the single smartest person in New York City, taught me to write in my younger days, and then rose to the challenge half a century later of painstakingly copyediting this manuscript (which, in case you are curious, included over 3,000(!) "suggestions for improvement"). While I take full responsibility for all remaining errors, without her ministrations I would have come across to you as a complete illiterate. My siblings, Joseph, Emily, and Gideon, have managed to mostly suppress their snickers during my decades-long entrepreneurial career and provided significant help in myriad ways at myriad points where it really counted. My three children—the prime focus of my life—have had the dubious privilege of putting up with decades of my entrepreneuring, investing, and pontificating. One has served as my primary entrepreneurial pupil and protégé, the second keeps me honest on Quora, and without the third I would never have actually finished writing this book.

Most of all, I am grateful to my wife, who has put up with me for well over 30 years, and is an enabler for someone who is as different from her as two people could possibly be. Once again, this is not the book she wanted to see—one consisting of only stories from my investing career—but never fear, that one will eventually be forthcoming!

New York
March 2016

Index